Secrets of the
World's Healthiest People

Your Key to Dropping Pounds, Healing Disease, and Feeling Fantastic

Elizabeth Shimer Bowers
and Steven R. Bowers, DO

HEARST

To our three children
–Marin, Lila, and Drew–
who patiently watched
Mom and Dad
work together to
write this book.

© 2018 by Hearst Magazines, Inc.

Printed in the United States of America

PHOTOGRAPHS BY Mitch Mandel

BOOK DESIGN BY Susan P. Eugster

Library of Congress Cataloging-in-Publication Data is on file with the publisher.

ISBN 978-1-63565-050-1 hardcover

2 4 6 8 10 9 7 5 3 1 hardcover

Contents

Introduction

As a family doctor and wound care specialist, I see the results of healthy—and unhealthy—lifestyles firsthand every day. I'm often surprised when I learn a patient's true age. A 38-year-old patient may look closer to 28 or, in some cases, 58. A 40-year-old may shuffle into the office for an infected wound that won't heal but is on the verge of a heart attack. A few minutes later, a 78-year-old may practically jog through the door and sum up his medical history in one sentence. I'm not trying to put too much emphasis on looks, but in many cases, outward appearance is a good indication of overall health.

Liz, my wife and co-author, has made some similar observations. As a health journalist, she sifts through science to tease out the health facts readers need to know. She interviews and writes about people who have improved their lifestyles and lost weight. In some cases, these people seemed to have aged in reverse.

We face these observations as we watch ourselves—and each other—age. We face them as we watch our friends and parents get older, too. I, unfortunately, watched my father lose a battle with pancreatic cancer at the tender age of 45. That's only 4 years older than I am now. This experience changed me deeply. It inspired me to become a physician and it motivates me to take the best possible care of my patients, as well as myself and my family.

Almost daily, both Liz and I ponder the question: Can we stay healthy and strong by living a healthy lifestyle—or will our genes ultimately prevail? Given two people of the same age, how can one radiate a healthy glow, while the other has a belly that's growing as fast as the bags under his eyes? What are the secrets to overcoming hardship, side-stepping illness, and remaining strong and supple into one's eighties, nineties, and beyond?

We decided to take a deeper look.

We'd, of course, heard of people who live in Blue Zones—Okinawa, Crete, and other beautiful areas of the world where people tend to outlive the rest of us by years, even decades. But there's a lot about Blue Zones that just can't be copied and used by the average person. For one, Liz and I don't live on a beautiful Greek island. We're not surrounded by a close-knit community with elders who are willing to watch our children or run our errands. Our grocery stores are not exactly bursting with fresh, line-caught fish and garden-picked, organic produce. And most people don't walk or bike to get from place to place around here. They drive.

Indeed, our city is probably the opposite of what you'd imagine when you think of a Blue Zone. In Bethlehem, Pennsylvania, the hulking skeleton of the now vacant steel mill is always visible. We're surrounded by strip malls, fast-food restaurants, and cars—and their exhaust.

Sure, Blue Zones can teach us a lot (and we've included some of those lessons in this book), but we can learn so much more from people who have managed to maintain exceptional health in places like Bethlehem and Charleston and a remote ranch in northern California. How did they live into their eighties, nineties, and beyond with strong bodies, firm minds, and indomitable spirits? That's what we set out to find out.

To find the world's healthiest people, we talked to friends and relatives, conducted internet searches, posted on social media, and racked our brains. We wanted to locate those rare people who seemed just like, well, anyone, but yet had defied the odds. And they weren't as difficult to find as we had first assumed. It seemed as if just about everyone knew someone who seemed to possess superhuman traits when it came to health. "You have to meet my friend _____," became a sentence we heard over and over. All told, we sat and spoke with more than 30 people, asking them questions about what they ate, how they exercised, and what they did with their free time. They ranged in age from 33 to 99 and they lived everywhere from California to Switzerland.

They'd completed marathons, jumped out of airplanes, deadlifted hundreds of pounds, and overcome cancer, depression, and heart disease. A few had lived decades past their "sell by" dates. Doctors, for example, had predicted that one woman would never live to see her 5th birthday. When we spoke to her, she was 33—and one of the oldest living people with her particular disease. Others had faced unimaginable hardship and had emerged stronger, happier, and more at peace. A few were doing things that defied our visions of people in their seventies, eighties, and nineties. Like cheerleading, running barefoot on the beach every morning, or completing 50 push-ups in just 45 seconds.

We talked to people who truly hadn't gotten sick—not even a stuffy nose—in a decade. We met a Corvette-driving 90-year-old, one of the world's top-ranked bridge players, as well as a famous surf photographer. One woman has saved hundreds of women and children from their domestic abusers. One 76-year-old woman totes a rifle, births calves, hoists 150-pound hay bales, smokes her own beef jerky, and grows, raises, and hunts for nearly all her food. Oh, and she is also famous for her cream pies.

We learned of people in their seventies who still wear the same size pants they did in high school, as well as a mother of four who proudly dons a bikini.

They have fully earned the title of World's Healthiest People. We wanted to know their secrets. So, we asked them, and they generously shared them.

And now we want to share those secrets with you.

Before we introduce you to the World's Healthiest People, however, we'll start by explaining the latest science behind what it takes to remain healthy. You'll learn about the role of your genes and the environment, and the interplay between the two. We will tell you about the pieces of DNA called telomeres, which scientists think may hold important data about how long we will live. And, we will discuss inflammation, which seems to cumulatively build as we age. We've created a quiz you can use to determine where you are in the aging process. Take it now, and again once you've incorporated some of the secrets into your daily routine.

Then, in Chapters 5 through 9, you'll meet the World's Healthiest People, learn their secrets, and get advice on how to put their secrets to work in your life. Toward the end of the book, you'll find our easy-to-follow 9-week plan you can use to incorporate some of the secrets of the World's Healthiest People into your own life. You'll also find an eating plan and recipes that show you how to eat like the World's Healthiest People, too.

As you'll soon discover, the Secrets of the World's Healthiest People includes a spectrum of health topics—nutrition, herbs and spices, fitness, mind-body, and so on—and they come to you backed by science as well as my experience in guiding my own patients to good health. Here's a little preview of just some of them:

- Eat blueberries every day.
- Be thankful and count of your blessings.
- Push out of your comfort zone.
- Surround yourself with people who encourage you.

- Challenge your mind in unique ways.
- Take a shot of apple cider vinegar daily.
- Do that one thing you've always dreamed about.

As you read the book, Liz will tell the stories and at the end of each tale, I will provide commentary on why these healthy habits have worked so well for each person. At the end of chapters 5 through 9, I'll also provide a "prescription" for achieving the overriding goal of that particular chapter. We think you'll find that not only do the World's Healthiest People inspire us, but they also teach us how to live and age with grace, health, and strength. They open our eyes to a completely different understanding of what it means to be 40, 50, 60, 70, 80, 90, and beyond. Rather than fearing aging, flu season, and yard work, we can see these as opportunities to live our best lives and grow stronger, happier, and healthier than we've ever been before.

One

The Secrets
of the Super Healthy

No one is exempt from aging. We're not, you're not, and neither is Pat Moorehead.

We interviewed the 85-year-old, along with his 70-year-old wife, Alicia, because they both love to jump out of airplanes. That's impressive, we thought, but one of the most profound things Pat told us wasn't about sky-diving. It was a story about how he chose his home.

"I hate moving," Pat said. "So, when I looked at the model of the home I was considering buying back in 1968 and saw it had two stories, I thought, 'do I want to be climbing stairs in my eighties?' "

Now, most people would likely answer that question with a no. But, Pat and Alicia are not like most people. Pat thought, "Yes!" and he got the house with the stairs.

Today, in his mid-eighties, Pat not only climbs those stairs but he purposely does so without holding the handrail "because that's cheating," he says.

He and Alicia were just two of the more than 30 people we interviewed in our quest to uncover the secrets of the World's Healthiest People. We knew about the Blue Zones, geographic areas where the longest-lived people call their homes. Researchers had already studied those areas of the world extensively and we didn't feel like we needed to duplicate their efforts. Instead, we sought out people much closer to home. We wanted to find people just like Pat and Alicia—people that any one of us could read about and think, "That person isn't much different from me."

We looked for people who personified what it meant to be:

Able: They sailed into their eighties, nineties, and beyond with firm, supple bodies.

Spunky: They lead full lives and exuded enviable energy.

Well: They rarely, if ever, got sick.

Unbreakable: They bounced back from unimaginable hardships and setbacks.

Fit and trim: They still wore the same clothing size they did in high school and weren't afraid to sport a bikini.

They taught us many secrets, but the most important and powerful one is this one: We all have the power to age well.

Though no one can stop time, we all have the ability to wake up tomorrow with additional wisdom and drive to make that day better than the day before. Every single one of us can fight back against aging stereotypes that steal our youth and vitality. We can learn how to enjoy the ride and explore what's possible rather than dwell on what's not. We can keep our immune systems strong, maintain our weight, and keep our joints flexible so we can forever climb stairs, if not do cartwheels.

We can also laugh with our friends, catch big waves, run marathons, and challenge our minds.

We, too, can become one of the World's Healthiest People.

The World's Healthiest People are not necessarily special. It may surprise you, but these inspirational people are not genetic anomalies. They are simply living their lives according to several secrets that the rest of us can adopt. By putting their secrets to work in our own lives, we can be healthy for the rest of our lives as well. Here, we've listed nine reasons why you have what it takes to be one of the healthiest people in the world.

1. You are aging and you are not alone. With all the uncertainty in life, one thing is for sure: When you wake up tomorrow, you will be a little older. The pretty girl who sat next to you in high school homeroom? She will be a little older too. Your first movie star crush who will be forever young in your mind? He will also be older. By virtue of being alive, we all get older every day. So, you have a choice: You can remain (or become) a healthy person who maintains your weight, exercises, and eats well, or you can throw up your hands for the next few years or decades and do what's easiest and most convenient—not exercise and eat lots of processed or fast foods. This book will show you how to take the healthy path as you reach this critical fork in the road.

2. **All-day energy isn't as elusive as you might believe.** Yes, life is tiring—and stressful. You just need to find and utilize the things that give you the biggest boost. Maybe it's a berry smoothie every morning for breakfast, a mid-day yoga session, a coffee break with close friends, or a combination of all these and other activities. By reading *Secrets of the World's Healthiest People* and the scientific reasons behind those secrets, you will become inspired to make the most of each and every day. And, with your newfound energy, you will have the get-up-and-go to volunteer, take a cooking class, or finally plan that trip to visit an old, beloved friend.

3. **You never want to be frail, infirm, or shut in.** Surely, you don't look ahead to older age and see yourself in a rocking chair grumbling about constipation. So, don't become that person! Instead, perhaps like Harriet Thompson, become someone who runs marathons in your nineties. Or, like Louise Gooche, pursue something you always wanted to try (in her case, shaking pom-poms on a senior citizen cheerleading squad). We all have what it takes to be happy and healthy; it's just a matter of harnessing those powers and channeling them in the right direction. As you read and embrace the stories of some of the astonishing individuals we met, you will take that important first step toward becoming the healthiest person possible.

4. **When it comes to exercise, it's never too late to start.** Whether or not you exercise, you know you probably should. Even if you've never worked out a day in your life, as you'll learn from some of our stories, you can start now, regardless of your age or shape. You will read about avid exerciser Steve Colwell, 84, who says, "Exercise is like going to the

grocery store or brushing your teeth. If you want to stay fit, you have to do it—there's just no way around it." Nearly every person we interviewed, from age 41 through age 99, exercises. For some of the World's Healthiest People we interviewed, exercise is the backbone of their existence. For others, it's a way to get some fresh air, keep weight off, and stay well. For all, physical activity plays an important role in their health.

5. No matter how in shape or out of shape you might be, you can still get stronger. If you're in your sixties or seventies (or beyond), you can still build muscle similar to someone in their forties, research shows, but the process of bulking up just works a little differently. Your muscles are made up of a few types of fibers. At middle age, some of those fibers die. What you don't use, you truly can lose, as dead fibers cannot come back to life. It sounds dire for sure, but this isn't the end of the muscle-building story. You can't get back what you've already lost, but you can increase the size of the remaining muscle fibers, which creates the same muscle-building effect. And, when you build muscle, you improve your balance and strength. Plus, because muscle burns more calories than fat, it helps you to maintain your weight.

6. Healthy eating and delicious eating are not mutually exclusive. In fact, healthy foods taste pretty dang sweet. Adopting the Mediterranean diet—which features plant foods, nuts, vegetables, and fish—may be the most protective dietary move you can make, according to a review published in the journal *Biogerontology*. What's on the menu? Olives, guacamole, grilled calamari, and homemade bread dipped in olive oil. The cuisines that everyone raves about when they travel to Greece, Spain, and Italy are the very cuisines that will help you to live a long, strong, healthy life.

7. You don't have to eat perfectly. Life is not the same without dessert, so, as you will discover, the World's Healthiest People do not eat perfectly, but for the most part, their dinner plates are worthy of respect. Everyone we interviewed consumes plenty of fruits and vegetables as well as limits their intake of processed and refined foods. Some eat a vegetarian diet while others go for diets higher in animal proteins. What stands out for all is that they care about what they eat and proudly talk about some of their favorite dishes. Those who drink alcohol do so in moderation.

8. **You can bolster your immunity so you get sick less.** Even if you spent this past winter with a constant runny nose, next winter can be different. As you age, your body becomes more inflamed, and an inflamed body is less able to fight off invaders. Sometimes it gets lazy and lets an unwanted virus or bacteria slip in. Or it might get confused and attack its own tissues and healthy cells. Either way, it's safe to say that, in general, our immune systems work less efficiently as we get older. The good news is that there are things you can do to bolster your immunity and the World's Healthiest People will show you how.

9. **Accept and embrace the aging process.** Yes, you really can. As Kathy Shaffer, 62, says, "Getting older is a fact of life—you can't stop it, so why get upset?" An important part of healthy aging is accepting that there are some things you can change and some things you can't.

The key to growing old healthfully is recognizing and accepting that you are aging—without obsessing or letting the negative stereotypes put a damper on the wonderful person that you've become over the years.

The stories in this book will help you accept, embrace, and celebrate aging. The truth is that all of us can accomplish incredible feats and be incredible people, no matter how many candles are on our birthday cakes. The later years of life can be the best—full of art, theater, writing, runs on the beach, and hikes, and gratitude for all of these blessings. Based on the advice of the World's Healthiest People, you'll find that you can love yourself, your body, and your life at any stage.

Two

The Science of Incredible Health

When we spot a new wrinkle or gray hair, we can't help but stop and think, "how did *that* get there?!" Other questions haunt us too, like, "Why does my friend who is 5 years older have more energy than I do?", "How come my one friend can eat ice cream every night and stay slender, but I can't even look at a cookie without gaining weight?", "What gives with that one person at the office who never gets sick, whereas I seem to be hacking up mucus every other day?" and "Am I destined to age like my mother or father—abdominal basketball and all?"

Life and health seriously seems, well, unfair, doesn't it? It's as if good health and bad health is random.

Or is it?

In this chapter, we will help you to understand the science of good health so you can make sense of the driving forces behind your weight, energy, immunity, and overall wellness.

Scientists don't know everything, but they are uncovering more exciting facts about our health every day. You'll read about the role of genes, environment, epigenetics (the study of heritable changes in gene function that do not involve changes to DNA), telomeres, inflammation, calories, and stress. You will also learn the difference between chronological age and biological age. This knowledge—together with the secrets to come—will empower you to maximize your emotional and physical health as you age.

What Causes Aging, Sickness, Spare Tires, Chronic Sniffles, and Fatigue?

Do we really understand what makes us feel old, sick, and tired? Not entirely, but we're learning more all the time. As researchers continue to examine the link between genetics and health, one thing is for sure: It's complicated. Many factors may be at play—some present at birth and others that we encounter throughout our lives. What we do know is this: Health is unfair and it's unfair in many different ways. Let's look at the top unfair truths of good health.

People age at vastly different rates. There's your chronological age, which is the number of candles on your cake. More important is your *biological* age, or where you stand in terms of your physical health and predicted lifespan. (We've included a quick test to help you determine your biological age in Chapter 3).

Here's the mind-blowing part: Your biological and chronological ages can differ by 5, 10, even 20 or more years! One study tracked 18 different age-related traits of 954 people from the same town in New Zealand for several decades. Published in the *Proceedings of the National Academy of Sciences*, the study tracked things such as weight, gum health, and kidney function. Get ready for this...at age 38, some of the participants' biological ages were in their twenties, and others were close to 60! The slow agers nearly stopped aging during the period of the study, had a stronger grip, and did better on brain function tests. The accelerated agers, on the other hand, did poorly on those tests and were aging at a rate of 3 years for every 12 months that passed.

Some people gain weight easily, while others seem to be able to eat whatever they want. Why? Metabolism. Your basal metabolic rate (BMR)—the energy required to keep your body functioning when it is at rest—is due in part to the genes you inherited from your mother and father. In other words, part of it is out of your control. Some people luck out and inherit genes that keep their metabolism revving high; others have slower rates, which cause them to more readily pack on pounds.

The slow metabolism folks aren't doomed though. Environmental factors—the calories you eat, your body fat percentage versus your percentage of muscle, and your level of physical activity—affect your weight and metabolism too. Of the dozens of people that we interviewed for *Secrets of the World's Healthiest People*, many had inherited genes that caused them to gain weight easily but they found a way to circumvent their fate. Not only were they able to shed stubborn pounds but they were also able to remain slender over time. How? Their lifestyles lend themselves to trim, healthy bodies.

Not everyone gets sick when confronted with a room infested with the cold virus. That's because immunity to colds and other viruses seems to be due to a combination of genetics and exposure—both past and present.

To understand how genetics and exposure interact, let's look at the hypothetical story of Adam and his best friend, Will. Let's say Adam was born with a robust immune system, whereas Will's genetics resulted in an immune system that just isn't as powerful as Adam's. If Adam and Will are both exposed to a toddler with a runny nose, Will most likely will get sick and Adam probably won't. That's the unfair part. However, let's say Will was sick just a couple of weeks ago—with the same virus that has caused the toddler's nose to ooze virus-rich snot. In this case, Will can probably generously wipe the toddler's nose and forget to wash his hands—and all would be well and good. (Note: we do not recommend trying this at home).

In this respect, being older can be an advantage, because the longer you live, the more viruses you come into contact with, and the less likely you will be to encounter a virus that your body has never been exposed to before. Scientists are learning more about the role of genes in immunity. In the meantime, your best bet is to avoid germy people and places, and wash your hands frequently. After all, it's impossible to tell ahead of time whether someone has the cold you've already had—or a new one.

Some people are pre-programmed to develop diseases. Just like you can inherit eye color and hair texture from your parents, you can also inherit the tendency to develop certain diseases and conditions. A tendency to develop diseases such as heart disease, diabetes, and cancer can be passed down from parent to child via genes. Humans all share the same genes, but certain people have different versions of these genes—called gene mutations—that put them at increased risk for developing certain diseases. Some mutations are present when a person is born, and others may develop later in life from lifestyle factors and exposure to toxins in the environment.

Energy levels vary from person to person, no matter what their age.
Energy appears to be linked to metabolism; people with higher metabolisms have more energy and, therefore, have a natural tendency to move more to burn it off.

A "couch-potato" gene may govern your level of get-up-and-go. Scientists think that they have pinpointed the genes that produce AMP-activated protein kinase (AMPK), an enzyme our muscles produce during exercise. AMPK helps control the way we convert food calories into energy. People with higher levels of AMPK tend to have more energy and those with lower levels are more prone to be couch potatoes, research suggests.

Couch-potato gene aside, as we all know, energy levels also have a lot to do with what we eat. Different kinds of foods convert to energy at different rates. Whole grains, lean proteins, and unsaturated fats convert slowly and steadily, giving you longer-lasting energy. Simple sugars and white starches, on the other hand, tend to give you a quick boost followed by a crash...and a craving for more carbs and sweets.

How Powerful Are Your Genes?

You have a lot more in common with your average fruit fly than you would ever believe. In fact, you and the fly share 60 percent of your genomes. That's why scientists value fruit flies so much when it comes to studying genes.

Thanks, in part, to those studies, we know that the human genome is made up of about 25,000 genes, with three billion base pairs of DNA. In one out of about every 1,000 base pairs, there is a genetic variation, or mutation. Some of these mutations may increase the odds of developing a specific disease. Others may boost your chances of living beyond 100. Using different methods, scientists are trying to pinpoint the exact genes and mutations that affect how you age and how long you live. They've studied short-lived animals such as the fruit flies mentioned, as well as worms, and found hundreds of genes that affect the length of their lives. From their findings, we can surmise that certain people may live beyond 100 because of the genes they were born with and not necessarily because of what they ate. These genes might have helped them to overcome diseases or fend off diseases from even taking hold. And, separate from disease, there may be genes that work to speed up the aging process or slow it down. By turning on or turning off these genes, we may be able to change the way we age.

Epigenetics:
Nature and Nurture Get Hitched

When identical twins are born, they are as genetically similar as they will ever be. As they get older and live separate lives, their genetic profiles start to differentiate. From a research perspective, that's where things get interesting.

If genes were the sole drivers of our health, we'd expect identical twins to die of the same diseases, around the same time.

But, they don't.

A 2015 review published in *Nature* looked at 14.5 million pairs of identical twins. They found that genes could only account for half the risk of developing various diseases. The other half was the result of environment. This is where the science of epigenetics comes in.

• •

Nine Ways to Live to 100 and Beyond

To find the most powerful secrets to a long life, researchers looked for geographic areas with the highest numbers of people who live to 100.

The regions they found—coined Blue Zones by Dan Buettner, the explorer and author who led the researchers who discovered them—include the Barbagia region of Sardinia; Ikaria, Greece; Nicoya Peninsula, Costa Rica; Loma Linda, California; and Okinawa, Japan. When you look at the lifestyle habits from these regions collectively, some interesting themes emerge. There are nine common denominators among those who live in Blue Zones, many of which, you will discover, overlap with the secrets you'll learn in this book.

1. They live in cultures that require them to move naturally with activities, such as walking to get places and gardening.

2. They wake up each morning with a purpose.

3. They know how to relieve stress.

4. They eat until they are only 80-percent full; leaving a 20-percent gap helps them control their weight. They also eat their smallest meal of the day last.

5. They eat mainly a plant-based diet. Those who eat meat do so less than five times a month.

6. They drink alcohol regularly, but moderately—about one to two drinks per day.

7. Most belong to a faith-based community.

8. They put family first.

9. They have strong social networks that also put a strong emphasis on healthy habits.

The study of epigenetics blends the two worlds—genetics and environment—that scientists have long thought of as on opposite sides of the camp. According to epigenetics, the question may not be nature *versus* nurture, but rather, how do nature and nurture work together to make us who we are?

The science of epigenetics looks at how your environment can affect your genes, as well as how your genes govern your development, health, and biological age. To many researchers, epigenetics represents the future of aging research.

Epigenetics revolves around the epigenome. Think of the epigenome as little scars on your DNA, like the ones you may have gotten from falls or the chickenpox as a kid. In the case of the epigenome, these marks tell DNA how to behave. Your lifestyle—what you eat and drink, pollutants you come across (including cigarette smoke), and whether you exercise—all affect these epigenomic marks. And, when the epigenome changes, the activity of your genes can change too. Some changes are harmless; others increase risk for diseases of aging. Scientists also think some of these environmentally induced changes can be passed on from one generation to the next.

Besides looking at identical twins, scientists study epigenetics by examining the lifespans of laboratory mice that are genetically identical and raised in the same space. Interestingly, even with the same parents and living space, some mice live longer than others. Researchers think that this may be due to differences in nurturing early on. The shorter-living mice may have had trouble feeding, gotten less milk or less attention from their mothers, and slept farther away from their brothers and sisters. This lack of nurturing may physically affect their genetic profiles and cause them to die sooner than their better-cared-for litter mates.

The science of epigenetics is an exciting area and there's *lots* more ahead. In the future, researchers hope to better understand how changes to the epigenome affect health and aging, how single events in your life can change your genome, and whether your age at the time of an event makes a difference in how your genes evolve.

THE INFLAMMATION CONNECTION

Inflammation is your body's natural defense mechanism against irritation, injury, and infection. It involves a boost in white blood cells, pain, redness, and heat.

In small doses, it's a good thing. Inflammation is what fights off the flu and what helps to heal a sprained ankle. The problem comes when inflammation goes on for too long and becomes chronic. That's when it leads to poor functioning, disease, and earlier death.

As your body gets older, it becomes more chronically inflamed, a process known as inflamaging. This chronic, low-grade inflammation increases risk for obesity, metabolic syndrome (a group of conditions, including high blood pressure, elevated blood sugar, excess abdominal fat, and abnormal lipid levels, that occur together and increase risk of diabetes, heart disease, and stroke), diabetes, heart disease, dementia, and cancer. It can also become a vicious cycle, where inflammation breeds even more inflammation, which is tough for the body to halt.

Unlike wrinkles and age spots, you can't see inflammation and many people suffer from chronic low-grade inflammation and don't even know it. But, there are ways to measure it. A simple blood test can reveal whether certain markers—C-reactive protein (CRP), interleukin-6 (IL-6), and tumor necrosis factor-alpha (TNF-alpha)—are elevated. If they are, there's inflammation somewhere in your body, whether you feel sick or not.

Short Guys Finish Last:
The Science of Telomeres and DNA

As researchers learn more about the science of aging, telomeres are becoming more of a household name. These segments of DNA cap the ends of our chromosomes. They're often compared to the plastic ends of shoelaces, and they protect the tips of chromosomes—preventing them from fraying. Without telomeres, DNA would fall apart and cells would malfunction, leading to disease and death.

Longer telomeres, research shows, indicate better health, slower aging, and a longer life. The shorter your telomeres, the "older" you are and the higher your risk for diseases such as osteoporosis, diabetes, cardiovascular disease, Parkinson's disease, Alzheimer's disease, and cancer.

It works like this: Each time a cell divides, it passes its genetic information on to two new daughter cells. With each cell division, the cell's telomeres shorten. When its telomeres become dangerously short, the cell does one of three things: It turns itself off and stops replicating (a process called senescence); dies (called apoptosis); or continues to divide in an abnormal way (potentially leading to cancer).

When cells start to die, tissues struggle to rejuvenate. This causes them to break down, leading to poor health and, consequently, a higher risk of ending up in a casket sooner than later, research shows. In one of the largest studies on telomeres to date, researchers looked at the telomere lengths of more than 100,000 individuals of different ages. People with the shortest telomeres were nearly 25-percent more likely to die within 3 years than the people whose telomeres were the longest.

So, how do you end up with long telomeres? Some of it is the luck of the draw, as some people are born with telomeres that are up to two to three times longer than other people's. But some of it is also well within your control. People who consumed a Mediterranean diet—characterized by a high intake of vegetables, nuts, legumes, unrefined grains, olive oil, and fish, and a low intake of dairy, meat, and poultry—had longer telomeres than those who did not follow a Mediterranean eating plan, found a study of 4,676 women that was published in the *British Medical Journal.*

If this research on telomeres intrigues you, you can discover the state of your telomeres by undergoing a simple blood test for as little as $99. Similar to the mail-in DNA tests, you just buy a telomere test kit, such as Teloyears, online or over-the-counter, send a little blood sample away, and get your results in 6 to 8 weeks. We sent away for ours. The waiting was a little anxiety-producing. What if the test revealed that Liz was still 28 while Steve was 70? Or vice versa.

When the results arrived, it was a relief: We were more compatible than we ever realized. We're both 41 in chronological years, and, according to our telomeres, we're also both 31 in biological years. Whew!

Calorie Restriction:
Do Fewer Calories Equal Fewer Biological Years?

One of the greatest ironies in human existence: You need food to live, but the act of digesting and extracting energy from food stresses your body. The more you eat, the more stress your body undergoes. In our world of super-sizing and all-you-can-eat buffets, it's easy to overdo it, which is probably why nearly 70 percent of Americans are overweight or obese. Obesity leads to a host of health problems, including cardiovascular disease, type 2 diabetes, and some forms of cancer.

Adding to the irony, the only surefire way scientists have been able to slow down the aging process in animal studies is by restricting how much those animals eat.

The first studies on calorie restriction and lifespan took place in the 1930s, when scientists found that laboratory rats fed a calorie-restricted diet lived up to 40-percent longer than mice fed a normal amount.

Since then, researchers have done more studies, and restricting calories has been shown to prolong life in flies, yeast, worms, and monkeys. In one of them, researchers put a group of rhesus monkeys on low-calorie diets and compared them to another group of monkeys who were allowed to eat as much as they wanted. When the study concluded 25 years later, the big-eaters were three times more likely to have died, compared to the dieting monkeys.

It's important to note that caloric restriction does not appear to increase lifespan in *all* animals (some calorie-restricted mice died sooner than mice allowed to eat all they wanted!) and research on humans is still in its infancy, although the results are promising. Calorie restriction does seem to drop fasting glucose, total cholesterol, body weight, body fat, and DNA damage. It may also help mitochondria to function more effectively.

Why does it work? One theory suggests that by metabolizing fewer calories, there's less oxidative damage—wear and tear—on the cells. Other theories suggest that the lack of nutrients caused by calorie restriction might cause the body to build up defense mechanisms that make it more resilient. And, other research still shows that calorie restriction might influence the balance of hormones, rate of cell senescence, or expression of genes that affect aging. Really, it's probably a combination of these factors and others yet to be discovered.

The biggest issue with calorie restriction is its practicality. To pull it off, you'd need to consume roughly 30 percent less than you are currently eating. A normal diet consists of about 2,000 calories per day for a woman and 2,500 calories for a man. Therefore, a calorie-restricted diet would be no more than 1,400 calories per day for a woman and 1,750 calories for a man.

Cutting a normal diet by 30 percent is challenging. Thankfully, there's an easier approach that may be just as effective—and you'll learn about it in Chapter 9.

Stress:
How Much Can We Take?

We all encounter stress in our lives, both psychological and biological. Psychological stress results from factors like a demanding job or a death in the family. Biological stress comes from the processes we undergo every day—eating food, breathing air, controlling our body temperature, eliminating waste, and so on.

Much like inflammation, a certain amount of stress is normal, even beneficial. Without a rise in the stress hormone cortisol, most of us would never find the gumption to get out of bed in the morning. And, this same hormone is what helps us to think clearly.

But, problems result over prolonged periods of stress. Mothers of severely sick children and caregivers of people with Alzheimer's disease, for example, have shortened telomeres relative to other people their age, a few studies have found.

Stress can also leave behind harmful by-products called free radicals, which are reactive atoms in the body that have one or more unpaired electrons. As we breathe, eat, and do all the other things we need to do to live, the mitochondria in our cells sometimes produce these free radicals—a process called oxidation. Environmental factors, such as sun exposure, tobacco smoke, and pollution can produce free radicals too. The immune system uses free radicals to attack invaders like viruses and bacteria. Free radicals also help nerve cells communicate. But, most free radicals cause damage to other molecules, such as proteins and DNA. Our bodies are capable of neutralizing these substances, but too many stressors that last too long may flood the body with more free radicals than the immune system can handle. Over time, the damage accumulates, producing even more free radicals and a vicious cycle.

Free radicals contribute to many diseases and conditions, including atherosclerosis, cancer, neurodegeneration (neuron death that can lead to diseases like Alzheimer's and Parkinson's), and cataracts, and they may also affect how we age.

The good news is that substances called antioxidants can help protect you from free radical damage. You can get antioxidants in your diet from foods like berries and fruits and vegetables high in vitamin C. Remember that Mediterranean diet we mentioned earlier? It's loaded with antioxidant powerhouses and we'll show you how you can eat more of these foods.

Three

Determine Your True Health Age

Your true Health Age doesn't always equal the number of candles on your birthday cake. Depending on your genetics and lifestyle, you can age much more quickly or slowly. Based on physical health, your energy level, and your appearance, your Health Age may be in the thirties, forties, or fifties, even if you were born more than 60 years ago.

One way to see where you stand is to take a telomere test, as Steve and I did (see page 14 in Chapter 2). An easier and more immediate way to determine your true Health Age, however, is to take the quiz below.

Keep in mind that your score on this quiz isn't set in stone. As you apply more secrets and advice from Chapters 5 through 9, retake the quiz and watch your Health Age drop.

What is your waist circumference?

A. I am a woman and it is greater than 35 inches (+15)

B. I am a man and it is greater than 40 inches (+15)

C. I am a woman and it is 35 inches or less (-7)

D. I am a man and it is 40 inches or less (-7)

How often do you exercise for at least 30 minutes a day (any activity that is moderate to vigorous counts)?

A. I'm kind of a couch potato (+5)

B. I take a walk now and then (+3)

C. I exercise once or twice a week (-4)

D. I exercise three to four times a week (-7)

E. I exercise five or more times a week (-11)

Do you strength-train?

A. Never (+2)

B. Occasionally (0)

C. About once a week (-1)

D. Yes, at least two times a week (-3)

How much alcohol do you drink?

A. I have more than 3 drinks per day, equaling more than 21 per week (+10)

B. I drink 8 to 20 drinks a week, spread evenly throughout the week (+7)

C. I don't drink during the week, but I usually have 5 or more drinks on the weekend (+7)

D. I have a drink less than twice a month (0)

E. I have 2 to 7 drinks a week, spread out evenly throughout the week (-1)

How often do you feel happy?

A. Rarely. I'm usually unhappy. (+2)

B. Sometimes (0)

C. Pretty often. I'm generally happy. (-3)

D. All the time. I consider myself a very happy person. (-4)

How would you rate your energy level?

A. I feel sluggish most of the time (+5)

B. Sometimes, I feel sleepy in the afternoon (+3)

C. Most of the time, I have energy to do the things I need to do (-4)

D. I have energy to spare at the end of the day (-7)

How many friends/family members do you know you can count on?

A. I tend to deal with crises on my own (+2)

B. I can count them on one hand (0)

C. About a dozen (-2)

D. I have lots of people to support me (-5)

Compared to people my age, I think I look:

A. Older than other people my age (+7)

B. About the same (0)

C. Healthy, vibrant, and younger (-7)

How often do you read, do puzzles, or engage in other activities that exercise your brain?

A. Rarely or never (+3)

B. A few times a month (0)

C. A few times a week (-3)

D. Every day (-4)

What do you do when you feel stressed?

A. Try to ignore it or raid the pantry (+5)

B. It depends on my mood–I've tried all of these things at some point (0)

C. Practice deep breathing exercises, go for a walk, or run (-2)

How often do you enjoy a burger, steak, or other red meat?

A. Every day–it's not a meal without meat, right? (+12)

B. One to three times a week (+5)

C. About once or twice a month (-2)

D. Never. I don't eat red meat. (-5)

What role do cigarettes or other tobacco products play in your life?

A. I smoke (+20)

B. I quit smoking, but have lingering health problems (+10)

C. I consider myself a "social smoker" (+9)

D. I smoked in the past, but I quit and feel good (+4)

E. None–I've never smoked (0)

Do you have any discomfort in your joints?

A. Yes, constantly (+10)

B. A little, but it comes and goes (+3)

C. No (-5)

How often do you eat fish high in omega-3 fatty acids (such as tuna, salmon, or mackerel)?

A. Never. I don't like fish. (+2)

B. Once or twice a month (0)

C. Once a week (-4)

D. At least two times a week (-5)

How many fruits and vegetables do you eat per day?

A. I don't eat many fruits and vegetables (+7)

B. One or two (0)

C. Three or four (-5)

D. Five or more (-7)

Do you volunteer in your community?

A. I don't volunteer (+2)

B. I donate money to charities once in awhile (0)

C. I volunteer once a year (-1)

D. I volunteer a few times a year (-3)

E. My calendar includes at least one volunteer activity a week (-4)

How much beauty sleep do you get?

A. It depends on the night; I frequently have trouble sleeping (+7)

B. Usually 4 to 5 hours (+5)

C. Most nights I get 6 to 7 hours (-3)

D. Whenever I can, I get 8 hours (-4)

How often do you go to the doctor?

A. Never (+3)

B. Only if I'm sick (0)

C. Once a year for a checkup with my family doctor (-3)

D. I go for all the recommended appointments and screenings for my age group (-4)

Do you have a pet you love and enjoy?

A. No (0)

B. Yes (-5)

How much water do you drink per day?

A. I don't drink water (+2)

B. One to seven glasses (0)

C. Eight or more glasses (-3)

How often do you eat sweets or other refined foods?

A. After every meal (+5)

B. Once a day (+3)

C. A few times a week (0)

D. Rarely to never (-5)

Do you eat organic foods?

A. No (+2)

B. Rarely (0)

C. Sometimes (-1)

D. As much as I can (-2)

E. I only eat organic (-3)

Are you making strides toward achieving lifelong goals (traveling, hiking mountains, running a marathon, writing a book, etc.)?

A. I don't really have any goals (+2)

B. I have active plans in the works (0)

C. Yes, I've already accomplished some of them! (-2)

TO GET YOUR RESULTS:

Add and/or subtract the numbers from each response to get a total score. Divide that total by 10. If the result is a positive number, add that number to your chronological age. If it is a negative number, subtract it from your chronological age. The result equals your Health Age.

For example, if you are 51 years old and your final score is -60, first divide 60 by 10 to get 6. Then, subtract that number from your chronological age. 51- 6 = 45. Your Health Age is 45!

Here's how Steve and I did:

With a chronological age of 41, I ended up with a Health Age of 34.6, which is quite close to the result of the telomere test. I attribute my low Health Age to my diet (I eat lots of vegetables and fruits) and exercise habits (I exercise every day). But, I'm not perfect, and this Health Age quiz helped me to see that. I need to work on a few things, namely the amount of sugar I eat, managing stress, watching the things that cause my joints to ache, and making sure that I'm moving toward achieving life goals.

Also with a chronological age of 41, Steve ended up with a Health Age of 35—again, a result that closely mirrored his telomere test. He's proactive when it comes to exercise, healthy eating, and setting and meeting goals. However, the quiz taught him to to be better about going for regular check-ups (ironic considering that he is a doctor, but not surprising considering he is a male). He is also a past smoker; there is nothing he can do about that now, but it did affect his Health Age.

Four

A Short Guide
to the Secrets

In Chapters 5 to 9, you'll get to meet the more than 30 of the World's Healthiest People that we extensively interviewed for this book. They range in age from 33 to 97, with the majority in their eighties and nineties. They're charismatic, engaging, and inspiring. We hope you enjoy reading about them as much as we enjoyed interviewing them. They were true joys to meet and know—and they have so much to teach us.

Based on our interviews, we culled the most salient secrets for living longer, better, and healthier. These secrets are not only based on the true tales of each person but also each secret is supported by the latest science, as well as Steve's observations in his work as an osteopathic physician.

Here, we offer an overview of what you can expect from the coming chapters, as well as give advice on putting the Secrets of the World's Healthiest People to work in your life.

Each chapter follows the same format.

It starts with the real-life stories of several of the World's Healthiest People. Each story reveals that person's secret, along with science and commentary from Steve that supports why it works and how to put it into practice. In the final section of each chapter, Steve includes an actionable prescription for becoming one of the World's Healthiest People.

Each chapter profiles people who fit into one of five categories, which correspond to the five traits of the World's Healthiest People:

Chapter Five: Be Able-Bodied. By far the biggest section of the book, this section shares the secrets of people in their eighties and nineties who are fit, happy, healthy, vibrant, and sharp. These are not your usual octogenarians and nonagenarians, however. Two of them regularly jump out of airplanes and bought a two-story house with steps...*on purpose*. Another one decided to start sprinting at the age of 95 and broke two world records just a year later. Yet another ran her first marathon in her seventies—and is still running them in her nineties. And, we couldn't help but fall completely in love with the 97-year-old who wears heels more confidently than many women in their twenties.

Chapter 6: Be Spunky. These people wake refreshed, think clearly all day long, and generally feel incredible and invincible. This chapter includes stories of people who have overcome issues with fatigue, anxiety, depression, and lack of focus.

Chapter 7: Be Well. The World's Healthiest People profiled in this chapter sail through cold and flu season without a sniffle, and they fend off (or bounce back from) health problems like diabetes, heart disease, osteoporosis, autoimmune issues, cancer, and more.

Chapter 8: Be Unbreakable. In this chapter, you'll meet people who have not let hardship stand in their way of living good lives. Whether they lost their eyesight, were born with a rare, progressive disease, or suffered a debilitating injury, the World's Healthiest People we interviewed for this chapter teach us how to overcome hardship and persevere.

Chapter 9: Be Fit and Trim. We profile people who can still fit into their high school jeans, as well as people who once gained weight, lost it, and have now kept it off for years.

How to Navigate the Stories

Everyone has unique strengths, weaknesses, and risk factors, and the people we talked to are no exception. The stories in this book cover the gamut. Some of the World's Healthiest People revealed just one overriding secret, whereas others offer many different paths toward optimal health. We suggest that you read the stories that speak to you. You might zero in on the people who closely mirror your life. Or, you might choose to read and then

re read the stories of people whose lives are vastly different from yours. You're in the driver's seat.

If you prefer a systematic approach, flip to chapters 10 and 11. In Chapter 11, you'll find a step-by-step plan that helps you to incorporate the secrets of the World's Healthiest People into your life. In Chapter 11, you'll find mix and match menu options that guide you in eating like the World's Healthiest People.

Yet another strategy: Just take one tip from a story that speaks to you and incorporate it into your life for 30 days. Then, reflect on how you feel. If you feel better, continue with the advice and try to make it a permanent habit. When you're ready, try another tip for 30 days, and so on.

The World's Healthiest People Index

To help you get to the stories that resonate with you the most, here's a quick cheat sheet.

IF YOU HAVE JOINT PAIN, READ:
Steve Colwell, page 46
Amy Morosini, page 169
Derk Richardson, page 181
Diogo Teixeira, page 174
Kari Dougan, page 190

IF YOU'RE STRUGGLING WITH YOUR WEIGHT, READ:
Natalie Jill, page 205
Jeanette Alosi, page 106
Deb Gordon, page 200
Dan Berlin, page 160

IF YOU ARE OLDER THAN 60, READ:
Steve Colwell, page 46
Charles Eugster, page 37
Honey Kimball, page 83
Pat Moorehead, page 30
Rick Connella, page 65
Ann Jarrett, page 78

Barbara Packman, page 156
Bob Morris, page 34
Harriet Thompson, page 43
Walt Hoffman, page 69
Murray Grossan, page 122
Jim Yenckel, page 141

IF YOU'RE DEALING WITH A SERIOUS ILLNESS OR HANDICAP, READ:
Ed Shimer, page 137
Louise Gooche, page 133
Sarah Doan, page 165
Amy Morosini, page 169
Dan Berlin, page 160
Jim Yenckel, page 141
Harriet Thompson, page 43

**IF YOU'RE BATTLING HEALTH ISSUES LIKE FATIGUE,
ANXIETY, DEPRESSION, OR OTHER MENTAL ILLNESS, READ:**
Natalie Jill, page 205
Deb Gordon, page 200
Amy Morosini, page 169
Sarah Doan, page 165
Allison Laframboise, page 100

IF YOU'RE STRUGGLING WITH HARDSHIP OR PERSONAL TRAGEDY, READ:
Barbara Packman, page 156
Kathy Shaffer, page 111
Ann Jarrett, page 78
Kari Dougan, page 190
Sarah Doan, page 165
Mary Etter, page 127

FOR DIETARY INSPIRATION, READ:
Filomena Warihay, page 195
Amy Morosini, page 169
Dan Berlin, page 160
Natalie Jill, page 205

Dan Berlin, page 160
Amy Morosini, page 169
Diane Silver, page 149

Of course, we hope you appreciate reading about these impressive people as much as we enjoyed meeting them, hearing about their lives, and writing about their secrets to being such vibrant, healthy individuals. Okay, let's get started!

Five

Be Able-Bodied

When Steve and I talk about the future (aka older age), we picture long walks, relaxing days by the ocean with our grandchildren, and a trip to a new country or surf destination now and then. Steve has always dreamed of opening a little beach café.

Never do we discuss Meals on Wheels, walkers, or other assistance we never think we'll need.

Surveys tell us that most people want to "age in place." In other words, we want to remain independent in our homes. But only 4 percent of people over 90 report being able to perform all their daily activities without assistance, according to a University of Michigan study of more than 8,000 older adults. This doesn't mean that the future is hopeless; you just need to plan for it. Succeeding or failing to live independently, in large part, requires you to make the right decisions at the right times in your life.

As these stories will show, there are so many things that we *can do* to make our later years as healthy—or, dare we say healthier?—as the first half of our lives. Not only will the stories amaze you, they will give you practical, actionable advice on how you can overcome age-related joint issues and stay strong and supple, just like these incredible people have done.

Pat & Alicia Moorehead's Secret

Grow Old Adventurously

. . . .

Attack your bucket list

Do acts of kindness

Buy a house with stairs—and never stop climbing them

. . . .

Pat Moorehead, 85, and Alicia Moorehead, 70, are not taking aging lying down. In fact, they're doing it while flying through the atmosphere at 13,000 feet.

"I've always been annoyed with the phrase 'grow old gracefully' because I think it gives people an excuse to sit down and shut up," says Pat. "As an alternative, I recently came up with the phrase 'grow old adventurously.' "

The avid jumpers met on a skydiving trip to Mexico 33 years ago, and they have collectively made nearly 10,000 jumps. (As two people who have never skydived but have considered it, Steve and I found this comforting. If they've done that many jumps safely, the perceived odds of surviving a single skydive just got a whole lot better). They've landed everywhere from a glacier in Switzerland, the Red Sea, and one of the Jordanian deserts. They've traveled to more than 200 destinations, including Syria, North Korea, Libya, Kurdistan, and Iraq, usually without booking a single hotel room prior to arriving. (What?!) They took sledgehammers and helped knock down the Berlin Wall. The couple have a sense of adventure that most 20-year-olds wouldn't dream of and they have no desire to slow down. "We plan to 'keep on keeping on,' " Pat says.

To Steve and I, the definition of "keeping on" is getting through the weeks without getting buried in laundry or missing one of our kids' activities. The Mooreheads' definition of "keeping on" makes us look like slackers.

Using Curiosity to Cross Cultural Barriers

An important part of the Mooreheads' grow-old adventurously mode is travel, specifically to countries that take them out of their comfort zone.

"We have visited many countries—more than 200—and there are still many destinations on our list. We will do our best to visit them as well," he says. They've been to places many would consider too volatile for a getaway, sometimes jumping right into the fire. "When we were visiting Greece, they were having a protest in the main square about austerity measures and economic problems, so we walked down to check it out...and ended up getting ourselves teargassed!" Pat recalls.

Throughout all these places that many would deem too dangerous or difficult, Pat and Alicia have met friendly people everywhere. "It doesn't matter if you speak the language or not—you can have a meaningful interaction," Pat says. "We made a rule a few years ago—if we see something that sparks our interest, we stop to look." It started as the couple was driving on the Autobahn and realized they were going in the wrong direction. "We pulled off to look at the map and Alicia pointed down a road and said, 'what's that?' It was the road to Lichtenstein so we just kept going to check it out!" That trip added another country to their list.

To keep their options open, they avoid booking hotel rooms ahead of time and, instead, choose to wing it so they don't miss anything. "We're prepared to sleep in our car, but we've never had to do it," Pat continues, though he then made sure to tell us about the one time they came close. "We were driving down this dark road in the outback of Spain and the prospects looked dim. Then we stumbled upon this tiny village and, right at the start, there was this magnificent restored castle that had a room available. We stayed the night and it was magical."

As Steve and I listened, we found this part of their planning most inspiring. Despite eye rolls from Steve, I'm someone who reads countless reviews on hotels before I choose one and I also spray the rooms down with Lysol before I let my family enter. It's a bit different from the Mooreheads' carefree approach and, admittedly, less fun. They have so much to teach me about living a good life. Perhaps, as you read, you are feeling the same.

What Goes Around Comes Around

In all their travel experiences, the couple enjoyed Buddhist countries Burma and Bhuton the most, probably because they mesh with their ideals. "In Bhuton, they don't measure gross national product; they measure gross national happiness—for real," Alicia says. Pat adds, "We are not particularly religious in this household, but we lean toward a Buddhist philosophy. We've stood on Buddhist pagodas (temples or sacred buildings that are typically multitiered) at dawn and dusk and the calmness is amazing."

One Buddhist belief the Mooreheads—particularly Pat—believe in strongly is karma. "Alicia and I are always kind and I think it's come back around for us," he says. "If you do good things, good things will happen to you...like finding a room in a castle down a dark road in the middle of the night."

As he approaches his 10th decade, Pat does admit that he has a few aches and pains. "The body breaks down naturally—it just does—but you don't have to succumb to it."

He had good foresight when he bought his two-story home back in 1968. "I don't like to move, so when I walked into the model and saw the stairs, I thought, 'Do I want to be climbing stairs in my eighties?' And I said to myself, 'Yes!'" Not only does he climb those stairs, he doesn't use the banister because he wants to continue to challenge his legs and balance. "People ask me, 'But what if you fall?' and I say, "If I fall, then I'll grab the banister. *Duh*!"

When we asked him how long they will keep on skydiving and traveling, the Mooreheads say they will do it as long as they can. "If we wanted to grow old gracefully, we might quit. But we choose to grow old adventurously, so we'll keep on keeping on."

Why It Works

When Steve and I sat down and talked about Pat and Alicia Moorehead, what stuck out was their refreshing approach to aging. They are truly living each day of their lives by taking risks, doing what they love, and embracing new experiences. More important, they are living their lives based on their felt age—and not on a stereotypical idea of what people their age should and can do.

Take Pat's plan to buy a house with stairs—and stay in it well into his eighties. That decision stands in stark contrast to what many people his age do: downsize into a ranch home with no stairs, no yard, and little upkeep. Yet, climbing stairs into older age can help keep the brain young, found a 2016 study published in *Neurobiology of Aging*. To get to their findings, the researchers used an MRI to look at the volume of gray matter in the brains of 331 adults ages 19 to 79. (Shrinking gray matter is evidence of the brain's aging process). They then compared the results to the participants' reported levels of stair-climbing and education. The more years of education and the more stairs climbed, the younger their brains.

Steve's Secrets

To maintain the physical dexterity and zest for life that the Mooreheads exhibit, do the following:

GET UP AND GO. Skydiving and traveling are popular items on a lot of bucket lists. Unfortunately, too often those lists end up in a drawer collecting dust. It's easy to say you will do something after this or that, but the reality is that you will always be able to find a reason to put it off. If you have a dream of doing something, the best time to do it is *now*.

IF YOU CAN, TAKE THE STAIRS. We all know that we should take the stairs, but sometimes, when our hands are full or it's the end of the day, it's all too tempting to jump in the elevator instead. We admit it—we do this too. Next time you have the choice, if you are able, go for the stairs, not just for your body but for your brain.

LIVE IN THE MOMENT. Talking to the Mooreheads opened up a dialogue in the Bowers' house about the importance of being present. We talked about how we notice that so many people (including ourselves and our kids, at times) are constantly thinking about the next thing instead of enjoying what's going on at that particular moment. This is unfortunate, because it leads to a pattern where we only get enjoyment from memories of experiences, not the actual experiences themselves. By not booking hotel rooms ahead of time and doing spontaneous things, like taking detours to Lichtenstein, the Mooreheads do a good job of this. Try to emulate this behavior by taking pleasure in the here and now.

Bob Morris's Secret

It's Never Too Late to Get in Shape

. . . .

Pick fun classes that you enjoy

Include a wide variety of fitness options

Exercise with other people

. . . .

*"It was my mother who first told me about Bob Morris.
As she puts it, "He's such a joy to have
in exercise class–he makes us all laugh."*

That would be Zumba class, by the way. Bob is the only man in the class. He also takes Pilates and he's the only man in that class as well.

"I asked the instructors to confirm that it didn't make the women uncomfortable to have a man in the class. Apparently, it doesn't. I actually think they love me," jokes the 80-year-old.

Bob's right; the women in his exercise classes love him. A former aerobics instructor, Mom raves about Bob's deep knee bends. "I don't know if I've ever seen someone get so low. He's amazing," she says.

As I talked to Bob, I started to understand why my mom and the other women in her exercise class find him such a nice addition. He is about as warm and pleasant as they come. As we spoke, his genuine enthusiasm for every aspect of his life—from his morning Cheerios with milk to the books he reads in the afternoon—shined through.

I got the sense that he has always been pleasant, but he hasn't always been so nimble. A few years ago, when he was 77, he was playing senior softball and saw his skills taking a plunge. He also had a few pounds to lose. So he recently added the YMCA to his list of pleasures and it's made a huge difference.

"Since I joined the Y 3 years ago, I feel younger, l look thinner; life is better!" he says. "I may be in the best physical shape ever. I've made wonderful friends, my blood pressure is lower than it's ever been, and

I've lost 25 pounds—I'm back at my high-school weight!" At 6'1", Bob weighs a svelte 172.

Pushing Harder Than the Average 80-Year-Old

Bob goes to the Y every day except Sunday, 1½ to 2 hours a day, for a total of 10 to 11 hours of activity a week. He has tailored his exercise routine to his preferences and body type. If he doesn't like a form of movement or an instructor, he switches to a different class.

"I tried tai chi, for example, and although I think it's a beneficial activity, it wasn't for me—it was too slow and not enough activity," he says.

When we talked, the breakdown looked something like this:

MONDAYS—Pilates and yoga

TUESDAYS—an hour of yoga, a half-hour balance class, and a half hour of cardio

WEDNESDAYS—a Fit N 50 class that blends cardio, balance, strength, core, and flexibility

THURSDAYS—cardio fusion followed by a chair yoga class

FRIDAYS—Zumba

• • • • • • • • • • • •

Exercising with AFib

At 80, Bob is in far better health than most men his age. "My doctors are pleased," he says.

However, a routine wellness exam 2 years ago revealed that he has atrial fibrillation (AFib), a quivering or irregular heartbeat that can lead to blood clots, stroke, or heart failure. "I never had shortness of breath, dizziness, or any of the classic symptoms, even when I was exercising, so it was a bit of a shock," he says. Luckily, the diagnosis has in no way slowed down his exercise routine. "I just take a blood thinner once a day and if it weren't for that, I wouldn't even know I had it. If this is my one condition at my age, I'll take it!"

You may wonder: should Bob be exercising to the level he is with AFib? Absolutely.

A review published in the December 2015 issue of *Canadian Family Physician* found a connection between increased levels of exercise and decreased incidence of AFib in women. The same was true in men who exercised at a low to moderate intensity. Of course, every person is different. If you are concerned about exercising with AFib, talk to your cardiologist.

One activity Bob does shy away from is heavy lifting. "I'm not into the barbell stuff—I don't need to be Charles Atlas!" Instead, he uses the 5-pound hand weights in his Pilates classes to get his strength-training fix.

Bob is quite proud of his routine—"I think I push myself much harder than the average 80-year-old guy," he says.

Why It Works

Whether you are 55 or 95, you're never too old to start working out, as long as you are healthy enough to do so.

A key factor for Bob is likely his enjoyment of his workout routine. He looks forward to his exercise classes and takes pleasure in every minute. Research shows that exercise is more beneficial when people enjoy it than when they sweat and bear it just to get it done. A 2014 study done at the Cornell Food and Brand Lab found that people who exercise for the fun of it are less likely to eat afterward than people who work out purely for weight loss. And, research published in *Preventive Medicine* found that adults who exercised in groups reported 1.4 times more activity than those who exercised alone.

Zumba is also a good idea for Bob. Researchers at the University of Wisconsin-La Crosse's Department of Exercise and Sport Science looked into the cardiovascular and calorie-burning benefits of Zumba and found the Latin dance to be more than just fun. Researchers found that participants were at an average of 64 percent of VO_2 max, which is neatly within the recommended range of 40 percent to 85 percent. In addition, Zumba dancers burned an average of 364 calories per class— beating out cardio kickboxing and step aerobics and coming close to boot camp. Plus, Zumba is full body and works most major muscle groups.

Steve's Secrets

Use this advice to ease into an exercise program at any age.

PERSONALIZE YOUR PROGRAM. Bob is smart to go for exercise classes that target all the factors he needs to work on at his age—balance, cardiovascular health, muscle strength, and flexibility. Most gyms and YMCAs have a variety of exercise classes for seniors. Try to attend a mix, so you work on all fitness elements and muscle groups.

Keep in mind that your muscles will probably feel sore for 24 to 48 hours following a new activity (called delayed onset muscle soreness or DOMS). DOMS is normal and should gradually subside as your muscles get used to the activity.

FIND SOME FRIENDS. Bob says that one of the things he likes the most about his Y routine is the social interaction. When you socialize with people in your exercise classes, you will make friends you can do things with outside of class, plus it gives you extra motivation not to miss classes.

IF YOU DON'T LIKE AN ACTIVITY, STOP. As the Cornell study showed, continuing a workout routine that you don't enjoy can be counterproductive. If you find that an activity or class is becoming tedious, stop. It can create the perfect *opportunity to try something new.*

Charles Eugster's Secret

Work Out As If You're Half Your Age

. . . .

Strength-train to maximize mental and physical health

Eat more protein

Avoid sugar and processed foods

. . . .

When I came across a photo of Charles Eugster, I just knew I had to talk to him. I had to find out how he did it! Was he a genetic anomaly? Or, did he possess a secret that I could copy—one that would allow me to wear a bikini at age 98 and walk down the beach proudly, knowing that my 98-year-old husband is sitting and watching me and thinking to himself, "Yes, that's *my* wife, and yes, she still looks fine."

Thankfully, we did manage to track him down and talk to him. Sadly, he died about six weeks later.

Still, I would bet you a million dollars that, in the months before his death, Charles could have beat me in a push-ups contest. He was 97 when we met—that's 56 years older than I am and 15 years older than Steve and my ages *combined.*

And, I'm pretty sure that he was fitter, slimmer, and leaner.

Charles' story starts 35 years ago, when things were going quite well for him. He had a thriving dental practice in Switzerland and was happily married, with two sons. "All was good, except I was a self-satisfied lump of lard," he told me, with his characteristic dry wit. So, he decided to do something about the physical condition he had put on hold for 40 years. He entered a rowing competition for veterans in their sixties and his love of fitness was reborn.

About 16 years later, at age 78, Charles started rowing internationally for the World Masters Regatta, which involved 6 days a week of training. He went on to win 40 masters gold medals. "But at about age 86," he said, "I began to notice that my body was deteriorating. Being the extremely vain person that I am, I wanted to do something about it." That's when his fitness career *really* took off.

At 87, Charles began training with the bodybuilding organization, Mr. Universe. The oldest category of competitors starts at age 50—37 years younger than Charles was at the time. He changed his diet and lost 12 kilos (the equivalent of 26.46 pounds). "By the age of 90, my body was completely rebuilt," he said. At 95, he started sprinting. At 96, he broke two world records, for the 200-meter indoor and 400-meter outdoor sprints. When he turned 97, he wrote a book about healthy aging. When we spoke, he was closing in on 98, and he still showed no sign of slowing down.

As we were interviewing Charles, Steve and I glanced at each other a few times in amazement. The man was doing 50 push-ups in 45 seconds and I can do a max of 10—on my knees. Steve's in decent shape and can do many more than I can, but still, we were humbled.

In addition to the push-ups, Charles still sprinted up until his death, and he spent several hours a week at the gym. (Another humbling moment: I don't even have a gym membership).

"At the moment, my trainer and I are trying to preserve my muscle. Losing your muscle mass is something that causes frailty in old age and can literally kill you," Charles told us. "My trainer believes in functional training, which is training groups of muscles rather than individuals ones." The ultimate goal of functional training is to perform activities that carry over into everyday living, such as balance exercises, stretching, and agility drills.

"With exercise, one should have a goal—it's extremely important to know what you are aiming for—not just to have a beach body." We heard similar advice from a number of the people we interviewed for this book. They don't necessarily find their motivation to exercise from wanting to look good in a bikini. They mostly get it from wanting to continually be able to climb stairs, hoist bags into overhead compartments, and perform all of the other tasks of daily living.

All of this said, Charles *was still* turning the heads of some young 70-year old ladies on the beach. "I think vanity in old age is an enormous asset," he said.

Powering with Proper Foods

In addition to his exercise routine, Charles credited his high-fat, Paleo-style diet for his incredible physique. "Our modern-day idea of nutrition is so completely different from anything in the past and it's having a devastating effect," he said. He pointed to the obesity and diabetes epidemics. "Obviously, we're doing something wrong," he said.

Charles ate his meals off a smaller plate—a dessert plate. On that plate, he served up fruit for breakfast, and for other meals, protein and fat. To keep his muscles strong, after exercising, he drank a protein shake containing a combination of whey protein and the amino acid leucine, which can help build proteins and muscle mass. Steve and I drink a daily protein shake too—one point for us!

"In order to build muscle, you need a lot of protein, and, in old age, your protein synthesis is reduced," Charles said. "Protein supplements are a good way to make sure you get what you need." Charles said if he could, he would develop a protein supplement specifically designed for older people who want to build muscle. Because the market for this may be limited (let's face it, the Charles Eugsters out there are few and far between), he settled for what's already out there.

Charles ate full-octane foods—nothing that is reduced fat or skim "I like cream, butter, cheese—all the things they tell us we're not supposed to eat. I find they do me good, because they supply me with energy for a long period of time. Of course, my energy expenditure is high," he added. "For someone whose expenditure is low, this diet would not be good."

Agreed, it would not be good for someone with a low-energy expenditure, and here's a disclaimer: Just like his workout routine, Charles' diet is extreme to say the least, particularly when it comes to the fat aspect. Steve doesn't recommend eating a lot of saturated, animal sources of fat. Instead, he prefers monounsaturated forms like olive oil and fatty fish.

But, back to Charles. As much as he sought out protein and fat, he avoids sugar. "It's an absolute no-no," he said. He also abstained from alcohol for the most part (unless he was drinking champagne with a pretty lady) and made sure to eat a variety of different foods and only fresh or frozen—nothing from a can.

Why It Works

As you age, you lose muscle mass—anywhere from 0.5 to 2 percent per year starting at age 50, to be exact. The good news is that you can fight back by eating more protein and getting plenty of exercise.

When it comes to amino acids, animal sources provide all we need. Other protein sources, like vegetables, grains, nuts, and seeds, provide some amino acids but not a complete set. Your best bet is to eat a variety of sources of protein, from poultry to fish to meat to nuts.

Charles was also wise to eliminate sugar from his diet. Cutting sugar can lower your risk of diabetes, heart disease, tooth decay, and weight gain. Too much sugar can also make your skin look wrinkled and dull, according to a study published in the *British Journal of Dermatology*. During a process called glycation, sugar in the bloodstream attaches to proteins to create harmful new particles called advanced glycation end products (AGEs). Eating more sugar equals more AGEs and therefore, more damage to the collagen and elastin fibers that keep skin elastic and firm. Without elastin and collagen, skin becomes brittle, dry, and saggy. As if that weren't bad enough, AGEs also make skin more vulnerable to sun damage, which is the biggest enemy to young-looking skin.

A low-sugar diet can also help your brain. Seventy- and 80-year-olds who consumed high-carbohydrate diets were nearly two times more likely to develop mild cognitive impairment (MCI) than people who ate fewer carbs and more protein and fat (a diet more like the one Charles followed), found a study done at the Mayo Clinic and published in the *Journal of Alzheimer's Disease*. Study participants with the highest sugar intake were also 1.5 times more likely to experience MCI than those with the lowest intake.

Interestingly, the same study found that the participants who consumed the highest intakes of fat were 42 percent less likely to suffer from cognitive impairment than those with the lowest fat intakes; those with the highest protein intakes reduced their MCI risk by 21 percent.

With his eating plan, Charles may have prolonged his already long life too. In a study published in the journal, researchers fed mice a standard diet or a diet containing 25-percent added sugar—the equivalent of humans consuming three cans of soda. The female mice on the sugar diet died at twice the rate of the female mice consuming the standard diet. The male mice were 25-percent less likely to reproduce and maintain their territory. In other words, they got lazy and their libidos went down.

Steve's Secrets

We have to admit, we were inspired by Charles' regimen and resultant age defiance, especially the part that involves avoiding sugar and processed foods. We've both become more conscious of empty calories since Charles came across our radar screens. But with that being said, we don't expect you—or us!—to turn into Charles Eugster; he was an exceptional human specimen. To get a little bit closer, try the following:

OPTIMIZE YOUR PROTEIN INTAKE. How much protein should I get, you ask? To find out your daily protein needs, multiply your weight in pounds by 0.36. So, if you weigh 140 pounds, you should eat 50.4 grams of protein per day.

Good sources of protein include a quality protein shake, poultry, fish, and meat.

Here's a quick breakdown of some foods and the protein they supply.

1 pork chop: 41 grams

6 ounces broiled Porterhouse steak: 40 grams

6 ounces wild salmon: 34 grams

½ cup peanut butter: 32.5 grams

3 ounces turkey breast: 29 grams

1 cup lentils: 18 grams

1 cup edamame: 16 grams

Remember that Charles's lifestyle—both his exercise and eating regimens—were extreme. The average person should not be shoveling down as much animal protein and fat as he did. In fact, a diet high in red meat is associated with higher rates of cardiovascular disease and death. In the Nurses' Health Study, for example, researchers found that, for every additional 3-ounce portion of unprocessed red meat the participants consumed, their risk of dying from cardiovascular disease rose 13 percent.

CUT OUT PROCESSED FOODS. Charles's diet plan was all about eating like a hunter-gatherer, long before there were packaged baked goods or Velveeta cheese. You certainly can't go wrong with eating a clean, unprocessed diet. Go for raw nuts, seeds, and fruits and vegetables in their fresh or frozen form.

ELIMINATE SUGAR. Cutting sugar out of your diet is one of those things that is easier said than done. (I have a pretty good diet, but I love chocolate and peanut butter ice cream, especially when I'm at the beach and paying more attention to fun than health.) Problem is, sugar hides in all sorts of products that you might not expect, including salad dressings, spaghetti sauces, breads, and ketchup. Here are some ways to cut back.

- *Look for aliases.* **You won't always see "sugar" on an ingredients label. It may hide behind high-fructose corn syrup, molasses, sucrose, or any other word ending in -ose, dried cane syrup, brown rice syrup, or honey.**

- *Go for foods that are unsweetened or have no sugar added.* **Avoid artificial sweeteners, such as aspartame and sorbitol, which can still stimulate weight gain.**

- *Add some spice.* **On foods where you would normally use sugar, such as on cereal or in coffee, try adding some cinnamon instead. We did this with our kids; not only do they love it, they think they're getting away with something at breakfast. With the flavor of this spice, you won't even miss the sweetness. As a bonus, cinnamon has been shown to help regulate blood sugar and control appetite.**

Harriet Thompson's Secret

Never Tell Yourself That You're Too Old–Because You're Not

. . . .

It is possible to run a marathon in your nineties. You got this!

Practice positive self-talk

Donate your time for a good cause

. . . .

Both Steve and I run. Steve is more off and on; I've run almost every day since I was 14. That's 28 years of about 30 miles a week, or a total of nearly 44,000 miles. But, I have to admit, running 26.2 miles in one shot scares the heck out of me. One of the reasons is that I think I'm too old.

Well, I ate my words when I talked to Harriet Thompson, who is 94. The woman decided to train for her first marathon at age 76! And, she was relatively a spring chicken. Twenty years later, at age 92, she became the oldest woman ever to complete a marathon.

"I don't understand why they made such a fuss over it—I wasn't going very fast!" she says with genuine modesty.

Uh, we understand the fuss...

Harriet proceeded to tell us she ran the San Diego Rock 'n' Roll marathon in 7 hours, 24 minutes, which beat the previous record for a woman 90 or older by a half-hour. That breaks down to just under 17 minutes per mile. That's not bad at all for a nonrunner more than nine decades old and more than five decades my senior.

"How do you do it?" I asked. I mean, I'm 41 and I've never run a marathon. I've never even thought of signing up for one. I can't imagine just getting up and running one at age 76—three-and-a-half decades from now. But, I also like to think of myself as someone who could get up and run a marathon at age 76—because the alternative of *not* being able to run one terrifies me. We all want to keep the option open, right?

Her answer: "I'm positive," she tells me. "I never let myself think

I can't. When I'm running, I think to myself, 'This is easy—I can do this!'" A classically trained pianist who played in Carnegie Hall, Harriet plays piano pieces in her head to help her get through the race. Maybe, if I ever run a marathon, I can pace myself by writing happy stories in my head?

Doing Good for Others Does Good for You

But, there's something else that fuels her every step—a cause that inspires her to her core. Harriet lost a brother and a few friends to leukemia and a brother-in-law to lymphoma. She's battled oral cancer three times—in 1985, 2010, and again in 2016. When we spoke, she was undergoing radiation treatments and had recently gotten titanium screws in her cheekbones to help her eat and talk.

"I have never thought of myself as a runner. I just do the marathon for the cause," she says. Her special cause is the Leukemia and Lymphoma Foundation, for which she has run the race 16 times and raised tens of thousands of dollars.

In the past 19 years, she's only missed one marathon. It was in 2016, when she was nursing a painful open wound above her right ankle that she suffered from radiation treatment for squamous cell carcinoma. She did her best to stay in shape throughout the ordeal, with her sights set on the 2017 race.

Harriet says she stays on track by meeting with the Leukemia and Lymphoma Foundation's Team in Training every Saturday morning. "Most of them are in their twenties, so I don't go as fast as they do," she says. "And, when they run 20 miles, I do 8."

During our conversation, in her sweet way, Harriet asked me if I was a runner. I am, and I've completed numerous 5Ks and a half marathon. However, I admitted to her that I'm scared to try the big race and I'm more than 50 years her junior. "So, what's my excuse?" I joked.

Her response: "I don't think running 50 miles is a good idea, but once in a while, a marathon doesn't hurt."

Well put.

When we talked, she was planning to do the Rock 'n' Roll marathon again in June of 2017, for lucky number 17. "I don't know how far I will be able to go, but I'm definitely going to take a stab at it," she says.

As for me? We'll see if I ever get up the nerve.

Why It Works

People who are physically active age more slowly than people who are sedentary, research shows. The benefits may be particularly strong for people who, like Harriet, train for vigorous athletic competitions such as marathons. Older adults who continue to train and compete in athletic events were significantly less likely to suffer from chronic diseases and physical dysfunction, found a 2014 review on the relationship between aging and exercise published in the *Journal of the American Academy of Orthopaedic Surgeons.*

But you don't have to go as far as training for a marathon to boost your health, the study authors concluded. As long as you exercise vigorously, any type of regular activity helps reduce decline in aerobic capacity—the heart and lungs' ability to deliver oxygen to muscles—by up to 50 percent, the data shows.

You might think, as I did, that all of that running might save your heart, while destroying your limbs. The research has just one word for that thinking: hogwash. Older adults who engage in vigorous exercise are less likely to suffer injuries than their non-exercising counterparts, no matter their age. Maintaining muscle strength increases balance and reduces risk of falls, and falls are one of the leading causes of injuries for seniors.

Harriet is doing other good things for her body with her running program too. Research shows it can help prevent osteoporosis, arthritis, and injuries to ligaments and tendons. It can also help older adults live independently. When it comes to chronic diseases, regular physical activity helps combat heart disease, high blood pressure, colon and other cancers, and diabetes. It also helps individuals with chronic conditions such as Harriet's squamous cell cancer, to improve their stamina and strength. In terms of emotional health, exercise wards off depression, anxiety, and boosts happiness and well-being.

Steve's Secrets

If you are as inspired by Harriet's story as we were, use these tips to make your goal to run a distance race a reality.

JUST DO IT. If you've always fantasized about running a marathon or a half marathon or doing a triathlon or any other kind of race, take an honest look at what is stopping you. Chances are, it's nothing that you can't overcome. Think of Harriet crossing the finish line for the first time at age 76 and go for it. And, like Harriet does, consider running for a charity of your choice. Having a sponsor will keep you motivated and make the experience more rewarding, because you're doing it for a good cause.

JOIN AN EXERCISE GROUP. Harriet credits her Saturday morning Team in Training group for keeping her on track with her running regimen and inspiring her to go faster. Smart move. When it comes to maintaining a training program, accountability is key. And, many people need to be accountable to *others,* not just themselves, to stick with it. To find running buddies, check out the Road Runners Club of America (rrca.org) or Dailymile.com or strike up a conversation with runners in your neighborhood or park.

RUN ON OPTIMISM. Just as Harriet says, "This is easy—I can do this!" Saying positive things to yourself during a run or race can make the difference between doing your best and dropping out. Tell yourself, "It's a beautiful day," "I'm so lucky to be able to run," "This is great for my body," or "I feel fantastic." Say whatever speaks to you and inspires your feet to keep moving or move a little faster.

Steve Colwell's Secret

Be More Than Your Bad Knee (or Shoulder or Hip)

. . . .

Don't let a chronic injury stop you

Diversify your workouts

Play social sports

. . . .

You play pickleball on what looks like a tennis court, but you swat at what looks like a Wiffle ball with a small paddle that will probably remind you of table tennis. It's a sport that requires lots of sprinting, squatting, lunging, bending, and starting and stopping abruptly.

On any given Thursday (and sometimes Tuesdays), this is where you'll find 84-year-old Steve Colwell. As he sprints across the court, you'd probably never guess that his left knee has zero cartilage left to cushion his movements. Nor would you assume that he has a torn right rotator cuff (that's the ring of muscles and tendons that help you to move your shoulders).

"Frankly, I don't know how it continues to operate, because there is no cushion in there," he says of his knee. I can't jump on it or do a side lunge...but I love pickleball because it works on my reaction time—one of the issues that tends to go downhill for seniors," he says. Plus, it's a social sport that gets him together with active friends.

And, it's just one of many activities that Steve refuses to stop doing just because of a bum knee and shoulder. In fact, as we talked to Steve, we were hard-pressed to find something that the man *doesn't* do.

"Rather than give into the parts of my body that aren't good, I do what I can to strengthen and enhance them," he says. In addition to pickleball, Steve plays golf, does yoga, strength-trains, cycles indoors and outdoors, swims, rows, and performs exercises for stability and balance. He also developed a successful fitness program for older people that he still runs.

Creatively, he writes music, plays guitar and sings in a band with his brothers, the Steve brothers, with whom he recorded for Columbia Records and later performed on six continents. He paints landscapes, writes articles on health and wellness, as well as a book called *The No-Nonsense Guide to Fitness: The Do Anywhere Anytime Exercise Plan that Puts Old on Hold* (for which he ably modeled all the exercises; order a copy of the book by emailing jscolwell@comcast.net), and runs a fitness program for seniors called Striders. He does work to improve Muslim-Christian relations in his hometown of Seattle. The list goes on and on. Steve is nothing short of a modern-day Renaissance man.

"I think I'm a pretty fit person," he says, adding his definition of what it means to be fit: "Fitness is the ability to perform tasks vigorously and alertly, with energy left over to enjoy leisure activities and meet emergency demands. It's the capacity to endure, bear up, withstand stress, and carry on when an unfit person could not. It's the basis for health and well-being." Wow—nice definition, we thought.

Move It or Lose It

To keep himself "fit," Steve relies heavily on a variety of physical activities that cover cardiovascular fitness, strength, flexibility, and balance. Because he has arthritis, he admits that sometimes it hurts to move. "It feels like movement will cause more damage, but really it's the opposite; exercise helps, not hurts, arthritic joints." He also does exercises to strengthen the muscles around his knees. "These muscles act like a shock absorber, the same as on a car," he says. When he does certain activities, he wears a knee brace.

To clean up his bad knee, Steve had arthroscopic surgery twice. "I'm thinking, at some point, I will need a new knee, but until I have a crisis, I plan to continue to use the one I have."

He says exercise is just like going to the grocery store or brushing your teeth. "If you want to stay fit, there's just no way around it."

Why It Works

Steve and I were equally impressed with Steve's range of activities and ability to stay so physically fit, despite his age and joint limitations.

• • • • • • • • • • • • • • • • • • •

Helping Others on Bended Knee

Aside from his physical pursuits, one of the endeavors Steve is most enthusiastic about is his work with Muslim-Christian relations. This work builds on the outreach he and his brothers did as musical founders of the nonprofit Up with People, which used musical shows to encourage peace, cultural understanding, and positive social change around the world.

The peace-making work started with a week-long interface conference about 10 years ago in Seattle, where leaders from all different faiths met, including the Dalai Lama and Archbishop Tutu from South Africa. "While I was there, I realized how important it is for our future for non-Muslims to get to know Muslims, especially Christians," Steve says.

Being a devout Christian, he's working with an Imam in the Seattle area to put on programs to get the groups together. "We've discovered that we have more in common than we have things that are different in our religions," he says.

When we spoke, he was getting ready to attend a meeting to address vandalism of a mosque in his community. "I can't say for sure whether we have brought change or not, but we are trying," he says. "I continue to keep my eyes, ears, and mind open." Good advice for all facets of life.

That being said, Steve was quick to point out that Steve's main complaint—osteoarthritis of the knee—is a common one in older people. And, aside from a knee replacement, which Steve has so far avoided, there is no cure.

Lucky for a zealous guy like Steve, gone are the days when physicians advised patients with osteoarthritis (OA) to rest the sore joint. Instead, people with OA should engage in regular aerobic activity and strength-training to improve symptoms of the disease.

In fact, numerous studies show that both types of exercise help patients with OA feel better, reduce joint pain, and improve their ability to complete daily tasks.

In a study published in *Rheumatology International*, researchers looked at the effectiveness of a home-based exercise routine, a walking program, and no exercise intervention on people with osteoarthritis of the knee. Group 1 received the home-based program, group 2 did the walking program three times per week, and group 3 had no intervention. At the end of 3 months, researchers evaluated the participants' pain, physical function, and quality of life. Pain and physical function improved more for the participants who did the home-based exercise or walked than it did for the participants who did not exercise. When it came to quality of life, the walkers ranked higher than those who exercised at home.

There is a caveat: If you experience pain in the affected joint during a certain activity, consider it a warning that you should stop doing that activity. Remember: Pain is your body's way of warning you that something isn't right.

Another one of Steve's regular activities that is good for osteoarthritis is yoga. When University of Pennsylvania researchers looked at the effects of 8 weeks' worth of 90-minute beginner classes on people with OA of the knee, they found that yoga improved pain, physical function, and mood.

Steve's Secrets

Talk to your health-care professional before you start an exercise program, especially if you have osteoarthritis. Once you get the green light, use this advice.

CHOOSE THE RIGHT ACTIVITIES. Steve Colwell's active lifestyle demonstrates that you can pretty much do any form of aerobic exercise, provided you can do it comfortably. The best activities for people with OA are those that limit pounding or twisting of your joints. However, it's very specific to the person. Some people with OA can run, play basketball, or, like Steve, play pickleball with no problem. Others have to be more careful. Listen to your body and find activities that you can comfortably enjoy.

STRENGTHEN YOUR MUSCLES. As Steve Colwell points out, strengthening the muscles that surround your joints can help to take pressure off the joints themselves. Do these activities at least 2 days a week, in addition to your aerobic exercise. If you aren't already following a strength-training program, try following Steve Colwell's program. Adapted with permission from *The No-Nonsense Guide to Fitness*, do two sets of 8 to 14 repetitions for each exercise.

Push-Ups

Steve Colwell offers several levels of push-ups, depending on your ability level. As you develop more strength, you can move up the level ladder. At every level, try to keep your hands shoulder-width apart and your head straight and in line with your spine, then go forward or down, depending on the level. Once you've gone as low (or forward) as you can, press back up.

▼ LEVEL ONE: Against a wall or against a countertop

▼ LEVEL TWO: On the floor, with knees touching the floor

▼ LEVEL THREE: On the floor, full body (traditional push-ups)

Be Able-Bodied

Upper-Back Exercise

Holding a resistance band, with your elbows up, hands holding the band about shoulder height, pull your hands in opposite directions to the sides until your arms are about straight.

At the farthest point to the sides, squeeze your shoulder blades together. Bring your hands back to the starting position.

Back Exercise

Sit on a straight-backed chair or on the floor with your legs straight out in front of you. Place the resistance band around the balls of your feet and hold the ends in either hand.

Bend forward from the hips, keeping your back straight. Make sure that there is little or no slack in the band.

Pull on the band as you return to an upright seated position, squeezing your shoulder blades together.

Lower-Back Exercise

Stand with your feet shoulder-width apart and place a resistance band under both feet.

Holding the band in both hands, bend forward at the waist until your upper body is parallel with the floor.

Keep your head up, in line with your spine, and your legs slightly bent.

With no slack in the band, pull up to a standing position.

At the full upright position, squeeze your shoulder blades together.

Do a count of 2 seconds up and 3 seconds down.

Shoulder Exercise

Stand with your feet shoulder-width apart and the resistance band under your right foot so the band comes from the right side of your foot.

Holding the other end of the band with your right hand, lift it to the side until your arm reaches shoulder height. Repeat with the other arm, with the band coming from the outside of your left foot.

Abdominal Exercise

Sit at the front edge of a firm, straight-back chair.

With your glutes (butt muscles) at the front edge of the seat, lean all the way back with your hands placed lightly on the back of your head.

Only touching the back of the chair lightly with your back, use your abdominal muscles, not your arms, to pull you forward.

Immediately go back to the starting position.

Squats

Stand with your feet shoulder-width apart.

With your feet flat on the floor, squat down, bend your knees no farther than 90 degrees. As you go down, raise both arms forward.

At your lowest point, your glutes should be back as if you were going to sit down in a chair and your weight should be on your heels.

If you are in the proper position, you should be able to raise your toes off the floor and you should be able to see your toes. Lower your arms to your sides when you return to the starting position.

Hamstrings, Buttocks, Lower-Back Exercise

Stand and place both hands on the back of a chair.

Lift one leg as high as you can behind you, keeping your upper body and the leg you lift as straight as possible.

After 12 reps with one leg, do the same thing with the other.

Biceps Exercise

Place a resistance band under your right foot. Hold one end of the band in each hand.

Bend your elbows as you curl your hands toward your upper arms. Pull up for 2 seconds, breathing out as you raise the band, then release for 3 seconds.

Make sure that you only move your arms, not your upper body.

Do six reps, then switch to the other foot and do six more.

For an added balance challenge, try balancing on one leg while you do the curls.

Triceps Exercise

Holding a resistance band with your hands about 6 inches apart, place your left hand at your right shoulder.

Place your right hand as high as possible at your ribs.

Checking to see there is no slack in the band, move your right hand back until your arm is straight and then return it to your ribs.

Switch sides, starting with your right hand at your left shoulder and repeat.

Calf Exercise

This exercise is most effective if you do it while standing on a step. In lieu of a step, you can do it while standing on the floor.

Stand with your feet together.

Rest one hand against a railing or the back of a sturdy chair for balance. Lift your heels and rise onto the balls of your feet. Hold for a second or two. Then, reverse the movement, this time dropping your heels down until you feel a stretch in your calves.

If this is not challenging enough after 14 repetitions, place one foot behind the other and rise up on one leg only.

Hip Flexor Exercise

Stand behind and to the side of a sturdy straight-backed chair, with the hand closest to the chair resting on the chair back.

Lift the foot farthest from the chair up slowly by bending your knee to a 90-degree angle, so your thigh is parallel with the floor, then lower it back down to the floor.

Repeat 14 times and then switch to the other side.

Balance and Flexibility Moves

Older people are at a higher risk of falling, especially if they have OA. To improve your balance and reduce your risk of falls, perform activities that improve your balance at least 3 days a week. These balance-promoting activities can be part of your aerobic workout or strength-training plan. Examples include standing on one foot, backward walking, heel and toe walking, and tai chi. Or, some gyms and community centers offer classes that specifically target stability.

In many people with OA, stiffness accompanies the soreness they feel in their joints. Daily flexibility exercises for all your major joints can help keep them supple and improve your overall range of motion as well.

Steve Colwell has a number of good flexibility exercises in his program. Here's a good one for the trunk and core and another for the hamstrings.

Twist

Place your left arm shoulder height across your chest.

Place your left hand against your upper right arm to anchor it in place.

Twist your body as far as you can to the left. Then, do the same thing on the opposite side.

Hamstring Stretch

Place your feet in a wide stance, about 3 feet apart.

Bend forward slowly, placing your hands on your knees first, then your shins, ankles, and finally the floor (if possible). Slowly return to a standing position.

Rick Connella's Secret

Don't Let Your Genetics Define Your Health

. . . .

Run barefoot at sunrise

Live openly, always willing to try something new

Ditch your TV

. . . .

Rick Connella, 80, starts every day with a hefty dose of nature. "At 6:30, I go down to the beach, even in the dark, and run on the sand for a half-hour. Then, I relax on the beach, and watch the dolphins and the sunrise. It's exercise with some relaxation mixed in," he says.

It's amazing enough that Rick still runs at age 80. As a runner, I envisioned myself running on the beach each morning four decades from now, as Rick is doing. It was a stretch. Then, he dropped a real bombshell: "I do it barefoot," he says.

"You do?!"

"Yes, I used to run in shoes, and would jam my toes all the time. One day, I decided to take them off and it felt so good, I never put them back on," he says. "I think it's actually easier on my knees too."

Rick's barefoot running is only one piece of his impressively well-rounded active lifestyle. He continues to play tennis and basketball, swims, water-skis, and partakes in other water sports. He still body surfs. And, he's always open to trying new things. When he was 76, he went to Nepal with a Himalayan Mountain guide and trekked to the 14,000 foot Annapurna base camp, hiked through the jungle of Bardiya National Park, and whitewater-rafted down a raging Himalayan river.

"And, with a push from my son Eric, I recently tried paddle boarding. I liked it so much that I just bought three boards to use with my 10 grandchildren!" he says.

Steve and I know both Eric. He's our financial advisor. When I told him that we were writing this book, he said, "You have to talk my dad— he's a real stud!"

No truer words were ever spoken. When you see Rick on the paddle-board, you'd think you were looking at a man at least 20 years younger. He's also one of those guys who exudes pleasantness—you can hear him smiling as he talks.

For a stud, he's modest, but Rick does admit that he's in good physical condition. "When I compare myself to my friends who are the same age or younger, I would say I'm more energetic than they are," he says. "I think it's mainly because I have a positive attitude and am receptive to new ideas and concepts." He says having a positive attitude and exercising are kind of like the chicken and the egg. "I'm not sure if I have stayed so active because I'm positive or I'm positive because I exercise. Either way, I'll take it," he laughs.

Fresh Water in the Gene Pool

Rick says that his drive to stay active and healthy comes from watching several of his family members succumb to poor health at an early age.

"My dad was a very social, energetic guy, but his side of the family wasn't healthy," Rick says. "They are from a southern Louisiana farming town and their diets consisted of many fried foods. Unfortunately, that diet didn't change much when they migrated to California," Rick explains. "My grandfather and his three sons—including my father—were all very obese for most of their lives."

This obesity affected their health. Rick's grandfather died of heart failure at 63. One of his uncles died from cirrhosis of the liver at age 43. Another uncle died from a brain aneurism at 39. "My father eventually died from heart disease at 69. I have four younger brothers—all of whom are rotund and one of whom survived heart failure in his forties."

Rick decided that he didn't want to repeat history, so he rewrote it. Not only is he one of the fittest 80-year-olds we know, he's also one of the healthiest. "The doctor is very complimentary of both me and my wife," he says. "Our blood pressure and cholesterol levels are very low—the doc says we should live into our nineties!"

Part of rewriting his family history rested on an astute observation. He noticed that older people who watched a lot of TV tended to be less healthy than older people who watched a lot less of it. So, he and his wife mostly keep theirs turned off.

Instead, he immerses himself in real life, the outdoors, and several hobbies, especially photography.

"I love taking pictures of scenery, especially old buildings," he says.

He also attends a men's Bible study he calls "philosophical—in addition to studying and discussing the Bible, we also critique it from a theological perspective." When his afternoons are free and the weather is nice (which is often in Southern California), Rick plays golf.

"Physical activity is so good for your body and your mind," he says. "When I skip my run because it's raining or I'm on vacation or something, my day doesn't go as well. I can't imagine starting my days any other way."

Why It Works

Humans were designed to run barefoot, so it only makes sense that it's good for the body. Of course, we were also given the brainpower to create running shoes, so there's an argument for both sides.

Despite all that goes into designing modern running footwear, 79 percent of shoed runners still get injured in a given year.

The research on barefoot running is limited, but what's out there is pretty positive.

One of the biggest plusses is the foot strike pattern. Barefoot runners tend to strike the ground with the forefoot first. This is associated with lower impact and wider stride, both of which help prevent injuries. In one study, barefoot runners sustained fewer overall injuries; however, it's important to note that they also ran fewer miles than the shoed runners. When the barefoot runners did get injured, they were more likely to get hurt on the plantar surface of the foot. The barefoot runners also reported fewer knee and hip injuries, as well as less plantar fasciitis than the group wearing shoes.

Overall, these results came out in favor of barefoot running, particularly the number of musculoskeletal injuries, which are of concern to runners as they age.

By putting his bare feet directly against the sand, Rick is in physical contact with the electrons on the surface of the Earth. Some research shows reconnecting with these electrons (a phenomenon called earthing or grounding) can produce all kinds of health benefits. These include lower inflammation, decreased stress, reduced pain, and better sleep, all of which may help reduce the risk for numerous diseases and perhaps even help slow down the aging process.

Steve's Secrets

If running barefoot on the beach in your eighties sounds as good to you as it does to us, use this advice to get started.

STEER CLEAR OF A SLOPE. Sand is a lot more forgiving than a concrete sidewalk, which makes it easier on the joints. But, if you choose to run on sand, make sure that it's flat; running or walking on a sloped beach can do your hips and knees more harm than good. Also, look for sand that's wet and packed down to create as firm and stable a surface as possible.

SHOP FOR BAREFOOT ALTERNATIVES. If running barefoot turns you off, you're in luck: There are running shoes particularly designed to mimic the sensation and mechanics of running in bare feet—without the risk of a sharp shell lodging into your toe. Some even have cutouts for each individual toe. Two of the most popular brands of barefoot running shoes are Merrell and Vibram. I have a pair of Merrell barefoot runners and swear by them—I will never go back to a standard running shoe. If you decide to go barefoot, it's a good idea to talk with your health-care provider first. Also, start on the softest surface possible, such as sand. It takes time for your feet to build up enough calluses to safely run on more rugged terrain. If you notice any discomfort in your feet or legs, stop and call your doctor. Not everyone is built for barefoot running, especially people with flat feet.

GET RID OF YOUR CABLE. Find Rick's desertion of TV inspiring? Consider canceling your cable service. Not only will you be less tempted to turn on the TV to fill time and instead consider something more stimulating, such as reading a book, painting a landscape, or taking photographs, you'll also shave some money off your monthly bills. If you can't bear the thought of parting with your screen (I must admit, I get panicky at the prospect), look into media-streaming services such as Netflix, Hulu, and Amazon Prime, which allow you to watch what you want when you want for a fraction of the cost of cable.

Walt Hoffman's Secret

Have Faith

. . . .

Volunteer your time for a cause you hold dear
Condition your body to be ready for anything
Realize that you're never too old to drive a sports car

. . . .

Walt Hoffman is not what I imagined when I learned I'd be interviewing a Christian missionary. At 91, he drives a 2016 white Corvette, fully loaded with red leather interior and it's quite the conversation starter.

"I was introduced to a lady in my church parking lot a few weeks ago," he says. "Our friend introducing us found it necessary to say to her, 'Walt's 90, you know.'"

" 'Oh my,' she said. 'Mmm, ah, are you still driving?'

"We were standing next to the cars, and, as we shook hands, I drew her a step toward my car. 'That's what I'm driving...still,' I said, pointing toward my glistening Corvette."

" 'Oh my,' she repeated."

People seem surprised to see this old dude driving a Corvette. It's a conversation starter for sure, especially when I explain that it was a gift from my sister...and that I travel the world doing missionary work."

Because you're probably as curious about this as I was, here's the backstory on the car: His sister bought him the Corvette when he moved from Hawaii back to the U.S. because it cost too much for him to ship his old Corvette overseas.

The WWII Navy vet came to his missionary calling at age 75, after running his own construction company, and later serving as a pastor in a Baptist church.

His training program required outreach in third-world countries.

"I had decided that I would like to see lots of different places...but not India," he says. "Low and behold, our first assignment was in the slums of India, where our group helped to construct a church for lepers," he says. There, they helped build the church, brick-by-brick, in hot and uncomfortable conditions. At night, they slept on a concrete floor.

Despite their discomfort, the mission was successful.

His second trip, to Taiwan, was less physically draining but more mentally so. "We taught ministry to some very sophisticated people who wanted to prosper in the world," he says. "We sat and talked with them about the Bible in coffee shops, to teach them Christianity, and to help them practice their English."

Other ventures included visits to primitive cultures in the Amazon region of Brazil and teaching at a base in Santiago, Chile. "All of the trips were quite a contrast to the relative luxury of our home in Hawaii, where we lived at the time," he says.

This grueling ministry work has served as a motivating force, helping Walt to get and stay in shape, "I want to be ready to serve, to answer a call, or do something helpful, whether it's to go and visit someone or do some teaching," he says. "And, that readiness takes energy, preparation, and physical conditioning."

He and his wife exercise with a personal trainer twice a week.

"I focus my exercise routine on stability and balance," he says. His typical exercise week includes daily unplanned, but deliberate, walking. "When driving to shop, I seek a parking space some distance from the entrance (probably in part to protect his nice new car). I'll climb one or two levels of stairs rather than stand around waiting for the elevator," he says.

The planned trainer sessions include 30 minutes of aerobics on an elliptical training machine. "This machine has metrics showing which muscles we're using, our step size, height climbed, distance, and heart rate," Walt says. "The training then includes several minutes of hands-on, extensive stretching. Then, I do a series of repetitions at different stations. Some of these stations are machines using interchangeable weights requiring leg pressing, squeezing, rowing motions, and arm thrusts," he says. "I also do cabled weight pulls, varied resistance stretch cords, and free weights, as the trainer works specific muscle groups."

Walt's trainer has been gradually increasing the amount of weight he lifts, as well as his number of repetitions. "I'm usually a little sore the day after the training session, but it's worth it because I see improvements in both my strength and stamina. And, so far, I've avoided a walker or a cane. Most people are amazed that I get around as well as I do," he says.

On Call for Spiritual Guidance

Walt's calling into spiritual counseling was literally that: a phone call that he received in the middle of the night.

"My son's friend called me at 2:00 in the morning because he desperately needed some spiritual help," he recalls. Two years later, the same friend called again, this time asking Walt to give the same guidance to others in need. "He said, 'I want you to teach them the Bible, just like you taught me,'" Walt recalls.

At the time, Walt's construction company had just contracted to work on the Queen Mary, so the timing was tough. "But, I decided to do it, thinking it couldn't last very long," he says. It lasted 17 years and turned into a full-blown active church, with Walt as the pastor. All the while, he continued to lead his construction company through its busiest period. His book,...*And Church Happened*, which he published at the age of 89, tells that story.

In everything, from taking care of himself to counseling others, Walt does so for the greater good. "God created each of us for His purpose and we must seek to fulfill that purpose as much as we can," he says. Walt is serving his purpose with the top down in his brand-new white Corvette, driving to churches started by members of his bible study, from Arizona to Vancouver to Seattle.

"As long as I am here on Earth, I want to be useful, engaged, and productive," he says.

Why It Works

There isn't much out there on the benefits of driving a sports car into your nineties, but there is no shortage of research on the welfare of religion and spirituality for both physical and emotional health.

According to a large review done by researchers at Duke University on the topic, 93 percent of Americans believe in God or a higher power, and 75 percent pray at least once a week. The review also revealed that religion is related to better physical and emotional health. Emotionally, it showed lower perceptions of stress, less depression, increased sense of happiness and well-being, and a greater sense of purpose.

In terms of physical health, the Duke survey showed that religious people tend to drink less, are less likely to smoke cigarettes, and are more likely to exercise than those who are not religious. Some of the studies also show that religious people weigh less.

If that weren't evidence enough, the review found that religious individuals have fewer heart attacks, fewer deaths from heart disease, lower blood pressure, fewer strokes, better immune function, lower stress hormone levels, longer survival with cancer, slower cognitive decline, and greater longevity. Lots of other research has yielded similar conclusions.

- **Jews older than 70 who regularly attended synagogue were more likely to be alive 7 years later than those who did not, found a 2007 study in the European Journal of Ageing.**

- **Religious people with Alzheimer's disease had a slower progression of symptoms than non-religious people with the disease, according to a 2007 study published in Neurology.**

- **HIV patients who boosted their spirituality or religion had higher CD4 counts and a lower viral load, as well as slower disease progression over 4 years than those who were not religious, according to a 2006 study in the Journal of General Internal Medicine.**

- **Depressed people who believe in a caring god, be it through Christianity, Islam, Taoism, or Buddhism, responded to psychiatric treatment more favorably than depressed people who were not religious, according to a 2010 study published in the Journal of Clinical Psychology.**

All in all, there have been more than 70 studies since 2004 that showed positive findings with respect to religion and good physical and mental health.

Steve's Secrets

Like exercise, healthy eating, and embracing new hobbies and experiences, it's never too late to adopt a religion or strengthen your practice. Here are some tips.

EMBRACE THE SOCIAL PARTS. The happiness that comes from religious affiliation stems largely from the social network that forms in a temple, synagogue, or church. Religion also helps you feel like a part of something good, which is beneficial.

MAKE TIME TO PRAY. Most major religions involve prayer. As the Duke review and other studies show, praying is good for your health. It can help ward off the negative effects of stress, increase your trust in others, and make you a nicer person overall. If you don't already incorporate prayer into your life, set aside time in your day or week to do so, even if it's only for a few minutes.

DON'T FORCE IT. If you don't identify with a formal religion, don't feel like you must move forward with a practice to achieve good health. There are other ways you can become more spiritual. Try mindful meditation, yoga, deep-breathing exercises, or take a daily walk on the beach or through the woods. Anything you can do to boost your sense of calm, tranquility, and peace.

• •

At a Glance: How to Remain Able-Bodied

→ Always take the stairs. That way, you'll always be able to climb stairs.

→ Embrace your adventurous side. Never tell yourself, "I'm too old to try that."

→ Consume a variety of protein foods, such as poultry, fish, nuts, and tofu.

→ Wean yourself off added sugars and processed foods.

→ Prioritize anti-inflammatory foods such as fatty fish, olive oil, citrus fruit, cruciferous veggies, eggs, and avocados.

→ Stay active in any way you can, even if your joints want you to do otherwise. If your joints hurt, try low-impact options, like water aerobics.

→ Embrace yoga to keep your body supple.

→ Use a strength-training routine to take pressure off your joints.

→ Occasionally walk barefoot, especially on soft surfaces.

→ Lean on your faith or spirituality to bolster your health.

→ Drop 5 to 10 percent of your total body weight.

→ Take 1,000 to 2,000 milligrams of fish oil, 1,000 to 1,200 milligrams of calcium, and 800 milligrams of chondroitin daily.

→ Soothe sore joints with a daily application of 0.05% capsaicin cream.

Steve's Prescription for Staying Able-Bodied

You've gotten great advice, straight from the mouths of some of the best role models for successful aging. But, some of you may want more. Perhaps you've been struggling with a sore knee, or you have a parent with osteoarthritis and want to know what you can do to help stave it off. Or, maybe you want some bonus tips on how to preserve your health and vitality as you advance into your eighties and nineties. So, here are Steve's top tips for staying healthy.

PART WITH A FEW POUNDS. Two out of three people in the U.S. are overweight and one out of three is obese. If you fit into either of these categories, it's time to think about losing weight. The good news: You don't have to lose much! If you drop as little as 10 percent of your body weight, not only will you look younger but you will also have more energy and give your joints a much needed break. Remember, every extra pound you carry puts *4 extra pounds* of stress on your knees. And, losing as little as 11 pounds can cut your risk of osteoarthritis of the knee in half.

BUILD STRONG BONES. Behind every healthy joint there is a strong bone. One of the best things you can do to keep your bones sturdy and prevent osteoporosis is to get enough calcium. The recommended daily amount is 1,000 milligrams for both men and women ages 19 to 50; 1,000 milligrams for men and 1,200 milligrams for women ages 51 to 70, and 1,200 milligrams a day for both men and women ages 71 and older. Some of the best sources of calcium include broccoli, kale, figs, salmon, yogurt, and milk. For extra insurance, consider taking calcium in supplement form.

LOWER INFLAMMATION WITH YOUR LUNCH. And, other meals too. Eating certain foods can help calm inflammation in your body, boost overall health, and help prevent joint pain. Here are some of the most powerful anti-inflammatory foods.

Fatty fish: Coldwater fish such as salmon, mackerel, and tuna are rich in omega-3 fatty acids. Research shows that omega-3s can reduce pain and swelling in arthritic joints. Try to eat oily fish at least two times a week. If you can't get that much from fish, consider taking a fish-oil supplement. In a 2015 Thai study, people who took 1,000 to 2,000 milligrams of fish oil once a day for 8 weeks saw improvements in knee pain and function.

Olive oil: Rich in polyphenols, compounds that have both antioxidant and anti-inflammatory perks, olive oil is a must-have staple of an anti-inflammatory diet. As a bonus, it's made up of about 70 percent oleic acid, a monounsaturated fat that's good for heart health.

Citrus fruits: They add a refreshing splash to your tea or lemonade and they also invigorate your body. Citrus fruits, such as lemons, limes, oranges, and grapefruits, can neutralize damaging free radicals, lowering inflammation and possibly helping to reduce cancer risk. And, because they contain lots of water, citrus fruits help keep you hydrated, which is great for preserving youthful skin.

Cruciferous vegetables: Crunchy green veggies such as cauliflower, broccoli, kale, collard greens, mustard greens, watercress, Brussels sprouts, and bok choy do more than keep your bowels moving; they also speed up detoxification in your liver, which results in lower levels of inflammation. Plus, they contain compounds called glucosinolates, which can help fight cancer.

Eggs: No matter if they came before or after the chicken, eggs are worth their weight in gold. The zeaxanthin and lutein in eggs help support eye health, and the choline they serve up is good for the heart and brain. They're also a great source of anti-inflammatory omega-3 fatty acids. Look for eggs that are certified organic, and, if you can find them, pasture raised—they contain the most omega-3s.

Avocados: Rich in phytosterols, alpha-linolenic acid, carotenoids, and polyunsaturated fats, avocados are research-proven to help reduce the pain associated with both osteo-and rheumatoid arthritis. Not sure how to eat avocados? Enjoy them by themselves, cut them onto your salad for a tasty topper, mash them into a guacamole dip, or spread them on a sandwich for a flavorful, healthy alternative to butter or mayo—they are a versatile fruit.

CALM INFLAMMATION WITH CHONDROITIN. A substance found in human cartilage, chondroitin can help relieve pain and swelling in joints affected by osteoarthritis. It's often mixed with another cartilage component called glucosamine. In the past, studies on chondroitin have been mixed, but results of a recent study published in the *Annals of Rheumatic Diseases* came out in the supplement's favor. Researchers gave 600 adults older than 50 who had primary knee osteoarthritis pharmaceutical-strength chondroitin sulfate (800 milligrams) plus a placebo; the arthritis medication celecoxib (200 milligrams) plus a placebo; or a double placebo daily for 6 months. At 3 months and 6 months, both the chondroitin and celecoxib groups had less pain than the placebo group. The researchers concluded that chondroitin was as effective as celecoxib at reducing pain and inflammation associated with arthritis, and that it should be considered as a first-line arthritis remedy.

WORK OUT IN WATER. Aquatic exercises provide the same benefits as those on land, without stressing your joints. Exercising in water can improve pain and physical function in people with osteoarthritis, according to a 2014 review published in *Physical Therapy*. And, a 2015 Dutch study found that attending a regular 45-minute circuit-training session in the swimming pool helped ease pain in people ages 46 to 77 with osteoarthritis of the knee. You can find an aquatic version of pretty much any exercise class these days, from straight swimming to jogging to classes that build strength.

FIGHT FIRE WITH FIRE. Capsaicin, the substance that gives hot peppers their heat, can also ease pain in sore joints. When applied topically, capsaicin taps out substance P, a brain chemical that stimulates the sensation of pain. The result: decreased pain in the joint. In a 2010 German study, participants who used 0.05 percent capsaicin cream for 3 weeks had 50 percent less joint pain.

Six

Be Spunky

So many people go to the doctor complaining of fatigue, insomnia, depression, and stress. Far too often, these people leave the doctor's office with prescriptions for drugs that don't address their underlying issues—drugs that have an array of unpleasant side-effects.

The amazing people you will read about in this chapter have all found another, better way. Because of their lifestyles, they've found the secret to lasting spunk. They are happy, energetic, and fun-loving.

You can easily steal their secrets and put them to use in your own life. Want all-day energy and a clear head? Who doesn't?! Read on.

Ann Jarrett's Secret

Become a Renaissance Woman

. . . .

Surround yourself with culture

Try a visual art, such as photography, painting, or drawing

Engage in lots of leisure activities

. . . .

Ann Jarrett, 88, has probably tried more new activities in the past year alone than my entire family combined.

She's learning how to meditate. She's crafting her grandfather's life story. She's taking a poetry class. She's taken her grandchildren on international trips and has traveled to more than 62 countries, some of them several times. She has season tickets to the Philadelphia Orchestra, which, she says, is "wonderful music for the soul." She also attends lectures, documentaries, and plays closer to home.

And, that's all on top of her ultimate life's love—art—which she takes with her wherever she goes.

"My kids say I never stop. In a way, they are right," she laughs. "But I'm busy doing things that I love and I often take time to smell the roses right next door at Longwood Gardens."

Traveling to Help People

The travel bug first bit Ann when she and her husband, a physicist, started traveling for his job at DuPont.

"Every 3 years, the company sent him to an international conference on magnetism," she says. Ann joined him and they always added independent travel. "One of the conferences was at Moscow University and we added a trip to the Asian part of the Soviet Union after the conference was done," she says. Other trips included Oslo, Norway, and Kyoto, Japan.

After her husband retired, the couple did international biking trips in Europe and Earthwatch trips to New Zealand, Venice, and Kenya.

More recently, she has been on intergenerational Road Scholar trips (formerly known as Elderhostel). "One of my grandsons chose a Harry Potter-themed trip to Oxford, and the other chose a service project where they planted pineapple and coconut trees and built energy-efficient stoves in Belize," she says. "In Belize, we stayed in individual huts and got to work every morning by taking a boat down the river. At the end of the trip my grandson told me, 'I learned that I like to help people,' which made it so worthwhile," she says.

Ann also likes to help people. When her fourth child went off to college, she went to work for UNICEF. "I loved it because that's where my values are."

She then went on to become head of peace and world justice for her Presbytery—a body of church elders that represents 55 churches. That work sent her traveling once again. "I went to Ghana, Kenya and Zimbabwe and Trinidad and Mexico. Each time, our goal was to study the impact that first-world economies have on third-world countries, so we could present workshops at home," she says.

But, of all the places Ann has visited in her life, she says that Antarctica was her favorite. "I just *loved* the variety of penguin colonies. We had 28 landings in Zodiacs to view them up close and observe the parent penguins' strong instinct to feed and protect their newly hatched chicks," she says.

Surrounded by Stimulating People

It doesn't matter the weather or what's going on in the world. If you ask Ann how she is, she'll reply, "Wonderful!" She's so positive that it's easy to make the mistake of believing that she's never survived a hard day in her life.

But, that's just not true. She doesn't dwell on them, but Ann has seen her share of difficulties. In 1997, she and her husband were in a terrible car accident while on vacation in Sanibel, Florida. It left him with a severe traumatic brain injury and she cared for him for 5 years before he passed away. "You learn from the tribulations too," she says softly.

She also survived breast cancer 5 years ago, and she suffered a brain bleed while on a painting trip in Camden, Maine. "These things give you pause because you realize that life isn't forever," she says. "My biggest worry was that I wasn't going to recover completely enough to continue to enjoy my quality of life. But luckily, I did. I like to challenge myself and keep up with current events, and I don't dwell on the negative. I figure as long as I can keep going and love what I'm doing and learning, why stop?"

Ann lives in a peace-making Quaker retirement community in Kennett Square, Pennsylvania, full of retired artists, college professors, and other like-minded individuals—"very stimulating people who also value peace-making, so I fit in very well," she says. Every Wednesday, she joins fellow artists in a friend's studio to paint.

Steve and I found her living situation encouraging. So there *are* retirement communities geared toward and inhabited by people who want to keep living and learning! I immediately called my mom and told her about Ann's residence.

Ann's also hard at work on her grandfather's memoir. It started when she took a memoir class given by a retired English professor from Hunter College in her community. "He gave us specific assignments, so I wasn't able to write my memoir in that class, but it did light the fire," she says.

With fresh tips from her class, she gathered all the pictures, genealogy files, personal notes, and memorabilia she could get her hands on, and got started. "My grandfather was a special man worth remembering. In 1891, at age 16, he went to sea as a cabin boy on a three-masted wooden ship and he finished his career as manager of the United Shoe Machinery Company for Northern New England," she says. "He had a big influence on my life—he was my father figure and he lived to 106!"

Ann's physical activities have also been all over the map. She has enjoyed yoga, tennis, skiing, hiking, and swimming.

Although she can no longer ski or play tennis, Ann still goes for walks and swims. "In the summer, I swim laps in the outdoor pool here at my complex as often as I can; swimming feels good because it doesn't bother my joints," she says. "In the winter, I swallow my pride and swim laps in the indoor pool and take an exercise class called 'healthy joints,' which exercises different parts of the body, also in the water," she says. "Two years ago, I started to add up my 1/2-mile laps. I'm up to 85 miles!"

Why It Works

When Steve and I discussed Ann, he said, "I feel like I should have more hobbies...." And, he has pretty many! He swims, surfs, plays the guitar, and loves to try new recipes. Lately, he's talked about adding kiteboarding and paddle boarding to his water-sport repertoire.

And, this is a good thing, as leisure activities reduce stress by 34 percent and sadness by 18 percent, according to a study of 100 adults that was published in the *Annals of Behavioral Medicine*. Adults who engaged in the most leisure activities also had a lowered heart rate and a decrease in stress that lasted for hours after they had completed the activity.

Leisure activities that involve the arts—like most of Ann's do—seem to be particularly beneficial.

A review of 31 studies found that dance, expressive writing, music, theater, and visual arts positively affect memory, creativity, problem solving, reaction time, everyday competence, balance, and quality of life.

Some of the most salient benefits of participation in the arts include pleasure in creative activities, social support, and mental and physical stimulation.

Artistic endeavors may help ward off dementia too, according to an April 2015 study published in *Neurology*. Individuals who drew, sculpted, painted, and practiced other arts were 73 percent less likely to suffer memory or thinking problems over 4 years than were people who didn't participate in the arts. Those who did crafts were 45 percent less likely to have mild cognitive impairment. And, those who participated in social activities, like theater, reduced their risk of memory problems by 55 percent.

The study results showed that activities that stimulate the mind and help develop fine motor skills at the same time, such as painting, drawing, and sculpting, had a more protective effect against memory problems than socializing.

Another positive thing that Ann is doing for her mental and physical health is traveling. Research has shown that traveling has numerous health benefits. For one, it's good for the heart. The Framingham Heart Study, the longest-running study on cardiovascular disease, found that men who didn't vacation for several years had a 30-percent higher risk of heart disease than those who didn't take time away. The same study showed that women who vacationed only once every 6 years were eight times more likely to develop heart disease or suffer a heart attack than women who vacationed at least two times a year.

Experiencing new environments and areas of the world challenges the brain, promoting resilience and brain health.

Additionally, scientists at the Pittsburgh Mind-Body Center, University of Pittsburgh, found that people who have more leisure activities, including travel, tend to have lower blood pressure levels, decreased levels of stress hormones, and smaller waistlines.

Steve's Secrets

It sounds obvious, but one of the best ways to get involved with more art and culture is to put the feelers out for it and attend events that promote artistic expression. Beyond that, here are some specific tips:

MAKE YOUR RETIREMENT STYLE FIT YOUR LIFESTYLE. Ann is lucky enough to live in a retirement community that supports resident artists as well as those who are interested in the arts with resources and space to create pottery, woodworking, painting, and other arts. The community also offers libraries, book clubs, classes, and transportation to concerts and shows. How great to have all of this at her fingertips. If you are in the process of shopping around for a place to live in your retirement, keep a community such as this in mind.

FIND SOURCES OF CULTURE IN YOUR AREA. Look into what's offered at your local community college or university. Many have visual arts classes, such as photography, painting, drawing, and sculpting. You can also take a class on writing, art history, or poetry. Local colleges and universities are great places to see live music, plays, musicals, and other shows. Community and senior centers often sponsor bus trips to big cities for larger cultural experiences.

TRAVEL OUTSIDE YOUR COMFORT ZONE. It's no surprise that there is research to show that traveling is good for older people physically and psychologically. It's good to open yourself to new cultures, foods, and adventures. For seniors looking to travel safely to new places, the Road Scholar program is a wonderful resource. Check it out at roadscholar. org. Other good travel organizations for seniors include Grand Circle Travel (gtc.com) and Collette Tours (gocollette.com).

Honey Kimball's Secret

Stay Fashionable

. . . .

Be ready to go out on the town

Remain current with fashion and technology

Embrace the tools that can improve your quality of life

. . . .

Honey Kimball is not your typical 97-year-old. When we met her, she was confidently wearing strappy heels and gold hoop earrings that brushed her shoulders. Her hair and nails were impeccably done, and she sported a chic metallic sweater. She looked gorgeous.

"Every day, I get up, do my makeup, and put on something nice in case one of my girls stops by and says, 'let's go out,'" she says.

As a middle-aged woman, sometimes I feel like it's an effort to put makeup on or even find pants without holes, especially when I'm in a rush to get my kids to the bus stop. Sometimes that (lazy) attire extends to the errands I run that morning. But Honey helped me to understand something important: When I pay attention to my appearance, I feel better about myself and am happier overall. It's not a matter of vanity or conceit; it's a matter of pride and respect for myself and those around me.

Beyond her clothes, Honey knows what's hot in technology too. While many of her silent generation friends wave their hands dismissively at tablets and smartphones, she embraces them.

"When I turned 80, my daughter bought me a computer and said, 'Mom, you are going to learn to use this thing—I want you to write about your life growing up in the South during the depression.'" At first, Honey says, she longed to take notes on a big legal pad instead. But she learned how to use the computer and has a 450 page memoir—*A Southern Girl Looks Back*—to show for it.

Now she's a tech virtuoso. She reads a lot—mainly on her iPad. She talks and texts on an iPhone, and messages family and friends with her email and Facebook accounts.

When she needs something from the store or has a meeting of the Navy Wives Club of America, Honey gets in her car and drives. "Only in safe areas and never at night," she says.

In nearly everything she does, Honey is as independent and open-minded as someone a quarter of her age, which is probably a large part of why she has lived so long and so strong.

"I certainly don't feel 97. When I say '97,' it sounds like I'm talking about someone else," she says.

From Rags to Stitches

Honey has seen a lot of changes in her 97 years, both in terms of trends and her personal life. She grew up in the South during the Depression, the youngest of 10 children in a house with no electricity or running water. Compare that to the large home she and her husband shared for 60 years, and more recently, the comfortable five-bedroom ranch house she lives in by herself, a half-block from two of her four daughters. "I have someone who comes in and cleans once a month, so there's not much heavy work," she says.

But Honey has never forgotten her roots, which give her a pleasantly feisty edge and a hint of a Louisiana Southern drawl.

Her upbringing is also at the heart of one of her most salient passions—pretty clothes. "I watched how my seven older sisters dressed, wore makeup, and fixed their hair; when the camera came out, they wouldn't be caught without lipstick. They were girly girls, like me," she says.

Honey's love of clothes deepened when she learned to sew. As a young adult, she took a job doing alterations, which gave her an inside look at pieces from famous designers. "I would rip out a seam to alter a skirt or blouse and look at the way it was done. Then, when I sewed my own pieces from scratch, I would imitate what I learned."

She took that knowledge and created a successful sewing business, where, for decades, she made custom clothes, including formal dresses and gowns. "I had my little business cards printed and I just loved it!" she says.

Her last big project was her granddaughter Susan's wedding gown in 2006. (Susan, my friend and neighbor, is the one who suggested we talk to her spunky, stylish grandmother for the book.) "It was so much fun because it gave Susan a reason to visit me when she came for fittings. We changed the dress so many times, but I didn't mind—it meant more visits!" she says. "I took notes about the whole experience, which I'm going to put together for Susan as a nice memory."

Today she puts just as much love into smaller sewing projects, including stuffed animals for her great-grandchildren. "I make them out of soft fleece and they come with a matching blanket," she says proudly.

Walking Forward, Looking Back

Honey remains in remarkably good health. "The only time I ever stayed in the hospital was to have my four daughters and once for a broken elbow," she says. "I rarely even get colds—I'm blessed."

She does have osteoporosis and stenosis, which have affected her posture in the past few years. "I use a walker; I admit I don't like it, and it took me a while to get used to the idea. *But*, it *is* sparkly and pink with a lime green print—my daughters helped me pick it out."

She may have gotten it reluctantly, but Honey says the walker has done wonders for her life. "If I stand for too long, my back hurts. I learned when I was grocery shopping that the grocery cart gave me just enough support to walk around the whole store," she says. "I found that I can do the same with a walker and walk faster than I can without one."

In fact, Honey has gotten so comfortable with her sparkly pink walker that she thinks of it more as an accessory than a tool. She takes it to the fashion hub—the mall—where she walks 3 days a week. As she walks, she glances at store windows, where she looks at the latest fashions.

In her nearly 100 years, Honey has seen countless fashions and technology trends come and go, and many friends and relatives as well. "I'm the oldest person I know—it's weird to say that," she says.

It might feel weird, but it feels good too. For everything she talks about in her life, Honey is truly grateful. "I thank God every day that I am healthy and that my family is well and attentive—they keep me young," she says. "I also pray that things will work out for the best. So far, they have. It's been a good life."

Why It Works

It may sound simple, even trivial, but by getting up every morning and dressing nicely, Honey's opening all her options. If one of her daughters stops by and asks her to go shopping or to lunch, Honey is ready to jump in the car—a proactive move to prevent becoming a shut-in. And, as I discovered, the better you look, the better you will feel.

She is also keeping up with technology that can help keep her safe. Smartphones offer a few different ways to help you instantly connect with friends and loved ones, whether you are having a crisis or just want to check in. Facetime, texting, and special apps that remind you to take medications or show up for doctors' appointments are all wonderful resources too, especially if you live alone.

Another wise move was giving in and getting the walker. Seniors who use a walker or wheelchair not only boost their safety and mobility, they also report participating in more daily activities they enjoy, found a study in the *American Journal of Public Health*. The seniors also reported being just as happy as they were before they got the extra help.

When Steve and I talked about devices like walkers and smartphones that can improve quality of life, he said, "It's kind of a no-brainer; if it helps you get around and do the things you love, while also helping to prevent falls and possible injury, you should get one. And, of course, if you can find a walker that is sparkly pink and lime green, even better!"

Honey also made the right move when she relocated to a ranch house right down the street from two of her daughters, complete with a monthly cleaning lady. Living near family or friends gives an aging person the comfort of knowing someone is just a few minutes away.

Steve's Secrets

To mimic the joyful, easygoing example of healthy aging that Honey embodies, consider this advice.

STAY OPEN-MINDED. An important secret to aging in place (at home) is staying flexible and receptive to help and change. We thought about the happy, healthy older people we know. They're not against trying a new restaurant, TV show, or vacation spot. Whether it's a new technological device, a new housekeeper, or a new assistive aid like a walker, don't dismiss it—these are the things that can keep you in your own home.

GET A SMARTPHONE. If there's one piece of technology that can single-handedly do the most for older people, it's a smartphone. If you keep your smartphone with you at all times and download the right apps, there are so many things it can do to help keep you safe and secure. For one, it can take the place of a traditional medical alert system, providing you instant access to everyone in your contact list. There are also some great smartphone apps for seniors. The best apps include:

- **Fade fall detector, which alerts a loved one if there is a longer than normal period without movement**
- **HeartWise Blood Pressure Tracker that monitors blood pressure**
- **Pillboxie to help people keep track of their medications**

Look for a phone holder that straps around your waist (some of the more fashionable options include hip bags and festival belts).

CONSIDER A VIDEO MONITORING SYSTEM. Honey is lucky to have two of her daughters within walking distance of her house. For those whose friends or loved ones are farther away, a video monitoring system can be the thing that keeps them successfully living at home. The technology has improved and the prices have decreased, making video monitoring systems feasible for many people looking for the security they provide. The cameras are small and cover a wide view. Some of the best options include Nest Cam (nest.com), Piper NV (getpiper.com), and SimpliCam (simplisafe.com).

Peggy Kaplan's Secret

Never Stop Learning

. . . .

Engage in activities that challenge your mind

Pick social hobbies

Play games that you enjoy

. . . .

Top-ranked bridge player Peggy Kaplan was up against the highest-ranked competitors in the world. At the third quarter, she and her teammates were ahead by 28 points. It came down to one card.

It knocked Peggy and her team out.

"If that card would have been in a different place, we would have won," she says.

But, she lost.

And, she was thrilled.

Peggy tells me this story after I've asked her to describe the most exciting moment in her bridge career. Evidently, for her, it's not about winning. I'm surprised. I'm not a terribly competitive person, but I like to win, especially at things that mean as much to me as bridge means to Peggy. She goes on to tell me that she left that memorable tournament exhilarated by the level of competition with her opponents and the way she and her teammates played. "For me, playing the crème de la crème of bridge players is really the biggest thrill," she says.

As a Grand Life Master—a title only the very best bridge players hold—Peggy is a member of the elite crème de la crème herself. She's one of the top female players in the world, having played with big names like Warren Buffett and Bill Gates, who she says "are good bridge players and very nice guys."

Besides the thrill of playing with talented, high-profile teammates, Peggy loves the challenge of bridge. A trick-taking game that uses a 52-card deck, bridge is played in groups of four, split into pairs, with partners sitting opposite each other at a table. It requires a strong memory and the ability to predict your partner's next move. The best players remember every card played. Those who don't fall behind and lose the trust of their team members.

"One of the best things about bridge is that, no matter how many times you've played, you're always learning," she says. "New things always come up, which helps keep me sharp as I'm getting older."

Sharp indeed. Talking to Peggy, you would think that she's 30 years younger than she is, which is 65, or Medicare age, as she calls it. When I contacted her about being interviewed, she got back to me in about 60 seconds via Facebook messenger. She's warm and engaging, with a spunky hint of don't mess with me...I'm tough. She conducts her life and her real estate business like she plays bridge—quickly, efficiently, and with very few mistakes.

Well-Suited for the Game

Peggy's aunt introduced her to bridge in 1978. "She invited me to a tournament and I placed in every event," Peggy says. Her aunt fixed her up with some friends to play a team event later that weekend and again, Peggy's team won. "That kind of hooked me," she laughs.

My grandmother played bridge, but that's about all I knew about the game, so I asked Peggy about what her title of Grand Life Master really means. With a tone of genuine modesty, Peggy admitted, "It's a big deal. There are about 168,000 members in the American Contract Bridge League and only 450 are Grand Life Masters." To become a Grand Life Master in bridge, you must win a national event and accumulate at least 10,000 points—both of which are incredible feats for people who play bridge. Peggy has won *four* national events. "Women make up a very small percentage of that—I think I am ranked in the mid-thirties for women in point totals, so not a bad showing," she says.

Most of the other women on that list play professionally. For these women, bridge is their job. For Peggy, bridge is a hobby, although she does fill in for professional players on occasion. While many people at her level play in tournaments every week of the year, Peggy plays in only seven or eight. In between, she plays virtually, using software some of her bridge friends invented that allows players to compete against other real players in real time.

She admits that online bridge is no match for live tournaments though. "There is something about live bridge—the tension, the body language—it's exciting and adds a dimension that you cannot have when playing on a computer," she says. "Plus, when we are not competing, we are able to socialize!"

Peggy has friends from all over the world and has teamed up with players from Japan, China, Iceland, Europe, and South Africa. "It's a fun challenge to put together your system when one of you speaks only a little English and your Chinese is zilch!" she says.

Keeping Her Mind Keen

Despite her world-class bridge status, Peggy modestly calls herself a jack of all trades, master of none.

"Bridge aside, I have lots of activities that are challenging, interesting, and keep me engaged," she says. "I can't say no."

She adds that this is a common trait among bridge players. "Most people who play bridge are very intelligent people, who are involved in a variety of intriguing and challenging professions and hobbies apart from bridge," she says. "So, learning about the people, their interests, and jobs—not to mention discussing bridge—absolutely helps keep my mind keen."

Peggy's own personal list of activities includes photography, writing, and volunteer work. She takes pictures at the big tournaments and writes for the online newsletters that cover bridge.

"Before I started doing it, there were very few photos of bridge players, so no one outside of the bridge world really knew who they were. I thought it would be good promotion for the players and for bridge, as a whole. Plus, it's fun," she says.

She's also a matchmaker. "I like to fix people up on dates, in partnerships, and on bridge teams—I seem to have a knack at knowing which two people will get along."

When it comes to her full-time profession, following in the footsteps of her father and grandfather, Peggy chose real estate, a business she says uses some of the same skills as bridge. "In both worlds, the nicer you are and the more you respect people, the better your outcomes will be," she says. Both also require her to be flexible, creative, to think on her feet, and to keep her emotions in check.

"Some people get very upset and angry when they are playing; I rarely do that," she says. "And, I know that there are times when things have worked out better in a real estate deal because, although I felt mad inside, I didn't let it out," she says. In business and bridge, she's very much like her friends Warren Buffett and Bill Gates. "I try hard to be a nice person and it's paid off for me," she says.

Why It Works

By playing bridge, Peggy is exercising her brain. The brain is like a muscle—you have to exercise it to keep it strong.

Bridge is a great game for people to play as they age because it involves the unique combination of patience and speed—a combination that pretty much describes Peggy's approach to life.

Bridge also requires concentration, organization, and problem-solving skills. For all of these reasons, playing bridge can help ward off dementia, research shows. In a 2013 French study published in *BMJ*, researchers followed 3,675 people without dementia for 20 years and found that those who played board games were 15 percent less likely to develop memory problems than those who did not.

In a related study, researchers looked at the connection between playing games like puzzles, checkers, and crosswords and increased mental acuity in people in their fifties and sixties. People who played one or more of these games at least every other day did better on memory tests and other tests of mental function. When participants underwent MRI scans, those who played the games had more tissue in the areas of their brains related to memory than those who did not.

In addition to being stimulating to the brain, bridge is a great social game that attracts players from all different backgrounds and skill levels. As Peggy mentioned, she's made connections with many interesting people at the bridge table and these social interactions help slow the aging process by lowering levels of interleukin-6, an inflammatory chemical that increases the risk for osteoporosis, cardiovascular disease, Alzheimer's disease, and certain types of cancer.

Steve's Secrets

As Peggy's story demonstrates, there are many mental, social, and physical benefits to be gained from mind-bending activities like bridge. To get in the game, do the following.

FIND A GAMING CLUB IN YOUR AREA. A bridge club will help you meet new people with whom you can get together and have fun playing bridge. The American Contract Bridge League has a bridge club search form on their website to help you find one near you (web3.acbl.org/findalist/club). Bridge not your thing? You can find other gaming clubs as well. Check out findgamers.us/find-groups.

GAME ONLINE. If you are a somewhat experienced bridge player and want to play against real opponents in the comfort of your living room, check out acbl.org/clubs_page/play-online-for-masterpoints/. For computerized versions of bridge and other card games, go to aarp.org/games/bridge/.

PLAY GAMES WITH FRIENDS. You don't have to become a member of a formal club to play more games. Meet friends for Bunco, checkers, poker, or canasta. When you are by yourself, pick up a crossword puzzle or Sudoku, or deal a hand of solitaire.

Sandra Ramos's Secret

Stand Up for Your Beliefs

. . . .

Volunteer for a cause you value

Express yourself

Don't lose sight of what's important

. . . .

Sandra Ramos likes to tell off jerks. She likes it so much, in fact, that she's made it her life's work.

"It's not really work; it's my passion," says the 75-year-old. She is on call 24 hours a day. When we spoke, it was 10:00 at night and she put me on hold several times to field calls alerting her of women in need. "The phrase 'after work' isn't in my vocabulary, but I'm fine with that," she says.

That work started decades ago, when a forlorn woman knocked on Sandra's front door in Ringwood, New Jersey, asking for a safe place to stay. The woman, whose children Sandra taught at Sunday school in her Unitarian church, was scared and desperate to get herself and her kids away from her abuser. Sandra wanted to help, but it was 1970 and long before the age of women's shelters and other resources. So, she took the family in.

Soon after, word spread and more women knocked on her door. "At one point, I had 23 women and children in my home," she says. That was in addition to her own three children. "It was chaotic at times, but we all supported each other, and the women stayed as long as they needed," she says.

The city officials weren't as compassionate as Sandra. The building inspector came to Sandra's home after receiving complaints from neighbors about the abused women and children living on their block. Soon after, Sandra was threatened with jail. She stood her ground, refusing to throw the families out. And, for the next 6 years, she marched, staged sit-ins, threatened legal action, and defied court orders, all in the name of protecting women and children from abuse.

"I think that the most important things people can do are to follow their consciences and not be sold out," she says.

Eventually, the city stopped fighting her.

"They offered me a job (working for the city) running shelters for three times what I was making at the time," she says. And, she needed the money. But, there was a catch. "I could get the funding, but not have a say in who was coming to the shelter," she says. I asked her who the city would want to keep out of the shelter? You know—the people you would expect them to want to keep out, she tells me. I take that to mean the women society is way too fast to reject—minorities, those with mental illness, drug abusers, and women who've had trouble with the law. "If I would have agreed to what they were asking me to do, I would have been dead in 3 months—I would have been miserable."

So, she turned it down. Instead, she went out on her own and formed a nonprofit called Strengthen Our Sisters. At first, she rented a small apartment. Then, she built up enough funds through grants and donations to rent a house. In 1990, she found a farmhouse that needed renovating that included a cottage and 10 motel units on 4.5 acres— perfect! So, she sought additional funding to buy the property, and she got it.

The current organization now has space for 150 women in seven different shelters. In addition to grants and donations, her shelters run thanks to the kindness of volunteers, including herself. She currently has only 13 women who work purely as volunteers. "They are wonderful, but they have to make money somewhere, so they are limited in how much time they can give," she says. The shelters offer a computer school where women can sharpen their skills, two thrift stores, a car donation program, two daycare centers, and a food pantry. In all of these places, Sandra is a fixture. She serves meals to the women and children and runs sessions and support groups to give the women the emotional and practical tools they need to get back on their feet. "Only when you are healthy yourself can you have healthy relationships," she says.

True to Sandra's original mission, the women she helps are of different backgrounds, races, ages, and situations. "Domestic violence is an equal opportunity employer," she says.

Sandra is eclectic and she fits into no mold. She's a lesbian. She loves wearing colorful purple dresses and scarves. She refuses to use email or the Internet—only the phone. She doesn't like money and she doesn't place value on material things. If she has enough money for her next meal, she's satisfied. But, she does like to express herself. "The outside of my house is decorated with snakes and goddesses, and my hair—like my clothes—is purple," she says.

Some of the women she helps are fellow lesbians. "I used to think lesbian women could never be battered, but it happens," she says.

With all her zeal, Sandra has made fighting for battered women her mission, not because she was battered herself (she wasn't), but because she has such a strong desire to do what's fair. "I have always disliked injustice, even when I was a kid—I want to do what is right."

When the phone finally stops ringing and Sandra's day is done, she says that what makes her happiest is knowing she is helping women get strong and feel good about themselves, "so they don't have to depend on some schmuck." Sometimes, the women successfully break away and sometimes they go back to the batterers on whom they are dependent. But, Sandra goes to sleep knowing that she's done everything in her power to help, "which keeps me healthy," she says.

Why It Works

By devoting so much time to her cause, Sandra may be adding years to her life. Volunteering is healthy, not just for the conscience and mind, but for the body as well. Adults over 50 who volunteered on a regular basis were less likely to develop high blood pressure than people who didn't volunteer, found a 2013 study published in *Psychology of Aging*. High blood pressure is a chronic condition that increases the risk for heart disease, stroke, and death.

Volunteers are also happier. When compared with people who didn't volunteer, volunteers were 7 percent more likely to report being "very happy" if they volunteered once a month and 12 percent more likely if they volunteered every 2 to 4 weeks, and 16 percent more likely if they volunteered weekly, found a study done at the London School of Economics and published in *Social Science and Medicine*.

Sandra is also doing herself and others good by standing up for what she believes. A 2016 study published in *Psychophysiology* found that standing up for your beliefs is a positive psychological experience. Researchers looked at cardiovascular responses of participants put into a group of people who disagreed with them on an issue and given one of two goals—either fit in or be an individual. The participants who were asked to fit in showed cardiovascular responses consistent to a threat state, while the participants who were free to speak their minds did not.

Another thing we noted in Sandra's story is her disdain of money. She prides herself on living on just what she needs to get by. Research on the effects of money on happiness are mixed—and it probably comes down to the fact that it depends on the person. According to research by psychology professor Sonja Lyubomirsky, author of *The How of Happiness*, half of our happiness is based on our individual baseline happiness level—something we carry from birth. Life circumstances—including wealth—contribute to only 10 percent of total happiness. The other 40 percent comes from "intentional activities."

In Sandra's case, these things include serving battered women, swimming in a stream, listening to jazz, and donning purple scarves.

Steve's Secrets

Want to make yourself and others feel good at the same time? Volunteer your time to a cause you believe in—it's simply one of the best things you can do as you get older. Use this advice to make it work.

CHOOSE YOUR CAUSE. Volunteering in and of itself is healthy, but it's particularly beneficial if you donate yourself to a cause that's meaningful to you and spend 2 hours a week doing it, finds a 2011 study done at Stony Brook University School of Medicine in New York. In the study, 68 percent said that volunteering has made them feel healthier physically and 96 percent said volunteering made them happier. Volunteers also reported less anxiety, less trouble sleeping, and stronger social networks than people who do not volunteer. Love animals? Spend some time each week petting cats in an animal shelter. Want to fight homelessness? Find an organization in your area that helps get people off the streets. Most nonprofit organizations need volunteers so the possibilities are endless.

SPEAK YOUR MIND. It's healthier to speak up and defend something you believe in than it is to stay quiet and avoid rocking the boat. Don't be afraid to defend the topics and causes about which you feel strongly. To do this without seeming aggressive, try the following.

- **Always keep in mind where the other person is coming from—and respect their perspective. You don't have to agree with it, but respect it. Try to put yourself in his or her shoes and imagine what that person is going through.**

- **Speak your points clearly in a way that's not overly defensive or self-righteous. When you're trying to explain your position on a matter, it's best to stick to the facts and leave emotions and opinions out of it.**

- **Remind yourself that your perspective matters. No one has the authority to invalidate you and you have the right to stand your ground.**

TRY NOT TO FOCUS ON MATERIAL WEALTH. In general, people who prioritize material things over other values, such as good health and a strong social network, are significantly less happy than those who value more simple pleasures, such as a pretty sunset or hot shower. The next time you are thinking about buying something, ask yourself, "Will this change my life in a good way?" If the answer is no, leave the item on the shelf and keep more money in your savings account.

Tom Servais's Secret

Do What You Love

. . . .

Find something that you are passionate about and do it as much as you can
Gravitate toward activities (and a career!) that force you to stay in the moment
Log your workouts

. . . .

Tom Servais always wanted to be a professional athlete. Throughout his life, he played basketball, baseball, football, tennis, and golf, and he also windsurfed, snowboarded, and surfed.

He was never good enough at any of these sports to go pro and make money doing what he loved to do.

But, that didn't stop him from marrying his passion with his career. Since he couldn't compete in those industries, he decided to work on the sidelines, as a photographer. He's since taken one of the most famous surfing pictures of all time.

"It's the photo of Tom Curren—Backdoor," Tom says. In the photo, legendary surfer Curren glides on a massive blue-green wave, a sparkling sea spray creating a perfect frame behind him. The photo is just one in Tom's impressive five-decade portfolio.

Getting many of those shots required Tom to put himself in the same precarious waters as the surfers themselves. "I've swum out at the big pipeline; I admit, there were a few times I was scared," he says.

To get some shots, surf photographers must swim out into the huge waves worthy of the world's best surfers, all while holding an expensive waterproof camera. Tom shoots some of his photos from the water and some from the beach—whatever's necessary to capture the best angle.

He may have been scared, but at age 64, Tom shows no signs of slowing down. He still makes a living shooting photographs of surfers on 10- to 20-foot waves.

"I'm a lucky person and I've been lucky to have gotten great photos, some of which are iconic shots that people have never forgotten," he says. "I'm also genetically lucky because I'm very healthy and have never had any serious injuries or illnesses. I'm probably healthier than 98 percent of people my age."

A person can enhance or detract from his genetic makeup, he says. "I think I've mostly added to mine because I've always been into sports and enjoyed being active. I've put a good base down. I'm smart enough to know that I have to exercise once or twice a day to keep it up. I like to get my heart rate up. Otherwise, I picture my blood pooling in my body and growing algae—I like to keep it flowing."

Tom says that what he loves so much about sports and his job as a surf photographer is that both aspects of his life help him live in the moment. "When you are playing a heated game of tennis, you're not thinking about that fight with your girlfriend—you are thinking about playing your best," he says. "If you are snowboarding, you are looking down the mountain at the run. If you are surfing, you are enjoying the water, watching the sun go down, talking with friends, and catching waves."

To stay motivated, Tom keeps an exercise log. "I write down the activity and how long I did it, and I have different highlighters to high-light each activity in its own color," he says. "If I have to skip a day due to a surf competition or travel, I use a red marker—I try to keep red days to an absolute minimum."

Despite being in great shape, Tom is also healthfully realistic, and he admits that he feels his body slowing down...just a bit. "We are all fighting Father Time and I can tell I'm not as strong as I used to be," he says. "But was Jack Lalanne as strong when he died as he was at 45? Probably not."

Why It Works

When I proposed talking to Tom, Steve was totally enthused. As a surfer himself, Steve has admired Tom's photos, as well as what he had to do as a surfer in and out of the water to get them. Plus, in addition to all of the exercise and healthy eating, Tom has a career that combines two of his loves—surfing and photography."

Workers perform better and have happier moods on the days they exercise compared with the days they don't, found a study published in the *International Journal of Workplace and Health Management*. Exercise improved their overall well-being and competitive advantage in their jobs.

There's also a connection between job satisfaction and happiness and health. In fact, career fulfillment matters more to your contentment than does money or social class.

And, when Tom's workday is done and he can finally surf purely for the enjoyment, he's boosting his mental health even higher. A study done at the California State University, San Marcos, and reported at the American Psychological Association found that surfing for 30 minutes was associated with a decrease in negative feelings and an increase in positive ones.

Steve's Secrets

When it comes to life satisfaction, Tom has it all figured out. He splits his time between his two favorite activities—sometimes, combines them—and gets paid. Of course, we made the point that money doesn't buy happiness, so here are some tips from Steve on how to find the richer kinds of joy and ultimately reap the health benefits that result.

FIND A JOB YOU LOVE. To find career happiness, you don't have to take award-winning photos while dodging humongous waves. Just find something that makes you feel fulfilled. This could be an occupation you do for your entire life or something you choose to do part-time in retirement. The good news is that people tend to appreciate their jobs more as they get older. In a study done at the University of Chicago, researchers looked at a 40-year history of the General Social Survey, one of the most comprehensive polls of American attitudes, and found that 63 percent of workers aged 65 or older expressed deep satisfaction with their jobs, compared with only 38 percent of young adults entering the workforce.

TRY SURFING. As someone who surfs, I say you are never too old to learn. Surfing is fantastic exercise—it promotes balance and core strength, reduces stress, and is a good cardiovascular workout. You can find surfing lessons in any beach area. Rent the equipment and try it out before making the full investment. And, start with a longboard—it's easier than a short one.

If you find surfing intimidating, another option is stand-up paddle surfing, which can be done in the ocean or a lake. Paddle surfing is a great total body workout.

EXERCISE IN A VARIETY OF WAYS. Try to do something different with your exercise routine every day of the week. By mixing up his workouts between surfing, tennis, mountain biking, and yoga, Tom is keeping his muscles stronger and younger. If you perform the same exercise in the same way over and over, your body will adapt and you will stop gaining benefits. When your workouts are varied, you will also avoid boredom, which can lead to less-intense or shorter workouts. To keep your mind and body interested, do activities and exercises that you enjoy.

Allison Laframboise's Secret

Do Yoga

. . . .

Stop and experience the present moment
Face every emotion—good or bad
Employ drumming and other relaxation techniques

. . . .

Twenty years ago, Allison Laframboise, who is now 42, was a victim of her own thoughts. "I was going through a hard time. My longtime, long-distance boyfriend had just been diagnosed with cancer, I was grappling with sexual abuse from my childhood, and I dealt with all the madness by trying to perfect my body, which led to body-image issues," she says. Then, she found yoga.

"Boston University, where I was going at the time, offered yoga as an elective, so I decided to go for it. It was love at first try," she says. "After my first yoga class, I felt present—in my body and out of my head for the first time in so long. I had broken my cycle of obsession and depression, if even just for a small amount of time..."

That small amount of time became a big amount of time. Allison has not stopped practicing yoga since that first time. She does it every day, teaches Kripalu yoga, leads yoga and drumming retreats with her husband in the Massachusetts Berkshires, and designs and sells inspirational jewelry (called Prasada) that reflects her personal philosophies.

"What I like most about yoga is what it does to my body and mind," says Allison, who is also co-author of *Pranayama: A Path to Healing and Freedom*, a book about yogic breathwork. Physically, she says it helps release tension in her muscles, "so I feel more fluid and free and less painful and achy." Mentally, it makes her a happier person and a better mom.

It also makes her look and feel much younger. "Yoga reduces stress, increases a state of presence, and offers physical activity that keeps blood flowing, organs active, and immunity high. It also increases my self-knowledge, so I can make the choices necessary to live the life I want to live," she says. All of these benefits help keep her young in body, mind, and spirit.

The Fountain of Yoga

As Allison and I talked about the benefits of yoga, she told me a story about her dermatologist: "My derm said for a while, whenever older patients looked particularly youthful and could hop up on the exam table with ease, he would ask them how they stay so nimble. They would almost always say, 'yoga.' So now, when patients come in looking particularly healthy and physically agile, he says, 'I know what you do!'" she tells me. Her dermatologist was so impressed that he became a yoga convert.

"Last time I saw him, he commented on how much it has helped his back pain," Allison says.

Yoga has also helped ease physical discomfort for Allison. For her jewelry business, she sits a lot—either working at the computer or designing her pieces. "Sitting is horrible for our bodies—my hips get really tight, which leads to back pain and other discomfort throughout my body," she says. "It has been said that sitting is the new smoking in terms of the health problems it causes." Yoga helps counter the pain and tightness by keeping her body more flexible and free moving.

It helps keep her attitude more flexible too, which can be challenging for a mom of two young boys.

"Yoga reduces stress by giving us accessible tools to be in the present moment," she says. "Relaxation is important because stress contributes to all kinds of diseases and early aging," she says. One of those tools is deep breathing, which shifts us out of fight-or-flight mode. "It helps me to take a moment before I react," Allison says.

Being in the present moment affects the way she approaches her kids as well. "After teaching yoga or doing my own yoga practice, I see my children like the miraculous beings they are. I see the expressions on their faces so clearly. I hear their voices, feel their skin, and notice all their movements," she says. "I can't be in this mode 100 percent of the time, but I can get there sometimes—it's a miracle and a gift I hope to never take for granted!"

Searching for the Experience of Being Alive

Like many yogis, Allison quotes the wisdom of American mythologist Joseph Campbell. "He says that we're not looking for the meaning of life, but rather the experience of being alive," she says.

Another important part of being alive is facing every emotion, good or bad. "If I experience sadness, I let it flow through me and part of me watches it without wavering, knowing it will pass and another emotion will come," she says. She calls this tool an inner witness. "With our inner witness, we can step back and be present to an emotion without having to shut down or numb ourselves."

Plus, when we see fears and limitations clearly, we can address them instead of letting them control us. "For example, I had a lot of fear about starting my own business and being able to generate enough income. Because of my self-awareness through yoga, I could see that fear, take responsibility for it, and figure out how to work through it."

And, when we feel negative emotions, heal old wounds, and shift dysfunctional patterns, we are better able to release them, which makes us healthier.

As much as she loves yoga, Allison admits that the practice isn't for everyone. "I think it's important for people to try what they are naturally drawn to," she says. "If yoga isn't completely your thing, there's something out there that's a better fit—you just have to look for it. I do believe that mind-body practices have tremendous benefit when it comes to staying healthy and young. Find something that helps you be more present, calmer, more alive," she advises. "Some examples are tai chi, meditation, and mindfulness."

Why It Works

When he heard the story about Allison's dermatologist noticing yogis are more agile, Steve could relate. He's seen the same benefits in his patients who do yoga.

Yoga offers many health benefits, including increased flexibility, improved muscle strength and tone, better energy, increase in cardiovascular health, protection from injury, and help with weight reduction and control.

In terms of mental health, as Allison points out, yoga helps improve relaxation and reduce stress, which is known to cause all kinds of physical problems, including trouble sleeping, headaches, back pain, drug abuse, and problems with concentration.

For all these reasons, research shows that yoga can help slow aging. In one 2014 study published in *Evidence-Based Complementary and Alternative Medicine*, researchers looked at the effects of intensive yoga practice on two important substances linked to longevity and youth—growth hormone (GH) and dehydroepiandrosterone sulfate (DHEAS). As we age, levels of these two substances drop significantly. GH is a hormone that stimulates cell growth and reproduction, and DHEA is a hormone produced in the adrenal gland that improves immune function, heart health, and other functions in the body.

In the study, researchers assigned 45 participants ranging in age from 34 to 53 to either a yoga group or a waitlist control condition. The men in the yoga group performed yoga practices 6 days a week for 12 weeks, increasing their intensity as they went along. Those in the control group went about their usual daily activities. At the end of the 12 weeks, the yoga group had significant increases in both GH and DHEA levels. They also had notable decreases in their body mass index (BMI). This study was small, but the results do suggest that yoga has benefits for keeping the body supple, strong, and healthy.

Other research has linked yoga with improved heart health and more balanced levels of brain activity and hormones, including lower levels of the stress hormones epinephrine and cortisol.

The study results indicate that yoga may help prevent age-related degeneration, including the protection of heart health.

An additional important finding from the study: Yoga appears to increase levels of a protein called brain-derived neurotrophic factor (BDNF), which affects mood, brain plasticity, and memory. Low levels of BDNF have been linked to depression, cognitive problems, dementia, and Alzheimer's disease.

It seems as though the effects of yoga on the brain are similar to those in the body—it helps keep things flexible and strong. So, in addition to keeping your heart young, yoga may help to keep your mind sharp too.

Steve's Secrets

Once reserved for Hindus and Buddhists, yoga has fully hit the mainstream. Professional basketball and ice-hockey players, rock stars, and triathletes all recognize the benefits of yoga and are practicing the ancient art.

Here's how to get started and reap the most benefits from yoga.

UNDERSTAND THE TYPES. There are many different forms of yoga, each with their own approach to the practices. Almost all yoga in Western culture falls under the umbrella of Hatha yoga. Hatha yoga is a broad term that refers to a physical practice of yoga, meaning it focuses mainly on yoga postures (as opposed to breathwork and meditation). A class described as Hatha is usually a basic class, where students are guided into a posture to hold it for a few breaths and then they're guided out of the posture. This is a great pace for beginners, as you have time to learn safe alignment and become comfortable in the posture. The other yoga styles that follow are specific types of Hatha yoga.

Hot yoga. As its name suggests, hot yoga exposes class members to temperatures between 85° and 105°F. The goal is to make it easier for the body to get warmed up to move and to release toxins by sweating. To avoid dehydration, drink plenty of water before you do hot yoga. And if you feel dizzy, lightheaded, nauseated, or have trouble breathing while doing hot yoga, move to a cooler area.

Vinyasa. Vinyasa yoga flows quickly between postures, usually moving into a new position with each inhale and exhale. This will elevate your heart rate and provide a stronger exercise element.

Iyengar. Named after the founder of this style, B. K. S. Iyengar, this approach focuses heavily on alignment detail.

Ashtanga. Ashtanga is a very traditional practice that includes six specific posture sequences. A student progresses from one sequence to the next over time. It can be physically demanding and is therefore not recommended for those with injuries or medical conditions. This is good for people who like things that are regimented and predictable.

Anusara. Anusara yoga encourages creative expression and includes playful elements.

FIND A GOOD CLASS. You can find yoga classes at health clubs, gyms, community centers, spas, and yoga studios in your town (more and more pop up all the time). Most venues offer beginner or gentle yoga classes, which are a great way to get started. Not only will a beginner's class teach you the basic tools you need to build on but it will also surround you with fellow yoga rookies, which will make you feel more comfortable. Another important tip: Make sure that you like the instructor. Because of its effects on the mind/spirit, yoga can become a very personal experience, so it's helpful to find a teacher who you resonate with. If you try a class and don't like it, don't give up. The quality of yoga varies tremendously. Try a class somewhere else or with a different instructor.

GET THE ESSENTIALS. To get started, all you need is comfortable clothing that allows you to move with ease. If you want to purchase a basic yoga mat you can, but most facilities that offer yoga provide mats for you to use. If you are trying yoga at home, you can do it right on your carpet if you don't have a mat.

TAKE IT ONE STEP AT A TIME. Whatever style you choose and wherever you decide to practice yoga, keep the following tips from Allison in mind:

- **Take it slowly at first**
- **Never force anything**
- **Listen to your body and honor what feels best for you**
- **Remember, yoga should never hurt**
- **Use yoga to increase attunement with your body and mind**

Whether you are experienced with yoga or just getting started, Allison offers free yoga resources through her website (allisongemmellaframboise.com) and her YouTube channel (youtube.com/channel/UCWetxAYmbQHjaKd4-rFzeNA).

Jeanette Alosi's Secret

Try Ayurveda

. . . .

Eat your main meal at noon

Consume what's in season

Realize that it's never too late to try something new

. . . .

Jeanette Alosi wasn't always so strong and vibrant. "In my twenties, I ate processed food, rarely exercised, and drank alcohol more frequently than was healthy," she says. Those habits, three pregnancies, and hypothyroidism caused her to feel sluggish and gain weight.

"After I had my three children, finances didn't allow for a lot of extras, so I started to pay attention to the quality of food I was eating," she says. When she returned to school to become a respiratory therapist, she learned even more about how to eat for good health.

But, it was when she discovered yoga and Ayurveda in the early 2000s that things really started to change for the better. "Ayurveda specifically reminded me that I am part of nature and therefore affected by nature's laws," she says. "The season of the year, time of day, foods I choose, when I sleep, relationships I am in, are all significant aspects of my health and well-being."

Eating with Gratitude

Ayurveda has taught Jeanette how to eat—and when to eat—which has made a tremendous difference in her weight and how she feels.

"According to Ayurveda, the main meal is best eaten at noon, when the digestive fire (juices, enzymes, etc.) is at is strongest," she says. When she eats her biggest meal in the middle of the day, Jeanette says she sleeps better, has more energy, and approaches the day with more happiness and strength.

She also eats according to the 80/20 rule presented by her Ayurvedic teacher, where 80 percent of food should be for life force and the other 20 percent should be for pleasure. "I eat non-GMO, organic, fresh, and local," she says. "Do I do that 24 hours a day, 7 days a week? No. Sometimes, I eat lunch out and drink a craft beer. Do I beat myself up over that? Emphatically, no!"

Jeanette stays true to Ayurveda's teachings in that she eats foods that are in season—fruits and lighter vegetables in summer and heavier root vegetables and grains in winter. "I eat no refined sugar and a very small amount of white flour," she says. "Instead, I use rice or wheat pasta, and I make my own bread."

She starts each day with a glass of warm water and lemon, along with half-decaf, half-regular coffee. "I add cardamom when brewing to help counteract the effects of the caffeine," she says.

Jeanette also rarely eats meat. When she does, she makes sure that she knows where it came from. "The source of meat is important for a variety of reasons. Not only is it important to know the chemicals, hormones, and food it ingested, but also how it was raised. We also absorb energy from the food we eat and energy from animals that are not raised humanely would not be digested in a healthy manner," she says.

This is what a typical day of eating looks like for her.

BREAKFAST. She eats small portions, usually a poached egg on rye toast or oatmeal with raisins, sometimes with maple syrup. "I sprinkle the oatmeal with turmeric and cinnamon for their astringent, bitter, and pungent taste," she says.

SNACK. A snack consists of cut-up fresh fruit topped with lemon or lime juice, turmeric, and cinnamon. "Ayurveda recommends eating fruit separate from a meal because it aids in digestion," she says.

LUNCH. Lunch may be beans and rice, salad, or fresh vegetables. "I eat meat or fish with lunch four or five times a week," Jeanette says. Sometimes she makes kitchari, a blend of yellow mung bean, basmati rice, cilantro, coconut, and spices. "When cooking with fat, I use ghee (a clarified butter commonly used in South Asian and Middle Eastern cuisine that I make myself) and Ayurveda recommends sunflower oil for my body type—kapha." There are three body types in Ayurvedic medicine—kapha (water energy), pitta (fire energy), and vata (wind energy), each of which have unique shapes and dietary needs.

DINNER. Dinner can be leftovers from lunch or sometimes a soup made with veggies. For everything she eats, Jeanette is grateful.

"Dr. Carrie Demers from the Himalayan Institute once said more important than what you eat is how you eat. You should be thankful for what you have and eat with a positive attitude rather than obsessing over whether everything is organic," she says.

Like a Kid Again

Jeanette also practices Ayurveda's sister science, yoga, and meditates every day.

These practices have opened Jeanette's spirit to new experiences. "When I was 49, my sister who is 10 years younger asked me to go skiing; I thought, 'if I don't try it now, I probably never will,'" she says. Jeannette had a blast. "When I told my husband how much fun I had, he immediately wanted to try it too. Now, it is something we do together and both love—it's the beauty of the mountains, being outdoors, and when you are skiing downhill, you actually feel like a child again," she says.

Since they started, Jeanette and her husband have made skiing an integral part of their activities together, traveling to Vermont, Canada, Wyoming, Montana, Colorado, Oregon, and most recently, Utah. Skiing keeps them in good shape in the winter and gives them motivation to do things that keep them strong and flexible throughout the year. "My husband has a goal to ski with our granddaughter when he is 80," she says.

Jeanette admits that the slopes haven't always been smooth. "In 2013, I had an accident at Mt. Bachelor in Bend, Oregon, that resulted in ACL reconstruction surgery, which took me off the slopes for close to a year." But, she credits a complete recovery to her yoga and Ayurveda practices.

"I think our response to pain and suffering and our ability to bounce back is a true reflection of our health and well-being. As we get older, there are going to be challenges to our bodies, minds, and emotions—it's how we respond to them that matters," she says.

In addition to her skiing trips, Jeanette walks three times a week and bikes occasionally.

"We also kayak in the summer and do some hiking," she says. "I believe in making exercise as enjoyable as possible."

In everything, Jeanette tries to follow the 80/20 rule. "If we practice healthy habits 80 percent of the time, we can consider ourselves successful."

Why It Works

Consuming the bulk of your calories earlier in the day, as Jeanette does, can help with weight control. A 2013 study published in the *International Journal of Obesity* looked at the timing of meals in relation to weight loss. The study included 420 overweight participants who ate a mid-day meal consisting of 1,400 calories or 40 percent of their daily intake. Half ate that meal before 3:00 p.m. and the other half ate it after 3:00 p.m. The early-eaters lost an average of 22 pounds and the late-eaters lost 17 pounds—evidence that eating earlier contributes to more pounds lost.

In a more recent 2016 study published in the *American Journal of Clinical Nutrition*, 80 overweight women were randomly assigned to eat their main meals at either lunch or dinner. Fifty percent of their calories were to come from lunch, and 20 percent from dinner, or vice versa. The types of foods the participants ate was essentially the same. At the end of 12 weeks, both groups lost weight, but the women who ate more of their calories at lunch lost more (13 pounds) than the women who had eaten more of their calories at dinner (9 pounds).

Jeanette also has the right idea when she seeks fruits and vegetables that are in season. Seasonal fruits and vegetables are picked at the peak of freshness and nutritional content. They are also free of the waxes, preservatives, and chemicals used to maintain out-of-season produce. By buying seasonal fruits and veggies, you also support your local farmers and save money in the process—in season, these crops cost consumers less. Plus, you can feel good about buying local freshly harvested foods because they travel fewer miles before reaching your plate. This cuts down on the amount of fuel used and, therefore, reduces pollution. In short, seasonal produce is best for your body and the planet—a win-win situation.

Steve's Secrets

Use this advice to alter your diet for increased energy.

EAT YOUR LARGER MEAL BEFORE 3:00 P.M. Whether it's lunch or dinner, if you're trying to lose or maintain weight, you are best to eat your largest meal earlier in the day. If you eat smaller, more frequent meals than the standard three, make sure that more of them are in the a.m. than in the p.m. The studies are pretty clear in showing that you burn calories slower if you eat them closer to the time you go to bed.

SPRINKLE ON SOME SPICES. The spices Jeannette uses to flavor and season her food—namely cinnamon and turmeric—have powerful health benefits. Some studies have shown that cinnamon can help lower blood sugar levels and reduce inflammation. Turmeric is a yellow-colored spice often used in Asian cooking. It's an ancient natural remedy used for a range of conditions, including arthritis, digestive problems, inflammation, headaches, diabetes, and autoimmune disorders.

These are also wonderful no-calorie alternatives to sugar and fat for flavoring food. Here are some creative ways to use them:

- **Add cinnamon to hot or cold cereal or in whole-wheat pancake batter.**
- **Throw a dash of turmeric into a hot or iced latte.**
- **Mix cinnamon in with some peanut butter and spread it on celery or apple slices.**
- **Add ½ teaspoon of turmeric to a breakfast banana smoothie.**
- **Stir in ½ teaspoon of cinnamon in with a cup of vanilla yogurt.**
- **Blend turmeric with chickpeas in a food processor for a tasty hummus.**
- **Use cinnamon as a rub for chicken or grilled fish.**
- **Throw some turmeric into a homemade vegetable soup.**
- **Sprinkle cinnamon over sweet potatoes or cooked carrots.**

PRACTICE THE 80/20 RULE. For eating, exercise, and other habits, this is a good rule of thumb. If you spend the majority of your time making the right health decisions, you will reap the rewards. Not only is the 80/20 rule an easy way to keep yourself balanced but it also allows you the occasional glass of wine, rest day from exercise, or piece of dark chocolate. Here are a few examples:

- **80 percent whole, healthful foods, 20 percent splurges**
- **80 percent productive activities, 20 percent reading gossip magazines and binge-watching Netflix**
- **80 percent water, 20 percent wine**
- **80 percent exercise days, 20 percent rest days**

Kathy Shaffer's Secret

Life Is Short–Live It Hard

. . . .

Practice giving to others

Spend time with the people that you enjoy being around

Dream it...then plan it...then do it

. . . .

Kathy Shaffer's mother passed away from non-Hodgkin's lymphoma at age 56, when Kathy was just 31. Not a day goes by that Kathy doesn't think of her. "She was the sweetest woman and the best mom—she took great care of my dad and her five kids," she says.

At first, Kathy took her mother's death very hard. "I couldn't eat, I couldn't sleep, and I ended up in the hospital with palpitations," she recalls. But as she worked through the "nasty mourning process," she emerged a stronger person.

"I thought, 'you can wallow in sorrow or you can get on with your life.' I looked internally, and as a young mother myself, the choice was obvious—learn from the mom who always told me, 'Live for today. Be happy!' "

Now 62, Kathy truly lives for every day. Even in her retirement, every one of Kathy's days is meaningful. She walks with her husband and dog, exercises, gardens, decorates her new home and the homes of her friends, and travels. She's practically overflowing with positive energy, and she has a twinkle in her bright blue eyes and a glow in her cheeks that make her appear at least 10 years younger than she is.

"Getting older is a fact of life—you can't stop it so why get upset?" she says. Because she lost her mother at such a young age, Kathy looks at aging as a privilege, not as a curse. "To me, older age is about doing all the things you always wanted to do. I feel lucky to be so healthy and active at my age that I can do them!" she says.

Life Is Short–Live it Hard

Kathy admits her definition of living for today doesn't look the same now as it did when her mother died. In her early thirties, it meant taking a hard, honest look at what she wanted to do with the rest of her life. "I realized how short life is," she says. Unhappy in her career and her home life, she made some difficult changes.

First, she went back to school to get her bachelor's degree. "At the time, that meant working full-time, coaching college basketball, going to school, and being a mom to two middle-schoolers—all at once!"

Eventually, she sold her car to minimize bills, so she could concentrate on school full-time, and she walked the mile and a half to Moravian College near her home in downtown Bethlehem, Pennsylvania. "I really wanted to get my degree. I didn't do it the easy way—I didn't graduate until I was 39—but it was worth it!" she says.

Worth it indeed. Kathy got her degree in psychology and business, which led to a very successful career in hospital administration. With her charisma and drive, she moved up the ladder quickly, peaking as administrative director. Her career gave her fulfillment and the independence she craved; she ended her 23-year marriage to her high-school sweetheart. "Perhaps we were too young when we got married; life changes," she says.

As part of her position at the hospital, Kathy reached out to the community and became president of the Board of Directors for the Adult Literacy Center in Allentown.

"I enjoyed helping non-English speaking students get their degrees. I could relate to them because I went back to school later in life to get mine." She says her community service work was partially the result of her mother's advice: " 'Give, give, give to others; if you give, you will be paid back twofold,' my mother would say. She was right."

A New Kind of Purpose

Today, living in the moment for Kathy means enjoying her early retirement with her second husband, Bud (to whom she is very happily married), and spending her days exactly how she pleases—"which is heaven," she says.

Instead of logging hours in her office, Kathy spends six mornings a week at the gym working out in classes and with weights. "I grew up in a gym," she says. "I always played sports or coached so fitness is part of who I am."

Kathy also spends lots of quality time with her girlfriends—women she's kept in touch with from different ages and stages of her life. "I'm still friends with some of the women I coached in basketball and managed at the hospital," she says. She is a leader among her friends and reaches out to them often. "You have to schedule time with the people you enjoy, especially as you get older. Even if you feel like you are always the one doing the planning—stop pitying yourself and just do it! I'm always happy I did."

Above all, the thing that seems to make Kathy happiest is time with her family. Together, she and Bud have four children (two from his first marriage and two from her first marriage) and three grandchildren. She lights up when she talks about them. "I spend every Thursday with my grandchildren and have the kids over for meals all the time. Any excuse to see them. I still take my daughter school shopping—and she's 40!" she laughs.

Recently, when her daughter-in-law fell and broke both of her ankles, Kathy dropped everything and stepped in to take care of her three grandchildren—ages 6 months, 3, and 5. "A mother of three young kids and she couldn't walk! So, I went to help—that's what moms do. It's what my mom would have done," she says.

When she's not helping with her grandchildren, she and Bud spend lots of time together walking their beloved golden retriever, hiking, biking, and planning their next few decades.

"We are both very passionate people, and I know that keeps us aiming high and working toward our dreams," she says. "More importantly, my husband lets me be me, which I'm sure isn't always easy!" she laughs.

She and Bud also travel all over the world together, most recently on a 15-day excursion to Spain and Portugal. "Those trips are amazing—we relax and relearn history at the same time. It makes us feel special as a couple."

Kathy talks about her life with the fervor of someone who is living a life of the rich and famous, because, in her eyes, she is. "I keep moving, keep planning, keep giving," she says. "I have worked hard to get to where I am. I learned the hard way that you live for today. A lot of people say that they live for the present, but they don't actually do it. I'm doing it."

Why It Works

Steve and I both know Kathy Shaffer and we agree that she models the way we would like to be in the future. She's definitely living for today, and doing what she wants, which is awesome.

The scientific term for living in the moment is *mindfulness*. When you are mindful, you experience your life, rather than letting it pass you by.

Research shows that mindful people tend to be more exuberant, empathetic, kind, and secure. They are also more confident, happier, and better able to laugh at and accept their own weaknesses. Sounds like Kathy to a T.

There's good science to back up that Kathy's approach to life may also help keep her thin. In a 2015 study done at Brown University in Providence, Rhode Island, and published in the *International Journal of Behavioral Medicine*, researchers found that people who live in the moment tend to have less body fat. The researchers looked at nearly 400 people, measuring their body fat as well as their level of mindfulness using a 15-question survey. They found that people with low levels of mindfulness were 34 percent more likely to be obese than those who reported being more present in their lives.

Living in the moment may also help Kathy stay emotionally well. In a study published in the journal *Science*, a group of Harvard psychologists collected information on the daily thoughts, feelings, and activities of 2,250 volunteers and found they were happiest when they were enjoying what was happening right then, right now. Thinking ahead, reminiscing, and daydreaming made people less happy, even when the participants were thinking about something positive.

Mindfulness may also support Kathy's relationships by making her less aggressive and more agreeable. In a study published in the journal *Aggressive Behavior*, researchers looked at the relationship between mindfulness and aggression. They recreated mindfulness by asking some participants to slowly eat a raisin. They then exposed both the raisin-eaters and a second group who hadn't eaten the raisin to a provocative situation. The participants who mindfully ate the raisin were significantly less likely to react aggressively than those in the nonraisin group.

Aside from her mindfulness, another positive thing that Kathy has done for her health is to carry on her mother's legacy, by showing a similar loving style to her children and grandchildren. Incorporating the traditions that you grew up with is a healthy way to deal with loss.

- -

At-a-Glance: How to Be Spunky

→ After 10:00 a.m., perk up with green tea instead of coffee or energy drinks.

→ Pick snacks that contain protein and fiber, but very little sugar. Good options include apples with nuts, string cheese with carrots, or plain yogurt with berries.

→ Get 7 to 9 hours of shut-eye every night.

→ Drink 91 to 125 fluid ounces of water a day. That's 11 to 15 eight-ounce glasses.

→ Exercise for at least 20 minutes at a low-intensity at least three times a week. Walking and yoga are great options.

→ Perform an act of generosity every single day.

→ Dedicate 2 hours a week to volunteering.

→ Find hobbies that make life exciting and worth living.

→ When something bothers you, say something. Don't keep it bottled up.

→ Prioritize your friendships and relationships over acquiring possessions and material wealth.

→ Exercise your mind every day by playing board games, doing crossword puzzles, or listening to quiz shows, among other options.

→ Embrace the 80/20 rule by focusing on healthy, wholesome foods 80 percent of the time and splurges the other 20 percent.

→ Consume the bulk of your calories before 3:00 p.m., making lunch your largest meal of the day and dinner your smallest.

→ Sprinkle healing spices–especially cinnamon and turmeric–onto what you eat.

→ Transform your work into something you love. It will help you to hop out of bed in the morning energized to face each day.

→ Don't lounge around in your pj's. Get dressed, even if you don't plan on going out.

Steve's Secrets

In the hustle and bustle of everyday life, we too often find that "the moment" slips away before we have a chance to savor it. To slow down and capture more of the fleeting gems the present has to offer, use this advice:

BREATHE. A good way to bring yourself into the moment is to focus on your breathing. Think about each breath, in and out, to place your awareness on the here and now. A great thing about this exercise is that you can do it anytime, anywhere.

GO WITH THE FLOW. Literally. "Flow" is total absorption in a task to the point that you lose track of time and everything around you. To achieve flow, first set a goal that is challenging, yet attainable. Depending on your abilities, it could be something as simple as reading a novel or writing a short poem or as complex as composing a piece of music. You must also set up the task so that you get immediate feedback. If you are playing a piece of music, you will know you hit the wrong note, for example. As you become more focused on your task, you will become less self-conscious and less aware of any distractions around you.

SAVOR THE PRESENT. Too often, people will be in the middle of a beautiful situation and think only about what comes before and after. "I hope the sunset is as pretty tomorrow night," or "This vacation spot is so nice—let's book it for next year" are two good examples. Instead, relish what you are doing at the exact moment.

Steve's Prescription for Having Amazing Spunk

To follow up the stellar advice you've gotten from our always-spunky wonders, here's some bonus advice from Steve on how to maximize your spunkiness.

BALANCE YOUR ENERGY BY BALANCING YOUR DIET. In my observation—both in my personal life and practice—spunky people tend to be busy. There's no harm in being zealous, but in all the hustle, it's important not to let your eating habits take a back seat. Make sure that all your meals are balanced and include plenty of fiber-rich vegetables, fruits, a lean protein, whole grains, low-fat or fat-free dairy, and a small amount of healthy fats. Remember—a balanced plate helps you tackle a full plate! For more info on how to build a balanced plate, go to choosemyplate.gov.

EXERCISE FOR SPUNK. When your energy is sapped, the last thing you might think of doing is working out. However, research shows that exercise is one of the best remedies for sedentary people who feel fatigued. A study published in *Psychotherapy and Psychosomatics* looked at 36 tired people who rarely exercised. As part of the study, one group did 20 minutes of moderate-intensity aerobic exercise (similar to a fast-paced walk up a hill) three times a week for 6 weeks. The second group engaged in low-intensity exercise (equivalent to a leisurely walk) and the third group didn't exercise. The low-intensity exercise group saw the biggest energy boosts—65 percent—evidence that you don't need to work out hard to increase your energy; you just need to exercise regularly.

EMBRACE YOGA. There's a reason that Allison Laframboise and Jeanette Alosi have energy to spare at the end of the day—their yoga practices. In a 2017 study, performing yoga poses increased participants' energy and self-esteem. Whether you are a yogi or not, the following poses will help increase your zest, especially if you do them in the morning. Keep in mind that these are just two of myriad yoga poses that provide a nice energy boost.

Cobra pose: Lie face down with your legs extended. Bend your elbows and place your palms on the floor directly under your shoulders. Hug your elbows against your ribcage. As you inhale, lift your chest as you straighten your arms. Keep the tops of your feet, thighs, and pubis against the floor. Take 5 to 10 deep breaths and then gently release back down to the floor.

Bridge pose: As a bonus, this pose stretches your hamstrings, glutes, and quads. To do it, lie on your back on a mat with your knees bent and your feet flat on the floor, about hip-width apart. Hold a block between your upper inner thighs. Squeezing the block between your inner thighs, lift your hips so that only your head, upper back, and feet are on the floor. Hold for 10 to 15 breaths and release, relaxing on the mat for a minute or two following the pose.

DRINK UP. It's a simple tip that goes a long way: Guzzle water throughout the day. Even slight dehydration can make you feel tired, both mentally and physically. As little as a 2 percent decrease in your body's normal volume of water can cause fatigue, headaches, and problems concentrating, reports a study in the *American College of Sports*

Medicine's Health and Fitness Journal. The exact amount of water you need depends on a number of factors, including your altitude, activity level, weight, and any health conditions you may have. As a general recommendation, the Dietary Reference Intake for water for adults is between 91 and 125 fluid ounces (2.7 to 3.7 liters) of water a day.

A great way to monitor how much you are drinking is to use a water bottle that displays the fluid ounces on the side. Liz and I tried this and have noticed a marked difference in how we feel. Plus, the added water has made our skin look plumper and less tired as well.

STAY AWAY FROM SUGARY ENERGY DRINKS. While we're on the topic of beverages, in the name of energy, weight control, and general good health, stay away from caffeinated and other soda, sugary coffee drinks, and energy drinks. (Yes, Gatorade counts). These drinks will give you an initial energy buzz, but the crash back down will be equally as robust. If you need flavor in your drink, add a few slices of lemon, orange, lime, or other fruit to your water.

GET GOOD SLEEP. This may sound like a no-brainer, but to sustain your energy level throughout the day, you have to get enough sleep the night before.

The National Sleep Foundation recommends getting 7 to 9 hours of sleep per night. We as Americans do pretty well with our hours—we sleep an average of 7 hours, 36 minutes, according to a survey by the foundation. However, only 12 percent report getting an "excellent" quality of sleep. And, sleep is one of those things where quality is as important as quantity. To sleep better, try the following:

- **Keep the temperature of your bedroom between 60° and 67°F.**
- **Try a white noise machine, fan, eye masks, or earplugs.**
- **Stick to the same sleep time schedule every day, including the weekends.**
- **Don't take naps during the day.**
- **Exercise daily, but not within 4 hours of bedtime.**
- **Avoid caffeine after 2:00 p.m.**
- **Finish your last alcoholic drink at least 2 hours before bed.**
- **Have kids and pets sleep in another room.**
- **If your mattress and pillows are sagging, flat, or more than 10 years old, consider replacing them.**

STOP DRINKING COFFEE BY 10:00 A.M. Although it contains some water, coffee doesn't count toward your liquid intake; in fact, it can actually dehydrate, rather than hydrate, your body. The caffeine in coffee is a mild diuretic, which means it encourages your body to *let go* of water. Plus, drinking coffee too late in the day can keep you up at night, sapping your energy for tomorrow. To keep your body hydrated and energized, a good rule of thumb is to stop drinking coffee and switch to water by 10:00 a.m.

BE SKEPTICAL OF ENERGY BARS. Some have as much sugar as a candy bar. Others are legit. To discern the truly energizing, look for the following on the label:

- **No genetically modified organism (GMO) ingredients**
- **Less than 200 milligrams of sodium per serving**
- **No sugar alcohols, refined sugars, or artificial sweeteners**
- **Fewer than 200 calories**
- **Protein content that's half of the carbohydrate content**
- **Less than 7 grams of sugar**
- **No more than 12 grams of fat**

GO AHEAD, HAVE A SNACK. If you do it right, snacking is an effective way to keep your energy levels high. The key is to munch on the right kind of food. A bag of cheese curls or potato chips can actually be worse than eating nothing at snack time. Instead, look for foods that contain a protein as well as fiber-rich carbs. Good options include a small bag of air-popped popcorn and a cheese stick, a handful of berries and some granola with almonds, or a sliced pear with a ½ cup of low-salt cottage cheese. In terms of portion size, snacks should be big enough to sustain you without being filling.

TAKE ENERGY UP A NOTCH WITH GREEN TEA. Drink a cup of hot or iced green tea and not only will you get a nice little energizing dose of caffeine, you'll also get catechins—antioxidants that help raise resting metabolism. Plus, the polyphenols in green tea have a whole host of additional health benefits, from cancer prevention to lowering high blood pressure to helping to prevent diabetes. Green tea is one of the healthiest things you can put in your body, hands down.

Seven

Be Well

Most of us know someone who never seems to get sick. Maybe it's a pastor who never catches a cold despite shaking hundreds of hands each Sunday. Or, perhaps it's an elementary school teacher who, despite getting coughed and sneezed on every day, never misses a day of work.

And, if you are the kind of person who seems to catch every single sniffle, you may understandably wonder: How do they do it? Are they born with bionic immune systems? Or, do they use tactics that can help the rest of us?

Well, get ready to learn the answers to those questions—as well as the answers to questions that you may not have thought to ask.

In this chapter, you'll read about amazing people who seem to have found the secret to lasting health. That's not all. You'll also get the flip side. We tracked down several people who got sick, took control, and fought their way back to permanent good health.

Murray Grossan's Secret

Don't Fear Germs

. . . .

Have a healthy sense of humor

Eat yogurt every day

Reduce stress with measured breathing

. . . .

Dr. Murray Grossan hardly ever gets sick. "I may have had a cold 10 years ago," he says. Wow, we thought. With three young, germy kids running around, we've barely gone a few months. As a physician, Murray offers an educated perspective on why he's so healthy.

"I think it's partially because I've had constant minimal exposure to colds, flu, and other viruses as part of my job," he says. "Many doctors build up a resistance because of this exposure."

He also gives some credit to dumb luck.

As far as the strategies others can benefit from, he points out the yogurt that he's eaten every day for the past 30 years.

"I also tell jokes and make my patients laugh, which makes me laugh too," he says.

Thanks to these tactics and more, Murray lives a very healthy existence, especially for a 94-year-old. He survived colon cancer back in 1976 and has been cancer-free since then. He still practices otolaryngology and runs the Grossan Institute in Los Angeles—several decades after most people would have retired. When Steve and I talk about retirement, we hope we can work until 70; 90-plus never enters our conversation.

"Yes, I still practice medicine; my wife shops," he jokes. He's also written several books, including *Stressed? Anxiety? Your Cure is in the Mirror*. The crux of his philosophy is that the first step toward better health should be to stop the stress and anxiety chemicals that impair normal healing. Obviously, he's onto something.

Laughing It Off

"When Norman Cousins lay dying at UCLA, the doctors couldn't help him," Murray tells us. "Then, his friends brought in a movie projector, hung a sheet on the wall, and showed him funny movies. He laughed and he got well."

The science of psychoneuroimmunology shows how powerfully emotions affect the immune system. Even just the physical movement of a fake smile can increase a person's immunity, some evidence shows.

Murray uses humor to describe an important cancer treatment he received nearly four decades ago. "After my cancer surgery, I enrolled in an experimental program where they injected my cancer cells into a sheep. The sheep developed antibodies and then I was given those antibodies," he explains. "The only complication was my strong desire to have sex with a sheep!"

On a more serious note, he adds, "It is utterly tragic that almost 40 years later, we are just beginning to develop this form of therapy."

A Yogurt a Day Keeps the Doctor Away

When it comes to his daily yogurt, Murray's not as concerned with brand as he is with ingredients. "We don't really know which brands are best," he says. It's the probiotics in the yogurt he thinks are helping him stay well. Probiotics are bacteria and yeast that are good for your health.

Researchers are studying the ability of the probiotics in yogurt and other fermented foods to treat a range of conditions, from eczema to inflammatory bowel disease. "If I were starting today, I would explore the sauerkraut and kefir stuff too," Murray says.

In addition to regulating the bacteria in his gut with probiotics, Murray makes a special effort to balance the stress in his life. "Nearly every issue of the medical journals includes new evidence that illnesses are either caused by stress or are made worse by it," Murray says. "The more stress hormones you produce, the more you age."

Murray combats stress with measured breathing, where he inhales for a count of four and exhales for a count of six.

"When you are stressed, you pant and breathe rapidly," he says. In the caveman days, this used to give us extra energy to fight—or run from—a tiger. With measured breathing, the exhale is longer than the inhale, which stops the production of the stress hormones adrenaline and cortisol, and sends a message to the stress center in the brain that there is no tiger, and everything is okay," Murray says.

He recommends that everyone practice measured breathing for 1 minute each hour. "Try this for 5 weeks and your blood pressure will improve," he says. "The act of counting is important, as it rests the brain too."

When we talked about measured breathing, Steve's ears perked up. "I do this every day!" he said. Huh—the things you learn about your spouse, even after 10 years of marriage!

Why It Works

Is dirt good for you? According to some evidence and a theory called the hygiene hypothesis, yes. The hygiene hypothesis suggests that people who toughen up their immune systems early in life tend to have stronger immune systems later in life. In the past, children lived in caves and fields, where they encountered dirt, microbes, bacteria, and allergens on a daily basis. Today, in our world of hand sanitizer and bleach wipes, childhood unfolds a bit differently, which is one explanation for the higher rates of allergies that we're seeing in today's children.

And, it's a hypothesis that seems to hold up to research, at least on mice. Researchers compared germ-free mice (mice that lacked exposure to microbes or bacteria) to mice living in a normal "germy" environment. The germ-free mice had inflammation in their lungs similar to that in people with colitis or asthma. Another interesting finding: When the researchers exposed the germ-free mice to microbes in the first few weeks of their lives, the mice developed normal immune systems that were able to fight off disease. When researchers introduced microbes to the germ-free mice in their adult years, they did not see the same effect; the mice's immune systems were not up to snuff and the mice got sick.

The upshot: the best time to get sick may be in childhood.

You may not be able to do much about that now, but you can steal a different secret from Murray: laughter. There's a reason you feel great after a hearty laugh. And, as Murray highlighted, laughter and humor have health benefits in the long-term as well.

More specifically, when you laugh, it activates and relieves your stress response, which makes you feel relaxed. It increases your intake of oxygen-rich air, boosts endorphins, and stimulates your heart, lungs, and muscles.

In a study done at Loma Linda University, researchers measured stress levels and short-term memory recalls of 20 healthy adults in their sixties and seventies. For 20 minutes, one group watched funny videos, while the other group sat silently, not talking, reading, or using their cell phones. At the end of the 20 minutes, participants gave saliva samples and took a test that measured their short-term memory. Both groups performed better after the break, but the humor group had a 43.6 percent improvement in memory recall, compared with only 20.3 percent in the nonhumor group. The humor group also had lower levels of the stress hormone cortisol after watching the videos, while the non-humor group saw their stress hormones go down only slightly.

A good sense of humor can also protect against heart disease, found a related study done at the University of Maryland Medical Center in Baltimore. To test the humor responses of 300 people, researchers used two questionnaires. One contained a series of multiple-choice answers designed to determine how much people laughed in certain situations. The second measured anger and hostility with true and false answers. Half of the participants had either suffered a heart attack or undergone coronary bypass surgery and the other half did not have heart disease. The results: People with heart disease were 40 percent less likely to laugh in a variety of situations than the people without heart disease—an indication that laughter may have a protective effect.

Murray's daily dose of yogurt has likely helped keep him illness-free too. There's increasingly more science to back up the power of the tiny bacteria in yogurt and other fermented foods.

Why are these foods so effective? The live bacteria seem to interact with the microbes in our intestines. These 100 trillion microbes produce vitamins, such as B_6, B_{12}, and K_2; they help fight bad bacteria such as *E. coli* and Salmonella; and they help keep the bowels moving (an important factor to people as they age).

In addition to safeguarding our immunity, regular yogurt consumption appears to also aid in weight control, found a 2014 study published in the *International Journal of Obesity*. Study participants who ate more than three servings of yogurt per week gained fewer pounds over a year than those who ate fewer than one serving per week. And, we know that proper weight management helps prevent numerous age-related conditions, including diabetes, heart disease, and certain forms of cancer.

Yogurt may protect your brain too. In a 2013 study published in the journal *Gastroenterology,* researchers examined three different groups of women—one group ate yogurt with probiotics twice a day, a second ate nonfermented yogurt twice a day, and a third group ate no yogurt products. After 4 weeks, the women who ate the yogurt with probiotics had better responsiveness in the regions of their brains that process emotion and sensation compared to the other two groups.

Steve's Secrets

It's no surprise that Murray is as healthy and happy as he is at his age— he has the outlook of a much younger person. Use this advice to put his mindset into play.

TACKLE YOUR I-DON'T LIST. Take Murray's advice when he says, "Practice creativity—try new dishes, new table arrangements, new places to go. If you never boiled an egg, take a cooking course. If you don't play cards, join a bridge club." And, as Murray points out in his book, tackling your "I don'ts" is a form of anti-aging.

LAUGH AS MUCH AS YOU CAN—AT LEAST DAILY. One of our favorite things to do—with each other and with friends—is laugh. Nothing makes us feel better. When it comes to your health, laughter is like berries and broccoli—you simply cannot have too much of it in your life. Whether it's at funny movies, comedy clubs, or inside jokes with loved ones or friends, try to laugh as often as you can.

LOOK FOR PROBIOTIC-PACKED YOGURT. Uninformed shoppers beware: Some experts say that fewer than 10 percent of yogurts live up to their label claims. To make sure that you are getting the bacteria bang for your buck, look for the words "live and active cultures." If a yogurt is a non-refrigerated type, chances are it isn't worthy of your purchase, because refrigeration is necessary to keep the cultures alive and fresh. Also, stick to brands that contain the bacteria lactobacillus (*L. aci-*

dophilus) and/or bifidobacterium (*B. bifidum*) in the ingredients—these two bacteria are the most potent and, therefore, the most powerful. Also, beware that some contain as much sugar and fat as an ice cream sundae. To choose a healthful one, look for the following:

- **A maximum of 200 calories**
- **No more than 4 grams of fat**
- **30 grams of sugar or less**
- **6 grams of protein or more**
- **At least 600 IUs or 15 micrograms of calcium**

BREATHE DEEPLY FOR 1 MINUTE EVERY HOUR. Measured breathing (also called relaxation breathing) automatically puts you into the present. To practice this breathing exercise Murray swears by (and I swear by too), try the following:

- **Count silently to yourself as you inhale—one, two, three, four. You will find that, as you count your breaths, you automatically breathe more deeply.**
- **Exhale slowly for a count of six. As you make the long exhale, concentrate on signaling your body to relax. Feel your shoulders droop and your jaw and abdomen loosen.**

Mary Etter's Secret

Live off the Land

. . . .

Stay busy

Get sunlight for vitamin D

Give to others

Eat natural, organic foods

. . . .

Each morning, rain or shine, Mary Etter wakes up, slips into her work boots and heads outdoors, where she spends the next 10 to 12 hours hoisting 150-pound bales of hay, walking miles up steep hills, chopping wood, filling troughs, repairing culverts, pruning bushes, cutting fallen trees into firewood, mowing, repairing fences and corrals, fixing water systems, feeding and attending to the needs of 90 cows and birthing their calves, and keeping her 500-acre ranch in Northern California in good condition. In case she startles a coyote, skunk, bear, or wild boar, she always carries a rifle.

This is the life she was born into 76 years ago. It's the ranch she's run almost completely by herself for 40 years. She has no intentions of slowing down.

"I like to keep busy," says a very modest Mary. Busy indeed.

When I spoke to Mary about her work on the ranch, I was amazed at the amount of heavy physical labor involved. It sounded daunting for anyone. I am three-and-a-half decades younger than she is and I have my doubts about whether I would last a full day on the ranch. By day two, I'd definitely be laid up with a hot-water bottle.

She lives almost completely off the land. She never buys meat. Instead, she raises chickens and she hunts—for deer (her primary source of protein) or pork from the wild pigs that roam her ranch. For fruits and vegetables, she eats what's growing in her garden or scavenges for foods like wild herbs and blackberries. In the original orchard in her backyard, which is close to 100 years old, she garners pears, numerous types of apples, figs, walnuts, and persimmons. And, she makes most of her food from scratch.

"She cans her fruits and vegetables as well as her meats and poultry, and makes pies from scratch—the fat for the crust comes from her wild pigs," says her niece, Bobbie Johnson. "She doesn't have a food processor—she does everything by hand."

Most of the outdoor ranch upkeep is by hand too. "The only modern-day tools Aunt Mary has are lawn-related: a string trimmer, string mower, and lawn mower. She chops her own wood for the fire and uses old sheep shears to trim the ivy along the walkways leading up to her house—about 20 feet on each side," Bobbie says.

Once or twice a month, she drives 1½ hours to the closest town of Eurekato to purchase the few items that she can't raise, scavenge, grow, or make on her own.

With my mouth dropped open, I asked Mary if she has any help. "On the day I sell the calves and vaccinate the cattle, a few local ranch-ers help out. And, a few cousins help me cut wood and tackle a project from time to time, but that's about it," she says. "To me, my life is normal, but I understand that it sounds like a lot of activity to others," she chuckles.

When I asked her if she plans to continue to run the farm as long as she can, Mary paused and said, "Yes…I suppose."

"Aunt Mary is modest and she doesn't like to brag about herself," says Johnson. But she thinks her aunt has some accomplishments worthy of boasting. "She truly is like the original pioneer women," she adds.

Except, she's more like a bionic pioneer woman. With no vaccines or antibiotics, true pioneer women from the 1800s had a life expectancy of just 40 years.

Mary, on the other hand, hasn't seen a hospital since surgery for Crohn's disease as a child. She's had the flu a few times and recovered fine. Her only chronic medical problem is potassium deficiency, for which she takes potassium pills daily. "The closest medical care is 1½ hours away," Johnson says. "Aunt Mary is lucky—she rarely needs it."

Life in a Time Capsule

Mary lost both of her parents at a young age. Her mother passed away when she was 7 and her father when she was 20.

"Because my mother died so young, I took over the household duties when I was still a child, including all the cooking and baking," Mary says. "Luckily, my mother taught me a lot before she passed away."

The ranch looks much like it did back in those days, nearly 70 years ago. "It's like Aunt Mary lives in a time capsule," Johnson says.

Mary's communication style is from back in the day as well. She calls friends and relatives on a rotary phone. She doesn't have a cell phone or even the internet. "She handwrites letters with beautiful penmanship," Bobbie says, then laughs. "She *does* have a fax machine." Mary did recently get access to the news channel on her TV with a satellite dish—a gift from her niece and nephew—which has taught her a lot about what's going on in current events and politics. She also enjoys the radio and listens to it all the time and reads agricultural and historical publications.

Giving off the Land

As Bobbie talks about her aunt, she does so with immense love and respect. "She is such a kind person and always concerned about others," she says.

To give an example, Bobbie talks about the homemade presents Mary makes for her family members at Christmastime. "She takes 300 pounds of icy, frozen meat, hand cuts it, and seasons it with salt, pepper, and brown sugar." Then she loads heavy trays of meat on the racks of the family smokehouse. "She stocks all the wood for the smokehouse and she has to be pretty agile, like a trapeze artist, to walk around the edges so she doesn't fall in the fire," Johnson says.

The fruits of her labor: 40 gift bags filled with homemade beef jerky. "Together, with her canned turkey and tuna (a local fisherman friend brings her fresh fish), that's her present to us and we look forward to those presents every year," Bobbie says.

Bobbie also pointed out that her Aunt Mary is big on her community and works on making it better. She worked for years on the Mattole Integrated Coastal Watershed Management Plan making maps.

Mary is also deeply involved with her church and loves socializing with all the other valley folks. One of her biggest contributions is her 14-inch pies that she makes for fundraisers. "She is famous for her cream pies—they are masterpieces," Bobbie says.

Why It Works

Several aspects of Mary's lifestyle contribute to her stamina and health. For one, not only does she stay busy but she stays busy doing physical labor. She's also doing most of her ranch work outside, which provides sun and fresh air.

When you perform physical activity outside, it's good for your mental and physical health, research shows. In a 2011 study published in *Environmental Science and Technology*, researchers found that participants who exercised outdoors enjoyed their workouts more and had lower rates of depression and tension than those who exercised indoors.

Another small study found that those who exercise outdoors—especially parks and green spaces—have lower levels of stress hormones than those who work out indoors.

Because of the sunlight exposure, outdoor exercise also boosts vitamin D levels. Low levels of vitamin D may increase the risk for heart disease, cancer, and osteoporosis and worsen symptoms of depression. Sun exposure is a natural way to increase levels of vitamin D.

By hunting her own food, Mary is also getting lean game meats. Wild deer and birds are generally healthier choices than farm-raised animals because they have more vitamins stored in their muscles and less fat.

She's also consuming fruits, vegetables, and meats that are organic—free of pesticides, antibiotics, and other potentially harmful chemicals. Her cattle roam free, so they are not cooped up or stressed. Nearly all of her food is from the land and prepared from scratch, with no preservatives or unnecessary processes.

Steve's Secrets

Most people don't have a 500-acre ranch to take care of. Mary's situation is unique, to say the least. That said, here are some ways to follow her lead.

GET A HEALTHY DOSE OF SUN. There are two main ways to get the vitamin D your body needs—exposing your bare skin to sunlight and taking vitamin D supplements. You cannot get all of the vitamin D you need from foods. The recommended daily amount of vitamin D is 600 international units (IU) in adults up to age 70, and 800 IUs in people 71 and above. According to a 2011 study in the journal *Nutrition Research*, nearly 42 percent of adults are deficient in vitamin D, which increases their risk for a number of diseases, including cancer and heart disease.

What's considered the right amount of sun depends on several factors—the time of year, the time of day, where you live in relation to the equator, the amount of skin you expose, and your skin type. Someone with fair skin may get their daily dose of vitamin D in only 15 minutes, while a person with darker skin may need closer to 2 hours. Per the Vitamin D Council, the general rule is, you can produce the amount of vitamin D your body needs in about half the time it takes for your skin to turn pink.

EXERCISE OUTDOORS. Even if you don't have a large cattle ranch to manage, try to do at least some of your physical exercise outdoors.

And, if like Mary, you can check something off your to-do list at the same time, even better. Here are some good outdoor exercises and the calories they burn per hour:

- Swimming: 476
- Hiking: 442
- Chopping wood: 340
- Mowing lawn (push mower): 340
- Gardening: 306
- Horseback riding: 272

THINK ABOUT THE ORIGIN OF YOUR MEAT. Few older adults are out on the range shooting their own dinner, but that doesn't mean you shouldn't do your homework and know where your meat comes from. Here's a quick crash course.

- *Organic:* To be certified organic, an animal cannot be confined for an extended period of time, kept in unsanitary conditions, overcrowded, or directly or indirectly exposed to antibiotics, hormones, fertilizers, pesticides, genetically modified organisms (GMOs), or other contaminants.

- *Grass-fed:* Means an animal has been fed a 100-percent grass diet or has had unlimited access to the range. Grass is much higher than grains in key nutrients such as B vitamins and omega-3 fatty acids. It is also lower in calories. This makes grass-fed animals leaner and more flavorful.

It's important to note that not every organic animal is grass-fed and not every grass-fed animal is certified organic. "Organic" means that the animal was not exposed to unwanted chemicals; however, organic animals may have eaten grains. "Grass-fed" animals have only eaten grass, but there's no guarantee that the grass wasn't treated with pesticides. Therefore, to get the best-quality meat, look for "organically certified grass-fed" animals.

Louise Gooche's Secret

Don't Let Your Age Stop You from Acting Young

. . . .

If you've always wanted something, go for it!

Model good health for others

Don't let negativity bring you down

. . . .

For her entire life, Louise Gooche wanted to be a cheerleader, but something always got in her way.

"I grew up on a farm, so I couldn't stay for cheerleading practice, because I had to take the bus to my country home," she says. When she was in nursing school, she was far too busy with classes. When she started working, she had even less room in her schedule.

It was at age 62, when she retired, that suddenly Louise had more time for the things she always wanted to do in life. She was watching a cheerleading performance when the lightbulb went off.

"I said to myself, 'I can do that!'" As soon as she got home, she put up flyers at the YMCA where she was a member, asking for people to join her senior citizen cheerleading squad. She didn't expect anyone to take her up on it though.

"Who would want to be a senior citizen cheerleader besides me?" she thought.

She wasn't even sure if she had the body or stamina anymore. Just a year before, Louise was finishing up 6 months worth of chemotherapy treatments for colon cancer.

"The chemo made me so tired," she says. "I remember lying in bed and praying for my strength to come back." And, even when she was young, she was never a natural athlete. "I was one of those kids who was the last to be selected for an athletic team," Louise says.

But she loved to talk, which made cheerleading seem like a perfect fit.

And, she soon learned that she wasn't the only older woman with a similar background who wanted to learn how to cheer. Nine ladies signed up immediately—and Durham Divas was born.

"None of us had ever been a cheerleader," Louise says. So, they asked an aerobics instructor to teach them a cheer routine. Louise and the other women learned how to do splits and cartwheels, and how to support one another for pyramids.

"Our first show was hilarious—we wore red T-shirts and white shorts and shook pom-poms we bought at the dollar store," Louise recalls. They were a hit. Members noticed and soon the Y offered to sponsor the squad.

"We've been shaking our pom-poms for 13 years!" Louise says with pride. Today the Divas are a well-oiled machine, with matching purple and white uniforms and silver sparkly pom-poms. They are 12 ladies and 1 guy, ranging in age from 62 to 79.

"When we come out and the audience sees we can shake it like we can at our age, they go crazy!" Louise says. Just like cheerleaders 50 years younger, the Divas perform dance moves, one-level pyramids, and cartwheels. Louise can do a full split.

The Divas perform for all types of venues in Durham, from kindergarten graduations to college basketball tournaments to the North Carolina Senior Games. "Whether it's to wide-eyed kindergarteners who can't believe a grandma is dancing in a cheerleading uniform or seniors who feel like their time has passed, it is so rewarding to communicate healthy living and inspire people to do the things they think they can't," Louise says.

Louise has taken her passion as a senior athlete to the state level. She's chairman of the board of the North Carolina Senior Games, a year-round health promotion and education program for residents age 50 and older. "Our message is you don't have to allow illnesses and emotional stresses to take your joy away—come out and do whatever you can at your own pace," she says. "Just because you're older doesn't mean you're going to die the next day. If you maintain a healthy lifestyle and pay attention to your emotional, physical, and spiritual health, you can do whatever you desire."

Three Cheers for the Golden Years

Louise is now in better shape and has more energy than ever.

When she's not practicing with the Divas, which she does Mondays and Wednesdays for an hour and a half, Louise does another form of exercise, be it an exercise class, walking, or weight training. She walks at least 2 miles a day and includes weight training one day a week. "I also started working with hula hoops because it helps with core strength and keeps my back in pretty good alignment," she says. She does Pilates, aerobics, and yoga as well.

It's all paid off. In addition to being in the best shape of her life, Louise is also in good health. She hardly ever gets sick. Her only issue is her prediabetes. "I check my blood sugar every day and it's doing quite well," she says. Following her bout with cancer, she's also proactive about getting everything checked. "I see a doctor…every 2 to 3 months and I don't complain—I'm doing really, really great, so I'll keep checking everything to make sure that it continues!"

In everything she does—with the Divas and beyond—Louise is amazingly hopeful.

"You have to stay optimistic because you can literally worry yourself to death," she says. In fact, she tries to avoid negativity, even from her friends. "If one of my friends starts complaining to me, I say, 'Stop right there. Number one, I can't do anything about it, and number two, you're bringing me down—I'm not an emotional garbage dump,'" she says.

Why It Works

Obviously, not many people start cheerleading in their sixties, so no studies speak directly to the benefits of Louise's pursuits. However, when we look at what she's doing more generally, we can find plenty of strategies working in her favor. Topping the list: she has a purpose, which is vitally important, especially during retirement.

The research on the effects of retirement on health are mixed, with some studies saying it speeds up illness and death (probably because a lot of people retire *because* of health problems) and others touting its health benefits.

What matters is what people choose to do with their newfound free time. If you decide to put your feet up on your ottoman and catch up on years of missed daytime TV, your health will go into freefall. On the other hand, if you look at retirement as Louise did—an opportunity to do all of the things you never had the time to do before—you can actually become healthier.

In a 2014 study published in *Psychological Science*, researchers tracked the physical and mental health of more than 7,000 adults ages 20 to 75 for 14 years. They found that the individuals who had a purpose or direction in life lived longer than those who did not.

A more recent 2015 working paper from the National Bureau of Economic Research found that retirement is likely to immediately boost health and happiness. The researchers discovered that life satisfaction improves right after retirement, and those health and happiness benefits last for at least the first 4 years. In their survey, 80 percent of retirees said retirement presented them with more chances to enjoy themselves, and 70 percent reported that retirement gave them a chance for new, fulfilling experiences.

Steve's Secrets

If retirement is looming and you're not sure whether or not you want to take the plunge—and how to spend the newfound time if you do—try these suggestions.

STAY BUSY. This is probably the most important piece of advice. My happiest retired patients are not the ones who are lounging or worrying, they are out and about every day, doing things that they enjoy. Retirement activities can include physical fitness pursuits like Louise's Divas, traveling, volunteering, or even a part-time job. The bottom line is that you need to be engaged in meaningful activities to stay happy and healthy.

GET TOGETHER WITH FRIENDS. Louise is lucky in that her involvement with the Durham Divas and senior games also provide her with a social outlet—she's killing two birds with one activity, so to speak. If your retirement interests are more isolating, make it a point to get together with friends and family members often. Nurture your existing friendships and stay open to new ones. Find ways to spend quality time with your children and grandchildren—they will benefit and so will you.

DO SOMETHING YOU'VE ALWAYS DREAMED OF. Louise's story is so inspiring because she recognized a missed opportunity and went for it. She didn't care that cheerleading isn't a typical senior sport. It's never too late to try something that you've always wanted to do and retirement affords you the time to try it.

Ed Shimer's Secret

See Health Setbacks as a Detour, not a Dead End

. . . .

Show your body who's boss

Stay in shape—even when you are struggling

Follow doctors' orders

. . . .

Ed Shimer approached his 60th birthday much like he had approached cancer 4 years prior—with a big f#*% you.

"When my doctor told me that I had stage 3 oral cancer and a 40 percent chance of surviving, I pretty much went deaf," he says.

Then, he got to work. "Still in the hospital, I ran down and talked to a doctor friend who used to treat head and neck cancer at Sloan Kettering because I needed to see through the fog. He said, 'Ed—you can get through this—you just have to do everything they tell you. You only get one shot.' "

Ed did everything, and then some, to fight. His regimen included 125 reps of swallowing and mouth-stretching exercises every day to keep his mouth and jaw open. "I did every single one of them and recorded them in my little cancer log," he recalls.

He also worked out as many days a week as he could and played doubles tennis every Sunday. "At my lowest point, I think I did only two workouts in a week," he says. One day in that week, he tried to do his normal 10 sets of 30 to 40 push-ups and could only do 6 per set. "Only 6?!! That's the day I broke down and cried," he says. That's when he realized that he needed to pay attention to his body and rest when he needed to.

It paid off. Ed's body withstood the chemotherapy and radiation treatments better than most, which amazed his doctors. "I went to radiation treatments 5 days a week for 2 months, just ahead of another guy who wasn't in very good shape when he started," he says. "Each session, I watched that guy deteriorate more and more. At the end, he was in a wheelchair."

Ed, on the other hand, completed the treatments on his feet. "My doctor really tried to get me to get a feeding tube; most people with my type of cancer have to because the treatments make it so hard to swallow," he says. "But I said, 'I'm doing 125 swallowing exercises each day—why the hell do you want me to stop trying to eat?'" At the height of his treatments, to prove he could swallow, Ed took his doctor to the cafeteria and scarfed down a cheeseburger right in front of him. "He said, 'alright, no feeding tube!'" Ed laughs.

Ed kept his thyroid as well. "In most cases, the radiation just cooks it," he says. He also retained most of his impressive full head of hair. The treatments also spared his salivary glands and teeth. "Most people who undergo radiation to their face have their teeth pulled prophylactically because the gums never heal and the saliva glands get fried," he explains. Ed rolled the dice and elected to keep his teeth; luckily, they stayed. "My oncologist, Dr. Sharma, called me his model patient," he says.

Despite being a model patient, Ed had some tough moments physically and emotionally as he faced his mortality.

He recalls a crisp fall day when he took a walk on the beach with his dog. "There was a brisk, offshore wind and the waves were real glassy— it reminded me of my days growing up surfing at the Jersey Shore, and I thought, 'I may never see another day like this again. I was scared,'" he says.

But, that scare reminded him of how precious life is, how much he wanted to stay with his wife and everyone and everything else he loves so much. "It's amazing how much you appreciate the simple things when you have the grim reaper following you around," he says.

Now cancer-free, he's seen many more good surfing days since then, in some of the best surf spots in the world.

And, he decided to celebrate his 60th birthday—and 4 years cancer-free—in a special way.

"As my 6-0 drew near, I thought, 'I could go to dinner or I could do something to show my body who's boss,'" Ed says.

He chose the latter and decided to train for his first-ever sprint triathlon. Most triathletes train for months in all facets of the event. Ed did not. Instead, he relied on years of exercise and just 3 weeks of training before he went for the big race.

Being a lifelong surfer, Ed admits he had an advantage in the swim. "There was a 3-foot groundswell in the ocean, which most swimmers can't train for," he says. He came out of the water in the top 25 percent.

"Then, on the bike, I saw guys with these fancy aerodynamic handlebars and solid wheels and looked down at my basic road bike…and peddled like a madman," he says. He peddled so hard that he couldn't feel his feet when he got off to do the run. "The goal is 75 percent exertion—I think I was at 99."

Ed didn't just do well—he won his age group and also beat younger athletes in the forties and fifties categories. "The person with the time closest to mine was 38," he says. His score qualified him for the National Olympic distance race the following year.

As he talks about his performance in the triathlon, Ed says he "didn't see it coming," which seems to be a theme in his life. In his 60 years, he's been blindsided by lots of things—his cancer, crushing waves and sharks on surf trips to exotic places, and personal ups and downs. Ed has approached each challenge with the toughness he did for the triathlon and he's won.

The thing that has helped Ed time and time again: He is in great shape. Starting with his days surfing from dawn until dusk at the Jersey shore, Ed has exercised almost every single day since his teen years.

"I play singles and doubles tennis, I run, I do P90X, I do hundreds of push-ups and pull-ups—I like to mix it up," he says. He also likes to have a goal. "When people exercise purely for endorphins or vanity, it's not as healthy," he says. "I stay in shape so I can play better tennis, run a 5K, or surf for hours on end," he says.

He also stays in shape to preserve his health, which he is more thankful for than ever. He advises others to take care of themselves too. "The stats don't lie—a lot of us are going to go through cancer. You don't know if it will be you, so try to stay as fit as you can, not just for good health but to survive cancer and perhaps more importantly, cancer treatment."

He says he looked at his little cancer log where he recorded his exercises and treatments just the other day. "It was depressing, but it also reminded me of where I was then (trying to muster push-ups) and where I am now, gearing up for an Olympic triathlon in my 60th year. It feels pretty good."

Why It Works

It's always a good idea to stay in shape, as Ed says, not just to stay in good health but to survive cancer and cancer treatment, in the event you become one of the statistics. Physical activity helps people survive cancer, not just before the diagnosis but also during treatment. In one study, moderately vigorous exercise was associated with a 50 percent lower mortality rate in breast cancer survivors. Tennis, swimming, and bicycling all fall into the moderately vigorous range.

Physically active cancer survivors also had a 4- to 6-percent higher rate of survival at 5 and 10 years, respectively—about the same benefit as chemotherapy.

Another thing Ed has gotten right is exercising toward a goal. Goal-setting helps boost performance in all types of exercisers, from recreational gym-goers to elite athletes. In one study published in the *Journal of Applied Behavioral Analysis,* researchers looked at the effects of goal-setting in college-level rugby players. They found that the players who set specific goals showed enhancements in the specific areas of performance they set out to improve.

Steve's Secrets

So, what's the best way to get yourself ready to physically and emotionally beat an opponent as intimidating as cancer? Use this advice.

DO WHAT YOU LOVE. It's much easier to stick to a workout routine when it involves activities you love. Being a surfer myself, I know this firsthand. If you love to surf or swim, dive into the ocean or pool for your workout. If you enjoy hiking, strap on your boots and head to the woods. And, if competitive sports are your thing, like Ed, play tennis, squash, or racquetball. No matter how you spend the time, aim for 150 minutes of moderately paced or 75 minutes of vigorous physical activity per week.

TAKE PART IN YOUR CARE. In all areas of health care—cancer treatment included—outcomes are generally better when doctors and patients have clear, open communication. Patients more involved in their treatment decisions are more satisfied with their results than are patients who were less involved, found a study published in the journal *Current Oncology.* Don't be afraid to ask questions about your treatment options and, if you're not satisfied, seek a second opinion.

STAY POSITIVE. Despite some scary moments, Ed stayed relatively positive throughout his cancer diagnosis and treatment. He refused the feeding tube not to be defiant but because he truly believed that he could continue to swallow on his own. He also maintained his fitness with an eye on a healthy future. The studies on the power of a positive attitude are somewhat mixed. But, it certainly can't hurt to stay as happy and strong as you can.

Jim Yenckel's Secret

Be Proactive about Your Health

. . . .

Get regular check-ups
Realize that feeling well doesn't mean everything is okay
Use every opportunity for physical activity

. . . .

At 80, Jim Yenckel is in near picture-perfect health. He runs, swims, strength-trains, eats an impeccable diet, and hikes some of the most difficult trails in the world. "I still wear the same size trousers I did when I left for college—a 32-inch waist," he says.

So, 3 years ago, when Jim's wife suggested that he go to the cardiologist "just to get checked out because of his age and activity level," he initially resisted. "I felt terrific," he says. "I was still running 3 miles most days, swimming a half-mile of laps weekly, and doing upper-body weightlifting (max 15 pounds per hand)." Did he really need a doctor to tell him that he was in good health?

"Thank goodness I agreed to go," he says.

At Jim's first appointment, the cardiologist ran some tests on his heart and the news, at first, seemed good. The doctor called his heart "strong." But his aorta was slightly larger than it should be. Jim had the beginnings of an aneurysm, which occurs when part of an artery wall weakens and then widens excessively or balloons out.

"Something to keep an eye on," the doctor said.

"Except for that, I was a healthy guy," Jim says.

To monitor the problem, Jim went back for an echocardiogram every few months. "It continued to be enlarged, but nothing alarming. Then, at my most recent visit in October 2016, they found my aorta had ballooned." Doctors scheduled him for open-chest surgery two-and-a-half weeks later, the soonest they could get him in.

"If they wouldn't have caught it, it could have burst fatally," Jim says.

He credits his fitness for his ability to recover quickly. "In the hospital, the nurses mentioned multiple times, 'he has strong legs,' as they helped me get up to use the restroom," he says. To prevent disturbing his healing sternum, the doctors warned Jim not to use his hands to push up from a chair or bed, and to instead keep them crossed on his chest. "Because I was so fit, I could quickly hoist myself out of bed using my strong stomach muscles (thank you, sit-ups) and my running/hiking legs to stand up."

When I talked with Jim, he was a few months into his recovery from surgery, with no plans of slowing down. "So far, I've had no problem completing the daily walks the doctor recommends." He was looking forward to his upcoming hike and getting back his regular exercise pace. "I'm going to continue to always look for ways to keep physically busy—and go max."

When we spoke, he was looking forward to a hiking trip with his friend John at Utah's Bryce and Zion national parks. He and his wife live in a four-level townhouse, which gives him plenty of access to stairs. "On top of all that, I usually walk to the post office, the bank, and Whole Foods for a backpack's worth of items," he says. "Mostly, I'm on the go from the time I get up until after dinner."

He encourages others to make exercise a priority, especially as they get older. "Use every opportunity for exercise. Being physically fit has been a big aid in my recovery."

Other than the aneurysm, Jim says he's been "quite healthy" in his adulthood—largely due to his exercise routine, he says—and that's how he plans to live the rest of his life.

Why It Works

If just for peace of mind, a check-up can never hurt. Even if you feel fine, regular doctors' visits are important, especially after age 65.

And at this point in the book, we probably are starting to sound like a broken record. But we'll say it again anyway: There is no question that physical activity makes you healthier and helps you live longer, regardless of your age. In one study, people who got some exercise but less than the physical activity recommendations of 150 minutes a week were 20 percent less likely to die over a 14-year period than those who did no physical activity. Participants who engaged in the recommended level of exercise were even more likely to extend their lives—they were 31 percent less likely to die during the study period.

Interestingly, there seems to be a sweet spot when it comes to maximizing health benefits of physical activity. People who exercised moderately for 450 to 750 minutes a week or vigorously for 225 to 375 minutes weekly were 39 percent less likely to die during the study period than non-exercisers. Exercising more than those ranges wasn't associated with any additional benefits.

Strength-training is particularly important. Older adults who strength-trained twice a week lowered their chances of dying by nearly 50 percent in one study.

Steve's Secrets

There are a few morals to Jim's close-call tale. These are the ones that are the most important.

EXERCISE THE RIGHT AMOUNT. For major health benefits, aim for at least 150 minutes (2 hours, 30 minutes) of moderate-intensity aerobic activity, or 75 minutes (1 hour, 15 minutes) of vigorous-intensity aerobic activity each week. Or, you can do a combination of both. Keep in mind that 1 minute of vigorous activity is equal to 2 minutes of moderate-intensity activity. If you are particularly motivated—like Jim—you can increase your physical activity to 300 minutes (5 hours) of moderate-intensity activity or 150 minutes (2 hours, 30 minutes) of vigorous activity each week. The more you exercise, the more benefits you will reap.

MAKE SURE THAT YOU HAVE THE RECOMMENDED IMMUNIZATIONS. Get a pneumococcal vaccine if you've never had one or if it has been more than 5 years since your last vaccine. Get the flu shot every year, a tetanus-diphtheria booster every 10 years, and shingles or herpes booster vaccine after age 60.

GET THE RECOMMENDED SCREENINGS. As Jim's story shows, it's important to monitor your health as you get older, even if you feel well. Use this chart to make sure that you've had the screenings you need.

SCREENING	FREQUENCY
Physical exam	Once a year
Blood pressure	Once a year
Cholesterol	At least every 5 years
Abdominal aortic aneurysm screening (the screening that saved Jim's life)	Once between age 65 and 75 for current or former smokers
Low-dose Computer Tomography (LDCT) to test for lung cancer	Once a year for current or former smokers
Colon cancer	Annually, starting at age 50
Diabetes	Every 1 to 3 years, starting at age 65
Dental exam	1 to 2 times a year
Eye exam	Every 1 to 2 years
Hearing test	Only if you have symptoms of hearing loss
Bone mineral density testing for osteoporosis	After age 70 for men, or age 64 for women
FOR WOMEN ONLY	
Mammogram	Every 1 to 2 years until age 75
Pap smear	Every 3 to 5 five years until age 65

Asha Mittal's Secret

Go Vegetarian

. . . .

Spice up your food with garlic, ginger, and pepper

Snack on real food (almonds, figs, and dates), not highly processed foods

Stay happily busy with volunteering and social engagements

. . . .

In 1968, Asha Mittal, 65, came to the United States and married a man she had known for less than 1 month. "We got engaged 24 hours after we met," she says. She was only 17. "It was an arranged marriage and a successful one—we've been married for 49 years."

In a foreign country with a new man, she held onto the food she loved from her native India, and she and the family she built here in the U.S. have been eating it ever since. As a bonus, it's helping to keep her always well.

"My husband and I are both vegetarians—we never eat meat," she says. "We eat a lot of lentils, vegetables, and fruits, and very little fried food." She bakes fresh whole wheat flat bread called Indian Roti or Chapati every day for burritos and makes stews from scratch. In everything, she adds spices from her home country.

Asha says her diet helps keep her youthful and gives her energy for her exercise routine. She thinks the combination of healthy eating and physical activity has boosted her vitality and potentially helped to keep her chronic asthma under control. "You need healthy food and it is especially important as you get older," she says. "If you eat junk food, it will stick with you."

Savoring the Taste of Home

For Asha and her husband, Faquir, healthy eating begins as soon as they rise. "In the morning, we have whole-grain cereal, a boiled egg, and a banana," she says. For lunch, they eat a sandwich and homemade soup, a salad, or tacos. "We eat a lot of basmati rice and brown rice, which goes with everything," she says.

For her soup, Asha puts lots of different lentils, onion, garlic, ginger, salt, and black pepper in a slow-cooker. "It's much better for us than having soup from the can." In everything she cooks, she adds plenty of vegetables.

After breakfast, lunch, and dinner, the Mittals have fruit—usually bananas, blueberries, or strawberries. "If we get hungry in between, we have almonds, figs, or dates," she says. When they do buy prepackaged food, they read labels and go by the motto, the fewer ingredients, the better.

One of her biggest goals with healthy eating is to avoid sweets. "There's nothing good about them," she says. When she does get a craving, she tries to satisfy it with fruit. Or, she eats a very small portion, like a piece of candy or dark chocolate—"dark chocolate is good for you!" she says.

Mixing It Up Is Good Medicine

The rest of Asha's life is as well-balanced as her eating plan. She works out 5 days a week, for about 2 hours. "I'm so thankful for my exercise— it's healthy for me, plus I look forward to it!" She goes to the gym at about 8:30 a.m. to walk on the treadmill, bike, and do crunches for 45 minutes. "Then, I take a class—chair yoga, Zumba, Fit N 50 or medita-tion, depending on the day. I like to mix it up."

In her free time, Asha enjoys volunteering. When her son attended Sunday school, she taught the class. More recently, she's worked in her local library. "I love books and read *a lot*," she says. "My husband and I enjoy reading about different things—he likes high-tech books and I like novels—but we always tell each other about what we've read."

Asha also has a fun group of nine ladies who she meets for lunch and dinner regularly. She visits her son, daughter, and grandchildren often. "I'm never bored," she says.

All of the healthy food, volunteering, and challenging her mind with books have left Asha in good health for her 65 years. The only health problem she struggles with is asthma. "It's genetic—my mother has it and my mother's father had it," she says. She manages it with steroid medication, coupled with her healthy lifestyle. "The symptoms do slow me down a little sometimes, but they don't stop me—I still exercise 5 days a week. I want to keep moving!" she says.

Why It Works

Research shows that, in general, vegetarians live longer than people who eat meat.

In a 2013 study published in the *Journal of the American Medical Association*, researchers looked at the diets and mortality rates of 73,308 Seventh-day Adventists between 2002 and 2007. They found that the vegetarians had a 12 percent lower mortality rate than non-vegetarians.

In a more recent 2017 review published in the *European Journal of Clinical Nutrition*, researchers looked at the Mediterranean diet–which is rich in olive oil, fruits, vegetables, nuts, and legumes–in relation to telomere length. (Telomeres are caps on the ends of chromosomes. Their length can give a snapshot of where you are in the aging process. Longer telomeres indicate slower aging.) Of all of the Mediterranean diet elements, fruit and vegetable intake is most strongly associated with longer telomeres and, therefore, longer life.

The herbs and spices used in Indian cooking may help ward off disease too. Here are some of the biggies.

GARLIC: people have used garlic as medicine for hundreds of years. In 18th-century France, gravediggers drank crushed garlic in wine to help protect them from the plague. Soldiers ate garlic during WWI and WWII to help prevent gangrene and it was used topically to help prevent wound infections.

Since then, research shows that garlic can help prevent atherosclerosis (hardening of the arteries), high cholesterol, high blood pressure, and some forms of cancer. Some studies also show that garlic can help boost the immune system. Garlic's medicinal powers seem to come from its antioxidants—substances that help fight harmful particles in your body called free radicals.

Garlic can also help fight the common cold. In a 2014 review, scientists found that people who took garlic every day for 3 months had fewer colds than people who took a placebo.

Because it boosts the immune system, garlic may help fight cancer too.

GINGER: In one study of 261 people with osteoarthritis of the knee, people who took ginger extract twice a day had less pain—and, therefore, needed fewer painkillers—than those who didn't take the ginger.

There is also some evidence that ginger may lower cholesterol, help prevent blood clots, and help control blood sugar in people with type 2 diabetes.

BLACK PEPPER: Another of Asha's favorite spices is black pepper, which also has powerful pro-health effects. In addition to being both an antioxidant and an antibacterial, black pepper helps with weight loss because it stimulates the breakdown of fat cells.

Steve's Secrets

If you've considered eating less meat or eliminating it from your diet altogether, perhaps Asha's story gives you some inspiration. Use these tips to swing more toward vegetarian.

CUT DOWN ON MEAT. If you eat meat every night for dinner, for example, try cutting back to three or four nights a week, and eat a piece of fish instead. Always have bacon with your breakfast? Substitute an extra egg or a piece of fruit. If you gradually cut back and find alternatives you enjoy, you won't miss it.

PACK IN FRUITS AND VEGGIES. The more fruits and vegetables you can pack into your diet, the healthier you will be. The USDA Dietary Guidelines for Americans recommend that you fill half your plate with fruits and vegetables at each meal. Half of your snacks should consist of fruits and veggies too. To get a healthful mix, eat a variety of fruits and vegetables of all different colors and textures.

ADD SPICES FOR FLAVOR. By adding lots of flavorful ginger, garlic, black pepper, and other spices to her soups and meals, Asha is doing her body good. Not only do herbs and spices offer healthier taste alternatives to calorie-laden sugar and fat but they also come with health benefits that can help lengthen your life and prevent disease.

Diane Silver's Secret

Befriend a Pet

. . . .

Enjoy the unconditional love of a furry friend

Take your beloved pet for walks for exercise and fresh air

Expand your social network by befriending fellow animal lovers

. . . .

Diane Silver hasn't been sick in 4 years. "And the last time, I wasn't even that sick—just a cold," she says.

Diane says she thinks that her super immune system has a lot to do with her 12-year-old Australian Shepherd, Nougat. "He calms me and brings great joy into my life," she says. "He is wonderful company and a good listener."

Diane works from home, which can be isolating at times. But, no matter if she is plugging away at her computer or in the kitchen making lunch, Nougat is by her side. "He follows me around the house and sleeps either on his comfy bed or under my desk while I work," she says. "It's physically and emotionally comforting to have him with me, which I'm convinced is good for my immunity," she says.

When Diane isn't working, Nougat gets her out and about in her neighborhood. "I have met many people who have dogs, some of whom have become friends," she says. "And, people always stop on the street to admire or pet Nougat."

Fellow dog owners in the neighborhood help each other out too. "We walk each other's dogs and keep them overnight when owners are away," Diane says. "These social interactions make me feel a part of the community and boost my overall sense of well-being." In addition to her daily walks with and without Nougat, Diane stays fit by going to the gym 3 days a week. One day, she works out by using the elliptical machine and stationary bike; one day, she takes a step aerobics class; and one day, she works out with a personal trainer. "The trainer workout involves *a lot* of strength-training," she says.

She and her husband also take regular outdoor vacations, where they hike and ride horses.

Diane knows Nougat is up there in years. "As he's getting older, he needs help with some things, like going up stairs. I value every day I have with him," she says.

She adds that she and Nougat have just completed the Animal Assisted Training program at the San Francisco SPCA that allows Nougat to be a therapy dog. "I was so proud of him at graduation when he received his AAT certificate. I think he has a lot to offer others too."

Why It Works

Anyone who has ever loved a dog or cat knows how much joy a pet can bring. Plus, the emotional benefits of having a pet can translate into physiological ones. When you feel attached to an animal, changes happen in your brain to reduce the stress response. Breathing rate, anxiety level, and blood pressure can all decrease as a result. You can almost feel this happening as you pet a dog or cat—it's relaxing and rewarding at the same time.

When you stare into a dog's eyes, your brain releases the bonding chemical oxytocin, found a 2015 study published in the journal *Science*. Oxytocin is a feel-good hormone that also plays a role in social bonding.

Dogs also get you moving, as just about any dog owner can tell you. Walk a dog once at 6:00 a.m., and, the very next day, the dog is reminding you to go for a walk at 6:00 a.m. Dogs *love* walking and their exuberance can be contagious. In one study, researchers found that regular dog-walking was associated with a lower body mass index (BMI), fewer visits to the doctor, more frequent exercise, and increases in social benefits.

Steve's Secrets

Already have a pet you love? Fantastic. By cultivating a relationship with Fluffy or Fido, you are supporting your mental and physical health. If you have a dog and are able, take him for regular walks. Remember: Exercise is important for your dog and it's important for you. Plus, by walking together, you will probably save yourself money in vet and health-care bills too.

If you don't currently have a pet, weigh the pros and cons before you decide to get one. Pets take a lot of time, effort, and money. According to the U.S. Bureau of Labor Statistics, the average pet owner spends $500 per year on a pet; other estimates say the yearly total is closer to $1,600. However, pet owners report lots of plusses in terms of companionship and there are health perks too. Researchers found people who currently or previously owned a cat had a lower risk of death due to heart attack or other forms of cardiovascular disease, according to a 2009 study published in the *Journal of Vascular and Interventional Radiology*. If the pros win and you make the decision to go for it, get your pet from a reputable agency, shelter, or breeder. Consider these factors:

SIZE: Do you want a small dog or cat, or is a large dog more your speed?

NOISE: Do you live in a condo or apartment where barking will be a problem?

PERSONALITY: Would you prefer a calm dog or one with lots of energy? Or, maybe a more laid-back cat is your speed? Does the animal need to be good with children?

AGE: Are you prepared to get up in the middle of the night, and when you're out, are you prepared to come home every few hours to let a puppy out? In many ways, puppies are like babies and require intensive care. If not, consider rescuing an adult or older dog, or a cat.

LIFESTYLE: Do you travel a lot? If so, do you know of someone who can watch the dog or cat for you while you are gone, or do you have the means to pay for boarding?

If you are unable to permanently adopt a cat or dog but would like to try having a pet, consider fostering a dog or cat. Typically, this allows a person to be with an animal for a limited amount of time and the facility pays all expenses for the animal's care while it is in a foster home.

Steve's Prescription for Staying Well

You've just read about people who embody what it means to be "well." Whether they've overcome a health problem or never stayed a night in the hospital, they value their good health and take measures to preserve it. Beyond their strategies, here are some tips on how to stay disease-free.

MEDITATE. By practicing mindful meditation, you can cut your chances of coming down with a cold by up to half, according to a study done at the University of Wisconsin, Madison. Researchers asked 51 people who regularly meditate to log their illnesses and sick days for one cold and flu season, and they had 13 fewer illnesses and 51 fewer sick days than a group that didn't meditate.

And, learning how may be easier than you think. For a few minutes each morning, just try following your breath in and out. Notice how the air feels warm as you inhale and cool as you exhale. Tune into the stretching sensation of your ribs and belly expanding on the inhale, as well as how those areas of your body feel as you let the breath back out. Don't worry if you get distracted easily. That's common. Whenever you catch your mind wandering, just bring it back.

• • • • • • • • • • • • • • • • • •

At-a-Glance: How to Be Well

→ Take 800 to 1,000 IU of vitamin D a day.

→ Include shiitake mushrooms in your repertoire of foods and consume vitamin C-rich foods regularly.

→ Wean off of added sugars.

→ Wash your hands regularly, especially before eating or after shaking hands, handling money, or using the restroom.

→ Meditate for a few minutes every morning.

→ Consider getting a pet.

→ Consume immunity-boosting spices, including ginger, garlic, and black pepper.

→ Eat more veggies and less meat. Make sure your meat is certified organic and grass-fed.

→ Exercise for at least 150 minutes a week, preferably outdoors.

→ Get the recommended check-ups and screenings for your age.

→ Surround yourself with friends.

→ Try new activities that excite you.

→ Consume a probiotic-rich yogurt once a day.

→ Practice measured breathing for 1 minute every hour.

→ Laugh every single day.

WASH. YOUR. HANDS. We say it to our kids and grandkids, but do we do it enough ourselves? Washing your hands often, especially after you've touched something or someone that might make you sick, goes a long way when it comes to preventing infection. Make sure to dry your hands well since viruses and bacteria are more likely to cling to wet hands than dry hands. Hand sanitizer is a good in a pinch, but it's no substitute for washing the germs off your hands and down the drain.

VACCINATE YOURSELF AND THOSE YOU LOVE. Despite the bad press (which has been disproven, by the way), I'm a big proponent of vaccination. It's a simple, easy step that can go a long way toward protecting your health and the health of those around you. As flu season approaches, getting a flu shot is the best thing you can do to prevent getting sick. Talk to your health-care provider about the additional vaccines you may need.

SHAKE YOUR SUGAR HABIT. Sugar may give you a short-term energy boost, but it makes your immune system depressed. In a landmark study done at Loma Linda University in California, after people consumed 6 tablespoons of sugar (sources included honey, orange juice, and sugary drinks), their white blood cells—the cells that fight infection—lost their ability to do their jobs, making them more susceptible to viruses and bacteria. This immune system suppression lasts for several hours after your last sip of soda or bite of cake. Therefore, if you consume sugary drinks and snacks regularly throughout the day, your immune system never gets a chance to return to full speed.

REVIVE WITH VITAMIN C. Vitamin C may do numerous good things to bolster the immune system, including stimulating the production and function of infection-fighting white blood cells and increasing blood levels of antibodies that can ward off invaders. The recommended daily amount of vitamin C for adults 19 and older is 90 milligrams for males and 75 milligrams for females. If you feel a cold or other acute illness coming on, you can boost your intake even higher. Here are some of the best food sources of vitamin C.

I yellow bell pepper: 341 milligrams
I mango: 122 milligrams
I papaya: 95 milligrams
I cup strawberries: 85 milligrams
I cup Brussels sprouts: 75 milligrams
I cup pineapple: 75 milligrams

MUNCH MUSHROOMS AS MEDICINE. Certain types of mushrooms, including reishi, maitake, and shiitake, encourage cells in the immune system to multiply, which boosts your body's infection-fighting powers. A 2014 study found that those who ate dried shiitake mushrooms experienced an increase in their number of immune cells.

BE VIGILANT WITH VITAMIN D. One reason we're more likely to get sick when the weather turns cold and we're holed up inside is low vitamin D. Low vitamin D levels are linked with an increased risk of respiratory infections, like colds and the flu. Aim for a daily dosage of 800 to 1,000 IU or get your levels checked to determine the best dosage for you.

Eight

Be Unbreakable

You can't expect to get through life without hardship. Loss and emotional pain, to some extent, are baked into this beautiful existence. Just about everyone, if they live long enough, has a story of suffering to share.

Because of this, attempting to avoid every type of loss—whether it's the loss of a job, the loss of someone you love, or the loss of your health—isn't realistic. What is realistic, however, is this: learning how to grow through your loss so that you can emerge stronger *because of it*.

Some of the most amazing people we talked to have had some serious low points in their lives. Not only did they overcome these setbacks but they also emerged even stronger than they were before they encountered them.

What's the secret to overcoming adversity? Let's hear from those who've done it.

Barbara Packman's Secret

Surround Yourself with Younger Friends

. . . .

The downside of excellent health is that you outlive everyone in your peer group

Meet people you like by doing the activities you like

Choose friends who lift you up and inspire you to be your best

. . . .

On Christmas Eve 2002 at 3:00 a.m., Barbara Packman awoke to loud banging on her front door. "I thought, 'who could it be at this hour?'" she recalls. It was three Atlantic City police officers. "They asked me if my son Craig had a heart condition. I said, 'no, he doesn't have a heart condition....' Then, they told me a few young men had come into the bar we owned where Craig worked. They'd shot him. He was dead," says the 87-year-old.

She tells the story slowly and takes deep breaths, as if she is reliving it.

"The officers asked if my husband could go down and close up the bar." Barbara climbed the stairs to the second floor of the family's four bedroom home, one block from the beach. She woke her husband, who had Parkinson's disease. She helped him get up to go close the bar that was now a crime scene. "I can't tell you how hard that was," she says.

Barbara is one of those naturally strong, resilient people who can tell you a story about losing her son with this overarching reassurance of "don't worry about me—I'm okay." "Luckily, the officers were just wonderful—a few stayed and comforted me while my husband was gone," she says.

Six months later, just as she was starting to emerge from her grief, Barbara's husband died. "The good thing was, throughout that nightmare of almost a year, I was still never alone—my friends took turns being with me. I couldn't have gotten through it without them."

Steve and I were both speechless. We haven't talked about it, but I know he would agree that losing a child is our worst nightmare, let alone losing your spouse shortly after. It was comforting to talk to someone who had emerged from this unthinkable tragedy so intact.

After the Rain Comes a Sunny Outlook

As I processed the gravity of the loss, I expected someone who had lost her husband and son to be withered within a 6 month period, with her loss evident by a heaviness in her face and body. Barbara, however, was the opposite. At age 87, she's got the spunk of a 30-year-old, a rosiness in her cheeks and a sparkle to her eyes.

Every morning she gets up and walks on the boardwalk, and we're talking *every single* morning. She's there in the rain. She's there in the snow. She's there in the ice. And, of course, she's there in the sun.

"The cold doesn't bother me—I just put on long underwear and bundle up," she says. The only thing that gets in the way is the wind, which can be wicked on the barrier islands of New Jersey. But, it doesn't stop her. "If it's too windy, I go to the Jewish Community Center and walk on the treadmill," she says. "I also go to Zumba classes 6 days a week and I lift weights."

How does she stay so motivated?

In a word: her friends, aka "the posse." She has a friend nearby just about any time.

In fact, she might be more social than I am. When it comes to exercise especially, I always go alone.

Although she's lost many of the good friends she grew up with, including her bridesmaids and high-school classmates, Barbara has made new ones who are just as true. "A long time ago, my mother told me, 'as you get older, you must make young friends because they will motivate you to get involved with more activities,'" Barbara says. "And, she was so right."

Finding People She Likes

Barbara took her mother's advice; many of the women she walks with on the boardwalk, lunches with, and tosses back cocktails with are more than 20 years her junior.

She met a lot of those friends enrolling in classes and going to lectures sponsored by her local university on topics that interest her, by playing bridge, and in her two book clubs (for which she reads multiple books at once!). She met others during her stint as an activist in the city of Margate at age 75.

"As you get older, if you want to stay healthy and fit, you must find the things that you like to do and then do them," she says. "As a bonus, when you do things that you personally like, you meet people that you like," she adds.

Today, more than 15 years after her losses, Barbara reflects on a full life by the sea—booming beach businesses she ran with her husband, lots of outdoor activity, and most importantly, her true friends. "There are acquaintances and there are friends. I have been lucky in my life to have many that I would call friends."

These friends are probably part of the reason why Barbara has stayed in near-perfect health. She is energetic and happy. Her vital signs are good and she takes only one medication for a tremor she inherited from her father's side of the family. "The tremor is in my hands," she says. "So, when I have the girls over for coffee, they have to fill the cups.... But, that's what friends are for."

Why It Works

When I marveled about Barbara to Steve, he understood. He says there's a pattern: His healthier patients tend to have a lot of friends. He pointed me to an important 2010 review that examined the connection between social relationships and mortality. The review looked at 148 studies and nearly 309,000 people, and it found a 50 percent lower risk of death in people with stronger social relationships than those whose social relationships were weaker.

More recently, researchers found a clear link between social relationships and good physical health. A 2016 study done at the University of North Carolina at Chapel Hill and published in *Proceedings of the National Academy of Sciences* found a lower risk of chronic conditions such as abdominal obesity, high blood pressure, and inflammation in people with more social ties. Over time, these conditions can lead to long-term health problems, such as cancer, heart disease, and stroke. This is more evidence that having a strong social network can improve your chances of living a longer, healthier life.

Having friends who are younger can boost these benefits. For one, nurturing others, research shows, is an important element to happiness. By befriending younger friends, you can encourage them and pass on important life lessons. In one of the largest studies on happiness, researchers found that giving back to others can boost your baseline happiness level by giving you a greater sense of purpose in life.

And, caring for and supporting others seems to keep blood pressure low, finds a Johns Hopkins University and University of Tennessee study that was published in *The International Journal of Psychophysiology*. Plus, having younger friends helps to keep you current and plugged in. Older adults who utilize the latest technology are better set up to "age in place," research shows.

Steve's Secrets

When it comes to scheduling her life, Barbara strikes a good balance. "My mornings are for exercise, and my afternoons are for socializing, other activities, and whatever I've neglected around my house," she laughs.

Here's how you can do the same.

KEEP A SOCIAL CALENDAR. Create a schedule that leaves room in your datebook for engagements that you enjoy. Within that schedule, set goals for yourself based on how often you like to socialize. For example, aim for three lunch dates a week, a Tuesday movie night, or one fun activity every Saturday.

GO FOR QUALITY, NOT QUANTITY. As Barbara says, there is a difference between friends and acquaintances. To get the most bang for your social buck, schedule time with the friends you hold dear—the people who make you feel stimulated, relaxed, and comfortable, rather than burdened with having to be socially "on."

MAKE THE MOST OF YOUR TIME WITH FRIENDS. Whether it's during a daily stroll on the boardwalk or a lunch at an elegant restaurant, make the conversations you have with your friends as meaningful as you can. Happy people engage in more substantive conversations—and less small talk—than people who report lower levels of happiness in their lives, research shows.

Dan Berlin's Secret

Stay Positive

. . . .

Accept what you cannot change and work on the things that you can

Tell yourself, "I can do this!"

Don't hesitate to lean on family and friends—they may just benefit from helping you

. . . .

Dan Berlin was on the beach with his kids. They covered him with seashells. Then, his 8-year-old daughter called out to her 5-year-old brother, "Hey look—barnacles on a beached whale!"

He maneuvered his hands through the shells and felt the jiggly flesh around his middle. It was clear. The shells were the barnacles. He was the whale.

He had an excuse that most people would find quite legit: He lost his sight due to a condition called cone-rod dystrophy and was now legally blind. "I felt useless and I was getting more and more angry about having to depend completely on others to get around. On top of that, I longed to be a normal dad, and go out in the yard and throw the ball with my kids. All of this made me feel quite low," he says.

So, he decided to turn this low point into an opportunity for change. He made a decision. No more whale. It was time to get back in shape.

The day Dan returned to Colorado, he slipped into sneakers, grabbed his cane, walked out his front door, and started jogging. He chose quiet, familiar roads. Within just a few minutes, he stopped dead in his tracks. Panic overtook him. Dan used his cane to jab at what looked like a solid object right in front of him.

"I thought I was going to run into something." It was a shadow from a lamp post.

The rest of the run was no easier, but he went for a second run, and then a third, and so on. "Eventually, I had to learn to just breathe and not let those moments of panic when I thought I might hit something affect my stride. When in doubt, I learned to just stop and reassess my surroundings."

Wow, and sometimes I use a little stiffness in my back as an excuse to skip my run or cut it short. Dan has already inspired me.

"Relying on other senses like touch and hearing, I was able to make it out and back home without hitting too many parked cars," he says. "It just felt so good to be outside, running."

So, he went again. And again. And again. He shifted from doubting himself to respecting himself as a runner, and eventually, an athlete. Since that brave jaunt, he's gone on to run many races—5Ks, 10Ks, half marathons, and eventually, full marathons, including Boston, one of the world's oldest and most elite marathons. Only the fastest of runners are invited to run it, and only after they've qualified by beating set times in other road races. He's also completed the Grand Canyon Rim to Rim to Rim and hiked Mount Kilimanjaro, the highest mountain in Africa.

What gave Dan the drive to go out for that first run—and what has kept him going since—is largely his optimism.

"I realize that I can't control what life presents, but I can control how I react to it," he says. "We are often a lot more than we think we are—the secret is trying new things with the right attitude, effort, and discipline."

Dan displays that discipline not only with his running, but with the rest of his exercise regimen as well. "For the past 4 years or so, I've been working out 7 days a week," he says. He runs 4 or 5 days, varying the intensity and duration; swims, cycles, or rows 2 to 4 days, depending on what he's training for; and does a functional training workout for 30 to 60 minutes, two to three times a week.

"This may sound like a lot of exercise," he says.

Ahh, yeah....

"It probably is," he continues, "but it is my downtime. Balancing exercise with my work and an active family gives me energy and joy."

He adds that intensive exercise helps him sleep better. "Our bodies heal when we sleep, so, if I am training during the day, I need to sleep and recover at night—it's yin and yang," he says.

That exercise also helps fuel his positivity. "As I started to choose more intense physical goals, my training followed suit and I've become an even happier person," he says. "In hindsight, it's amazing what a change in mindset and the simple act of accomplishing something as basic as running a race did to slowly change my attitude."

Helping Others

It was the day Dan decided to purchase a fluorescent running vest that his running started to turn into a movement. He asked the shop to print the word "blind" in block letters on the front and back.

"The guy who owned the sports printing shop is a triathlete. After I explained what I was looking for in the vest, he asked me to give him a call if I ever wanted a training partner," Dan says. "He became not only a training partner, but a guide in many races and a close friend."

A similar situation happened before Dan's first half marathon too. "I thought about how not to get in the way of other runners who put so much time into training for this race," he says.

He contacted the race director, who put him in touch with a now dear friend. "She guided me through that first half marathon, and became my running guide and mentor for many races, including my first Boston marathon."

Thankful for the people who have made his racing dreams a reality, Dan has given back as much help as he has received. Together with a few fellow athletes, he started Team See Possibilities to help children who are blind around the world. He also inspires people who aren't blind. "I get the comment all the time: 'If you can do it, I can do it,' and I say, 'of course, you can do it!' "

A Meaningful, Authentic Life

His workout and racing regimen has also given him the courage and confidence to try things beyond what he thought he could do. He's since co-founded Rodelle, a leading vanilla and baking essentials company. "Pushing the limit physically has taught me that I can almost always do more than I thought I could."

His blindness has taught his two teenage children to be more courageous too, as they look out for their dad. "I've always felt guilty because I can't go out and throw a ball with my son or teach my daughter to drive, like other dads can," Dan says. What he has done is taught them to be kind.

When his son was 8 or 9, he said, "Dad, I'm glad you are blind."

"Why?" Dan asked.

His son replied, "Because I get to help you."

As he looks toward the future, Dan sees many more challenges, both mental and physical, and he's excited to tackle them. "I'm in my forties, which means I have 40 more active years to go! I'm happy that I have the chance every day to live a meaningful, authentic life."

Why It Works

Despite dealing with a disability that makes his vision "older" than his 47 years, Dan is more vibrant than many men his age. Why? In part, because of his positive attitude and ability to accept adversity. Negativity toward adversity can increase your risk of becoming frail, which in turn increases your risk for dementia, depression, and numerous other age-related diseases and conditions.

People with negative attitudes toward aging lost more cognitive abilities and walked more slowly over 2 years than did older adults who reported more positive attitudes, found one study of 4,135 older adults.

Resisting negative stereotypes about getting older—which are prevalent—is important too. In a 2015 study done at the Yale School of Public Health and published in *Psychological Science*, researchers found that older individuals who were subliminally exposed to positive messages about aging experienced long-term boosts in strength, balance, and self-image.

In a different study, older adults who viewed age as a time of wisdom, self-realization, and satisfaction were 44 percent more likely to recover from a bout of disability than older people with a more negative view. All of these studies go to show that the way you approach the challenges you cannot change—such as aging—can make all the difference in terms of how you survive them.

Steve's Secrets

As a blind person, Dan has a unique take on surfing life's ups and downs. But, we can all learn from his resilience and optimism. Here are some tips on staying positive in the face of aging.

DO THE BEST YOU CAN WITH WHAT YOU HAVE. We all have our own sets of strengths and limitations, which may fade or become more pronounced as we get older. Instead of dwelling on a weakness, focus on how you can use it as a strength. You may not be the runner you used to be, but you can still raise money in charity races and have fun getting out there with running friends.

Similarly, when you feel your knees stiffening up or notice that you can no longer read the fine print on a pill bottle, don't look at it as something depressing about aging, but instead as a symbol of all the wisdom you've acquired throughout your years. Like Dan pointed out about his sight, you aren't going to change the fact that you are aging, but you can change your attitude toward getting older—and your attitude can make a tremendous difference in your physical and emotional health.

DON'T GET MAD, GET ACTIVE. Exercise is an excellent way to stay positive during adversity. In fact, a 2016 study published in *Medicine* found that exercise helped women overcome one of life's biggest hurdles—widowhood. (Widows are notoriously less active and more likely to smoke and drink, have trouble sleeping, suffer from depression, abuse drugs, and commit suicide than women whose spouses are alive).

Researchers looked at a large group of women and found that widows who exercised regularly added 4 years to their life expectancies and were 14 percent less likely to die than married women who were inactive. The widows also reported an increase in mental status, better sleep, less depression, and stronger social networks than those who didn't exercise.

SURROUND YOURSELF WITH POSITIVE PEOPLE. To stay upbeat, spend time with people who make you a better, happier person. Generally speaking, these people will make you feel like you have what it takes to overcome obstacles, support you, and help you reach your goals.

Sarah Doan's Secret

Accept Your Limitations

. . . .

Focus on your strengths, not your weaknesses
Have a reason to get out of bed every morning
Cherish the moment

. . . .

In the *Curious Case of Benjamin Button*, the main character ages in reverse, starting as an old man and ending as an infant. The movie is a fantasy, but Sarah Doan has experienced a similar fate in real life.

Soon after Sarah was born, doctors noticed that her esophagus wasn't done growing, so it was in two separate pieces, like a bridge in the process of construction with no middle. The culprit: a congenital disease called VATER syndrome that affects one in 10,000 to 40,000 babies. VATER stands for the different areas affected—vertebrae, anus, trachea, esophagus, and renal (kidneys).

Doctors told Sarah's parents that their 6-month-old infant likely wouldn't live past her 5th birthday. And, their prediction almost came true. Sarah was pronounced dead four times by the time she turned 3.

A critical turning point happened when Sarah was 3½. Her feeding tube fell out while she was playing and the family could not get her in to see a surgeon to replace it. "So," Sarah says, "my mom calmly, lovingly, but firmly took me into my bedroom and got down on her knees to be eye level with me. She said, 'Your tube fell out. It can't be put back in for a while, Sarah. So, I will make you whatever you would like to try, but I need you to start eating by mouth, like mommy and daddy and grandma. If you don't, you will die. Do you understand what I'm saying?' That conversation was a defining moment in my life and it's stuck in my head for 30 years now. We went into the kitchen and I asked for orange foods: steamed carrots, macaroni and cheese, and cantaloupe. I lived on those three foods for a long time."

Over the years, Sarah has undergone 34 surgeries, including 7 to rebuild her esophagus, correction of her severe scoliosis, a hysterectomy, and removal of her left kidney. Due to a botched surgery on her esophagus that nicked one of her lungs, Sarah has had pneumonia 12 times. "If I get it 2 or 3 more times, the doctors say I could die," she says.

Now at age 33, Sarah is, to her knowledge, one of the oldest surviving and highest thriving people with her disease. Her life is more limited than most. She has a lot less energy than other people her age. She has regular bouts of stomach upset and crippling back pain, and she can't eat certain foods. She also has a strained voice that resulted from having a trach tube in place for 2 years. It makes her sound both hoarse and out of breath. "My voice affects my everyday life a lot because I sound sick when I speak—people ask me about it multiple times a day. I can hide most things that have happened to me, but I can't hide my voice," she says. "I cannot work 40 hours a week and never will. I can't go from sunup to sundown without a nap. I cannot run a marathon and I cannot scream."

She has periodically struggled with bouts of depression because of these limitations, but, most of the time, she refuses to let them control her. "Instead, I focus on what I *can* do, and make the most of those things. I can do most things other people my age can do. I have to pace myself, but I kind of like that, because it has taught me to enjoy life and savor the moment."

Sarah gets some of her inspiration from active older people who refuse to allow the number of candles on their birthday cakes to slow them down. "I need to have places to go and people to see—a reason to get up every day," she says. "Even on the days when I'm in pain, my stomach is messed up, and my back hurts, I will purposely put on makeup and a nice outfit and try to go out. I like to feel pretty."

When we spoke, Sarah had a bachelor's degree in psychology and was going to school to get her PhD. But she was unsure if she wanted to proceed. She says her ultimate goal is to become an author. "I want to write, to tell my story, and to inspire people," she says.

Cherishing Every Moment

To stay positive, Sarah often puts her situation in perspective. "Things can always be worse!" she says, and remains thankful for what she has. "I take great joy in simple pleasures—a delicious cup of coffee, an exceptionally great hug from my boyfriend, my wonderful mom, the kids in my life, a great meal, a beautiful sunset, or even how good it feels to brush my teeth or pee without issues."

As I listened, I started to feel guilty. This woman's definition of a bad day is excruciating stomach pain; sometimes my definition is as trivial as forgetting to put the garbage out before the trash man comes.

On her good days, Sarah uses activities she enjoys for her exercise. "I run errands, cook, lightly clean, walk around the block, or window-shop," she says. Sometimes she will take a longer walk, do yoga, or dance.

She also maintains her sense of humor. "Studies have proven how healthy and helpful laughter is, and I love to laugh!" she says. And, she makes spending time with family and friends a high priority.

"I know how fragile life can be, how it changes in an instant, so I cherish every moment with those I love to the umpteenth degree."

But, although she accepts her limitations, Sarah refuses to settle for less than a good quality of life. "As much as I do see myself getting older and living into my eighties and nineties, I want the quality of life I currently have now. I have lived my life backward; I feel younger as I get older. God forbid something happens that would force me to live like I did as a little girl."

Overall, she is very positive and constantly reminds herself how lucky she is. "We all face challenges, but we can't let the "I can'ts" control us," she says. "Live your life to the best of your abilities—life like ultimately what you make it."

Why It Works

When people accept and adapt to life's losses, they are happier, finds a 2014 study published in the *Journal of Happiness Studies*. And, older individuals with more positive self-perceptions of aging live an average of 7.5 years longer than those whose perceptions of aging were less positive. The advantage remained even after researchers accounted for age, gender, socioeconomic status, loneliness, and functional health.

And, a 2009 study that stemmed from the Women's Health Initiative found that those with optimistic attitudes were less likely to suffer from coronary heart disease and more likely to live longer than the pessimists in the group.

Steve's Secrets

The rest of us aren't as close as Sarah is to aging in reverse, but there are some things we can do to maintain our youthfulness and vitality, and looking on the bright side is a good start. Use this advice.

WRITE IT OUT. When we spoke to Sarah, she had already sent us a detailed written account of her life with VATER Syndrome. The actual conversation consisted more of getting to know her and filling in the holes. She made it a point to tell us that writing the piece helped her achieve a new level of self-acceptance regarding her condition. This is a good lesson. No matter what type of adversity you're facing, be it physical, emotional, or situational, try writing about it in a daily journal. If you're not a pen-and-paper person, typing it out on a laptop or tablet works too. Sometimes, you don't know how you really feel about something until you write it down.

BE POSITIVE. Optimists are less likely to suffer ailments and better able to handle them when they do strike. Positive people are also fun to be with, which makes others more likely to invite them places and seek their company. So, when it comes to successful aging, it's much better to look at your glass as half full.

TRY NOT TO WORRY. A mistake I see a lot of patients make is obsessing about getting sick and when they are going to die. We're all going to die of something someday. You don't want to ruin your healthy days worrying about when the unhealthy ones may come.

Amy Morosini's Secret

Know for Whom and Why You Want to Be Strong

• • • • • • • • • • • • • • • • • • •

Start each day with a green smoothie and a shot of apple cider vinegar
Approach life like a marathon—one step at a time
Eat a plant-based, whole foods diet

• • • • • • • • • • • • • • • • • • •

Twenty years ago, Amy Morosini joined up with several friends for New Year's Eve celebrations. She drank too much—way too much. She decided to visit her boyfriend, who lived on the third floor of an apartment building. Her memory of what happened next is mostly just bits and pieces. She doesn't know why or how it happened, but she does know this: She fell out of his window.

"I had a crushed skull, broken hip, compound fracture of my left femur, two broken wrists, and a broken right elbow, jaw, and left foot. I also had extensive nerve damage down the entire right side of my body," she recalls. "When I first looked in the mirror after the fall, I didn't recognize my paralyzed and drooping face."

She'd suffered a traumatic brain injury. Her doctors told her that she would likely never walk again and would be in a wheelchair the rest of her life. "I was a typical single girl in her twenties who went out and partied with her friends sometimes. That one time I had way too much and made some bad decisions. All it takes is one time and your life can end or radically change," she says.

With a lot of hard work and physical therapy, thankfully, she did walk again. "It took 8 months, but I eventually relearned to put one foot in front of the other," she says. The nerve damage remains, and she has permanent weakness and a pins-and-needles sensation on her right side.

But, Amy's emotional health remained wounded. She battled panic attacks, anxiety, and depression for years. "I was so afraid one of my panic attacks would hit me in a social situation that I started drinking alcohol again, which I hadn't done since I fell," she says.

Instead of making her feel better, the alcohol fueled the panic attacks. "I would black out, and then worry the next morning about what I had said and done the night before," she says. "I also stopped working out and caring about what I ate; I pretty much gave up on myself."

About a decade later, married with three boys, Amy heard a doctor say the words, "Your son has autism and he will need care for the rest of his life."

"I hadn't been motivated like that since I heard a different doctor tell me that I would need a wheelchair for the rest of my life. I realized that I couldn't continue to live the way I was. The day that I heard my son's diagnosis was the first day I resigned to trade an unhealthy addiction—alcohol—for a healthy addiction to running, fitness, and a plant-based diet," Amy says. Today, her drink of choice is water—either straight from the tap or infused with lemon or mint leaves.

She signed up for her first race, a half marathon. It was the first of many. "As soon as I crossed the finish line, I was hooked," she says.

Amy has since completed eight half marathons, five marathons, and two Ironman 70.3 competitions. Eventually though, she was forced to make some changes to her fitness routine. "Training for endurance races is hard on a body, especially a body that's been broken like mine," she says. Together with her orthopedic surgeon, she decided her training regimen was taking was too much of a toll. "I have three sons that I need to be strong and healthy for, so ending up back in a wheelchair is not an option for me," she says.

So, Amy switched to yoga and strength-training, and the lifestyle habit that she values most these days is her diet—a clean, whole foods, plant-based eating plan. Amy's diet is 100 percent plant-based—no dairy or animal protein. "Good nutrition is like the ultimate endurance race because it lasts a lifetime," she says.

To sustain her plant-based diet, Amy dug an organic garden in her backyard. "I grow my own tomatoes, different kinds of peppers, two kinds of eggplants, two different types of zucchini, lettuce, cucumbers, and sunflowers (for the seeds)," she says. To season those veggies, she grows a bunch of herbs, including oregano, basil, sage, rosemary, parsley, and mint. "I also have three apple trees and a lemon tree. I love to cook using my own home-grown organic vegetables, fruits, and herbs."

Her go-to beverages include her green breakfast smoothies, a cup of morning coffee with almond milk, and a daily shot of apple cider vinegar. "Some people put apple cider vinegar in water and sip it throughout the day, but I hate the taste of it so I put it in a shot glass and throw it back like I'm doing a shot of tequila," she says. "Instead of sucking on a lemon afterward, I bite into a sweet piece of fruit, like a strawberry or tangerine. It's a healthy shot everyone should do!"

Now at 48, Amy feels younger and healthier than she did at age 30.

"My blood pressure and cholesterol have never been better since I started eating this way," she says. Amy has the energy and vitality to get through her busy days, which include taking care of her three boys, working out, and volunteering.

Amy admits that she misses racing, so she channels that drive into her work as president of the San Francisco Bay Area Chapter of Achilles International, a nonprofit organization.

"The mission of Achilles International is to enable people with all types of disabilities to participate in mainstream running events to promote personal achievement," she says. "I really believe racing saved my life, and I want to show people that they too, can cross a finish line."

Whether it's with nutrition, racing, or time with her family, Amy approaches everything she does with a deeper appreciation because of what she's been through. "Just like when you race, sometimes you have good days and sometimes you have bad days. Every day is a new chance to start over—life is a marathon, not a sprint," she says. "The key is to never give up."

Why It Works

When Amy realized that she needed to be there—in all ways—for her son, it was her turning point. That's when she became truly resilient. After all, some of the most powerful motivation to take care of yourself comes from a desire to take good care of someone else.

In terms of her day-to-day habits, the most salient in Amy's repertoire is her apple cider vinegar shot, and it has some merit. Some of the most promising studies on apple cider vinegar shows that it can help lower blood glucose. When people with diabetes took 2 tablespoons of apple cider vinegar before bed, along with an ounce of cheese, their blood sugar levels were lower the following morning compared to nights when they ate the cheese paired with 2 tablespoons of water instead, found one study published in *Diabetes Care*.

Apple cider vinegar also appears to help with weight control, another important factor as we age. In a double-blind study (one in which neither the participants nor the experimenters know who is receiving a particular treatment) published in *Bioscience, Biotechnology, and Biochemistry*, Japanese researchers split obese adults with similar body weights and waist measurements into three groups. Every day for 12 weeks, the first group drank a beverage that contained a ½ ounce of apple cider vinegar. The second group drank 1 ounce of apple cider vinegar. The third group drank a beverage with no apple cider vinegar. At the end of the 3 months, the two groups who drank the vinegar had less belly fat, lower waist measurements, lower body weights and BMIs, and lower triglycerides compared to the no vinegar group.

Another good thing about Amy's eating plan is that she eats—and grows—100 percent organic. That's because home-grown, organic foods are free from harmful chemicals and antibiotics, taste better, have more nutritional value, and are much gentler on the environment, found a review of 41 studies published in the *Journal of Alternative and Complementary Medicine*. Specifically, the organic foods had 21.1 percent more iron, 27 percent more vitamin C, 29.3 percent more magnesium, and 13.6 percent more phosphorus than conventional plants.

Plus, food always tastes better when it is from your garden. Gardening is also a wonderful, low-impact physical activity. A full-body workout, gardening involves a range of movements, including digging holes, pulling weeds, and carrying soil.

Another important step that Amy has taken is quitting her alcohol abuse. Binge-drinking—defined as four or more drinks for a woman or five or more drinks for a man—can damage every organ system in the body, including your heart, brain, skin, liver, and bones. We typically think of binge-drinkers as college-age, but the problem affects a significant number of people over age 65. In fact, the CDC reports that although there are a greater number of young people who report binge-drinking, older binge-drinkers claim to binge-drink *more often* than younger groups.

A much better choice, especially for those who tend to abuse alcohol, is water. A 2012 study published in the *Journal of Nutrition* found that even mild dehydration resulting from inadequate water intake can negatively affect mood, headache frequency, energy, and concentration. Amy is improving all of these factors by drinking her infused H_2O.

Steve's Secrets

Use this advice to put Amy's secrets to work in your life.

USE YOUR BLOOD WORK RESULTS AS MOTIVATION. This is what Amy did. "Get all of your blood work done and measure your blood pressure. Commit to a whole food, plant-based diet for 30 days, and then repeat those tests. You will be blown away at the results, not to mention how much better you will look and feel," she says.

START AN ORGANIC GARDEN. The best way to get the peace of mind of knowing where your fruits and vegetables are coming from is to grow them yourself. Here are some tips to help you get started.

- Choose your location carefully. For best results, find an area that gets full sun, out in the open.

- Put tall plants at the north end and short plants at the south end.

- Plan ahead and space plants according to how big they will get, not their size at the time of planting.

- Schedule time for watering, trimming, feeding, addressing pests (without pesticides, of course), and harvesting. If you have a busy schedule, go for plants that are less needy (your local nursery can help advise you).

- Choose plants according to the season (again, your nursery can help).

- Consider an automatic watering system.

- Don't get discouraged when you lose a few plants—it's all part of the gardening process.

- Find a good source of organic plant food (which actually feeds the soil). Steer clear of any organic product that contains inorganic fertilizers.

If you can't do a backyard garden, consider joining a crop share, or CSA (Community Supported Agriculture). When you sign up, you get a share of the weekly harvest at peak freshness delivered to your home or designated pick-up spot. On average, CSAs cost about $20 per week.

When my family and I joined a CSA, we had more fruits and veggies than we knew what to do with—they are well worth the investment, and from experience, they encourage you to find new recipes and ways to use the harvest. To find a CSA in your area, check out localharvest.org.

DRINK LOTS OF H2O. Drinking eight to ten 8-ounce glasses of water per day can help promote weight loss and boost your brain power. Water also causes skin to plump, causing wrinkles and pores to look less obvious. It also supports collagen, which protects skin's firmness and elasticity.

DO A SHOT OF APPLE CIDER VINEGAR. A couple tablespoons a day of apple cider vinegar is safe and may help with blood sugar and weight control. Can't stand the taste? Instead of downing it straight, try adding apple cider vinegar to roasted vegetables or as a marinade for chicken or pulled pork. You may also be able to hide a tablespoon in a smoothie or soup. Or, try substituting a little apple cider vinegar every time you have a recipe that calls for something acidic.

TAKE CARE OF YOURSELF SO YOU CAN TAKE GOOD CARE OF OTHERS. Take a moment every day to ask yourself if your needs are being met. If not, it's time to make some changes. Make time for things like training for a race, taking a class on a topic you enjoy, or another activity that challenges you and builds your courage and resilience.

Diogo Teixeira's Secret

Hike outdoors

. . . .

Do the thing you've always dreamed of

Exercise among pretty scenery

Say 'yes' to surgery that can improve your quality of life

. . . .

As he lay in a hospital bed following a spinal surgery, Diogo Teixeira, 71, just wanted to be able to do one thing. "I was just hoping to get up and walk," he recalls.

Diogo had suffered for years with arthritis of the spine. "I got my first epidural 16 years ago. When I got to the point that I couldn't walk, I gave in and had the surgery," he says.

During his procedure—called a laminectomy—surgeons created space in the spine by removing one or more of the laminae—the back parts of the vertebrae that cover the spinal canal. The goal was to enlarge the spinal canal to relieve pressure on Diogo's nerves.

The surgery worked and Diogo was completely back on his feet—and without pain—in 2 months.

That's when he began dreaming of hiking the Himalayas someday. "I love big mountains and hiking in the wilderness—it's great stuff," he says.

To prepare, he continued his twice-weekly sessions with his personal trainer and watched what he ate to drop 10 pounds. Three years later, along with his wife and a group of hikers who were also in their sixties and seventies, he helicoptered into Phakding. "From there we trekked to the Everest base camp," he says.

All told, he and his traveling partners faced a 5,550-meter trek. "It took about 9 days to go up, 7 to come back," he says.

He says the hiking part wasn't too difficult. "The yaks carry the heavy stuff and I was in pretty good shape," he says. The hardest part was dealing with the high altitude. "I didn't suffer any serious symptoms, but I experienced strange tingling in my fingers one day, and I had weird nightmares."

The dry air also put the hikers at an increased risk of dehydration. To combat the dryness, they drank plenty of water and used a buff—a cloth that wraps around your mouth and neck to keep dust away as well as traps moisture.

At night, the group slept in informal, unheated hotels called teahouses. "The central rooms were heated by a cast-iron yak dung heater, but the sleeping rooms were unheated—temperatures at night got down to about 30°F—cold enough for our water bottles to freeze," he recalls.

Along the way, the hikers bonded, learning about each other's lives and offering encouragement and support. "We made good friends—we've all kept in touch since the trip," he says. "It was the perfect way to celebrate my 70th birthday."

Diogo is very laid back and he speaks in a slow, chill way. But I could hear the subtle excitement and nostalgia in his voice as he recalled his hiking experience—even when he talked about the difficult parts.

Since hiking the Himalayas, Diogo has continued with his trainer sessions and gone on smaller outdoor hiking excursions. When we spoke, he was getting ready to start a camping trip in The Maze at Canyonlands National Park, the most remote part of the lower 48. "Later this year, I will be hiking the Kenai Peninsula in Alaska and in the Dolomites in Italy," he says.

To make sure that he's up for each hike, he makes regular visits to his doctor. "My doctor tells me, for my age, I'm one of the healthiest guys she sees." He takes no medications other than one for muscle spasms in his back. When I asked if he will make the Himalayan trek again, Diogo paused. "I don't know. I would love to go back, but we'll see. If not, I'm happy I did it once—it was a great experience."

Why It Works

One of the themes that came up repeatedly in my conversation with Diogo is his love of the outdoors. When he talked about backpacking out West in the mountains, he just lit up.

Exercising outside in natural surroundings like mountains gives you a dose of vitamin D from the sun. Plus, there's just something about sunshine and fresh air that lifts the spirits. Also noteworthy is that exercising outdoors—hiking, in particular—offers a complete escape. No phones, no laptops, no Facebook—just your hiking boots and peaceful surroundings. So, it makes sense that research has linked outdoor exercise with a more upbeat attitude. A study published in *PLOS ONE* found that hiking in nature can boost attention span and creative problem-solving skills by as much as 50 percent.

Hiking is great exercise to boot, burning up to 500 calories or more in 1 hour. And, long distance treks can lower levels of oxidative stress—a process thought to be an integral part of the onset, progression, and recurrence of cancer. Because it gives you a clear goal—completing the trek—hiking is also a wonderful way to challenge yourself and boost your self-esteem.

Steve's Secrets

After you've cleared your hiking plans with your health-care provider, use these to get started.

GET IN SHAPE. Getting in shape to hike is pretty much the same as getting in shape to run a race or improve your health—it involves a combination of cardiovascular exercise, strength-training, stretching, balance, and flexibility exercises. For the cardiovascular part, aim to engage in 30 to 60 minutes of moderate aerobic activity (like brisk walking) 5 or more days a week. For strength, perform resistance exercises at least 2 times a week. For the strength, balance, and flexibility necessary for hiking, try these exercises. Start with 5 pound weights and work your way up to heavier ones.

Modified Leg Curl

Lie on your back with your hips close to a bench. Place your left foot on the bench and lift your right leg up as high as you can. At the same time, press your left foot down into the bench, clench your glutes and hamstrings, and raise your hips off the ground. Do 10 reps and then repeat on the other side.

Lunge

Stand and hold equal weights in each of your hands. Step forward with one leg and squat until both legs are bent at 90 degrees. Push up and bring your rear foot forward. Repeat on the other side.

Band Walk

Tie a resistance band around the middle of your shins, tight enough that there's tension when you stand with your legs hip-width apart. Stand up straight, put your hands on your hips, and tuck in your abs, then take a step forward while maintaining the band's tension on your shins. Repeat on the other side.

GET THE RIGHT GEAR. Just because retail stores like Target, Wal-Mart, and Costco sell tents doesn't mean that you should buy one there. When it comes to hiking footwear, sleeping bags, tents, and rain gear, your best bet is to go to a specialty outdoor store. Salespeople at these stores are trained to talk to you about your hiking plans and match the gear to your goals.

USE A REAL-DEAL MAP. One of the biggest mistakes new hikers make is trying to use a road map or road navigation to hike the backcountry. Instead, if you are trekking a well-marked trail, go for a designated trail map that points out topographical features such as ridges, peaks, and rivers. For local trail maps, check bookstores or visitor centers. For popular U.S. recreational hiking spots, check out National Geographic's Trails Illustrated series. You can also use your smartphone to guide you. Some of the best apps for iPhone and Android include the following:

- **Yonder**
- **MapMyHike**
- **AllTrails**
- **Mountain Hub**
- **Gaia GPS**
- **Cairn (iPhone only)**
- **Geocaching**
- **Camp Finder**

Derk Richardson's Secret

There Is Life after Double Hip Replacements

· · · · · · · · · · · · · · · · · · ·

Recover by doing what you love

Consider Shintaido, aqua aerobics, and other gentle forms of movement

Overcome any hesitation to being the only man (or woman) in a class

· ·

What calms 67-year-old Derk Richardson? Swinging a 32-inch wooden sword. Derk practices Shintaido, a martial art developed in the 1960s. The name means "new body way."

Shintaido movements range from gentle and meditative to vigorous jumping, throwing, and rolling. Partners appear to fight each other, "but, it's much more of a peaceful and cooperative partner practice; our swords never actually touch," Derk says.

In fact, Shintaido is all about relationships. "The longer we practice, the deeper, subtler, and more sensitive our awareness of relationship dynamics becomes," he says. The art also promotes physical relaxation, flexibility, and fluidity of motion. "It develops an intimate understanding of our own bodies," Derk says.

Swinging Swords to Sharpen Listening Skills

A close friend first introduced Derk to Shintaido during a scuba-diving excursion to Midway Island in the Pacific in 1999. Also on the trip was Haruyoshi Fugaku Ito, one of the founding masters of Shintaido.

"When Ito demonstrated *eiko-dai*, something inside me cracked open," Derk says. (Eiko-dai is a kata, or movement pattern, which involves opening your arms outward, stretching them to the sky, and cutting them down in front of you as you run forward while yelling.) "I knew I had to try it," he recalls.

Derk lucked out. There was a class less than a ½ mile from his house, at the Lake Temescal Regional Recreation Area in California. The teacher, Shin Aoki, is the son of Shintaido's 'inventor' and founder, Hiroyuki Aoki. "I started practicing in Shin's class in June 1999, and he's been my teacher and close friend ever since," Derk says.

Despite using a symbolic wooden sword (called *bokuto*), as well as long sticks (*boken*) and karate throws, Shintaido fosters sensitivity. "In my daily life, I find that I'm often more aware of the energy flowing between myself and those around me," Derk says. "It might just be knowing when to listen and when to enter a conversation, and how to respond in beneficial ways. I'm also less fearful of new challenging situations." These are lessons we can all benefit from, at any stage of life.

This understanding helped Derk recover from two hip replacement surgeries within 5 years—one in 2011 and the second in 2016. Within 5 weeks after his second replacement, he was back to swinging *bokutos*.

"Several of the movements we do regularly in our karate class were especially helpful in restoring my strength and flexibility after the surgeries," he recalls. He adds that the warm-ups and stretches, especially the sequence of "health exercise" movements called *kenko-taiso*, were particularly helpful in advancing him down the road to recovery. "The results, in turn, bolstered my confidence in the progress of my rehab."

A few other exercises helped him integrate his new hips into his body as a whole. *Wakame taiso* (moving like seaweed), *tachi* jumping (a partner-led soft jumping exercise to loosen all the joints, lower your center of gravity, and decompartmentalize the body so energy moves freely throughout), were also instrumental in his rehab.

Derk healed remarkably well, but he understands that he can't turn back the clock. "My doctor told me I will never have the hips of a 16-year-old again, but I do feel like I have the hips of a 40-year-old, and I'm happy with that."

He's also happy that he can still perform the moves that support his physical and mental health as he gets older. "When we are received by and thrown by a partner in our karate practice, we actually gain energy as we roll softly on the earth and bounce up," he says. "This and other movements keep my body feeling younger than its 67 years."

Saturdays Are for Shintaido

To sharpen his Shintaido moves and stay in shape, Derk performs a varied workout routine. On Mondays, Wednesdays, and Fridays, he takes gentle movement aqua aerobics classes at his local YMCA in Oakland, California. "These 50 minute classes emphasize core strengthening, balance, and resistance; I usually get in the pool 10 minutes early or stay 10 minutes after to jog in the water, so I'm moving for a full hour," he says.

On Tuesdays and Thursdays, he takes a studio class, also 50 minutes, called low-impact Cardio Sculpt. It alternates aerobics with strength/toning exercises using dumbbells, kettlebells, weighted body bars, elastic bands, medicine balls, Bosu balls, and horizontal step platforms. "I am often the only man in these classes," Derk laughs.

He also plays co-ed slow-pitch softball once a week from April through October, where he is *not* the only guy.

He reserves his Saturday mornings for Shintaido. "December through March, we usually practice in a gym and focus on sword curriculum, called *kenjutsu*," he says. When the weather warms, they practice karate on the lawn by the lake.

Derk urges other people his age to find an activity they love as much as he does Shintaido. "Seek out exercises that are fun and suit your personality," he says. "Also, find a good instructor. I think having a good teacher becomes increasingly important as you get older. You need someone who will inspire you and guide you through techniques appropriate for your physical state."

Why It Works

Although there's no solid research on Shintaido, some studies have shown that martial arts, in general, can help people stay well.

Findings from a study published in the journal *BMC Research Notes* suggest that doing martial arts may help your body to avoid falling as well as to withstand one. Many martial arts address the art of falling, including how to roll and protect the head and other body parts.

Proper fall training is particularly important for people who suffer from osteoporosis, who are most at risk for injuries resulting from falls. This kind of exercise isn't right for everyone, however, so check with your physician before starting any new program.

In addition to protecting your bones, martial arts may also shield your brain. According to a study published in the *Journal of Alzheimer's Disease*, tai chi, an ancient Chinese practice of slow, deliberate movements that help with balance and relaxation, can help lower the risk of dementia.

Scientists from the University of South Florida worked together with Chinese researchers to look at the effects of tai chi on the brain. They split 120 elderly people from Shanghai into four groups. One group did tai chi three times a week, one group walked, one group increased their social interaction, and one group continued their normal routines. After 40 weeks, the group that practiced tai chi had the best improvements in brain volume (an important part of cognition, since gray matter in the brain usually shrinks as a person gets older).

Tai chi appears to have additional healing powers too. In a study published in *Cell Transplantation*, scientists at the Center for Neuro-psychiatry at China Medical University Hospital in Taiwan looked at three different groups of volunteers under age 25 for one year. The first group did tai chi for at least 2 hours a week, the second group walked briskly for at least 2 hours a week, and the third group didn't follow any specific exercise plan. At the end of the year, the group that practiced tai chi had the biggest boost in cells called CD 34+. These cells are markers for blood stem cells involved in cell self-renewal, which is important for proper maintenance and repair of organ systems—a process that slows down as we age. Researchers also concluded that tai chi may benefit the cardiovascular system by expanding blood vessel walls and increasing blood flow.

If that isn't enough to convince you, martial arts may also improve your emotional health, help give you better immunity, and lower your blood pressure.

Steve's Secrets

Ironically, martial arts like Shintaido can be some of the most calming, centering activities you can do. If you are interested, use these tips to get started and get the most out of your practice.

SEARCH OUT A SHINTAIDO OR ANOTHER MARTIAL ARTS CLASS. If Shintaido sounds appealing to you, look for a class in your area. Check out the practice locations listed on Shintaido of America web site, shintaido.org/docs/locations.htm. Keep in mind that Shintaido is an obscure martial art form and you may not be as lucky as Derk to find a class so close to your home. Another option is to find books and DVDs on Shintaido at ito.shintaido.org/publications.htm.

USE SHINTAIDO TO STRENGTHEN YOUR BODY AND MIND. Just about every movement and technique in the Shintaido curriculum can help you improve your comfort and confidence. Derk points to "greater awareness of the energies in the body; refinement of sensitivity and receptivity in our relationships with nature, other people, and universal energies; and an overall sense of free-flowing self-expression." As a bonus, you can find your own favorite technique that best suits your body and emotional development.

BRANCH OUT. Keep in mind that other more mainstream forms of martial arts—Karate, tai chi, Tae kwon do, Aikido, Judo—are beneficial for the mind and body too. A good place to start when looking for these classes is your local YMCA. Different Ys offer different martial arts classes, but most YMCAs offer free trial classes, so you can find the martial arts form that is best for you. Other good places to find martial arts classes are local community centers and martial arts schools.

DON'T GO ROGUE. Remember Derk's advice concerning the importance of a martial arts instructor. Because martial arts combines physical movements with spiritual elements and relaxation, you'll want to find a teacher that you get along with and respect. It's perfectly acceptable to ask for a trial class before you commit; if you and the instructor don't click, look for something else.

Steve's Prescription for Being Unbreakable

As a doctor of osteopathy, I haven't had formal psychological training, but I have overcome my share of hurdles in my life, and I've watched friends and patients do the same. So, in the name of good mental and physical health—and showing each other and ourselves what we're made of—here's my advice for nurturing resilience and being unbreakable.

REALIZE ADVERSITY IS A FACT OF LIFE. We all face challenges, be it health, family matters, natural disasters, or something else. If you expect your life will be perfectly smooth sailing, you will be sorely disappointed. So, the next time you suffer a setback, remind yourself that you're not alone.

PREPARE FOR ADVERSITY. The best time to bolster your defenses against life's blows is *before* they strike, not in the middle of a crisis. Knowing that challenges are coming, work on building your emotional strength, your courage, and your social support system of family and friends. Think through how you would handle certain situations should they arise. Investigate your options in terms of social services, including transportation, food, and cleaning, and have those contact numbers available in case a crisis strikes at any age.

DON'T WALLOW IN IT. While you do want to think about and plan how to handle the inevitable difficult situations that will arise, you don't want to become the Negative Nellie who constantly expects and plans for the worst. Try to strike a balance between realizing the inevitability of adversity and remaining optimistic about your future.

MEDITATE. Often, adversarial situations cause anxiety and depression—these emotions can cripple you and prevent you from dealing with the problem in a productive way. Sometimes, the best way to find a plan to overcome that problem is to distance yourself from it. Mindfulness meditation allows you to break out of anxious and obsessive

• •

At a Glance: How to Be Unbreakable

→ Embrace adversity. Rather than fear it, expect it, and see if you can learn from it.

→ Swap negative self-talk for positive self-talk.

→ Be willing to fail. It could be the best thing that happens to you.

→ Go for your dreams and don't expect them to be easy to achieve. Remind yourself that hard things are the things most worth doing.

→ Surround yourself with friends who lift you up, help you reach your goals, and support you when you most need it.

→ Meditate.

→ Journal about your experience.

→ Practice a martial art.

→ Challenge yourself with a long, outdoor trek. It will help you to see what you are made of.

→ Use exercise to burn off stress and negativity.

→ Use your strengths to your advantage, rather than dwelling on your shortcomings.

thoughts so you can move into a place of inner peace. With your new-found calmness and a clearer head, you can then gain the strength to overcome the adversity you face. It's important to note that you don't necessarily have to come up with solutions to your problems during your meditation sessions—just release the stress that's blocking healthy thought patterns.

Try sitting quietly for a few moments. Just watch your mind as if you are an observer. Think of your thoughts as clouds and your peaceful mind the blue sky behind the clouds. Rather than clinging to thoughts, allow them to just travel through as you gaze at the clear blue sky.

REMEMBER, THIS TOO SHALL PASS. It's a simple little phrase that speaks volumes. The next time you are in the middle of a crisis that seems like it will never end, remind yourself that it will.

NURTURE YOUR NETWORK. We all know that having a social network is good for your physical and mental health; it's also a good idea to have a strong one in place when the going gets tough. Having close friends and family members to lend an ear, cook a meal, and just be there for you can make all the difference between surviving and thriving in the face of adversity.

PURSUE YOUR PASSIONS. Nothing worth doing is easy. I learned this when I went through medical school. I learned it when Liz and I started our family at the same time I started my residency. It was so hard that, one time, I physically collapsed in a patient's room, but today I'm reaping the benefits of going for my dreams. Don't let fear hold you back from aiming for your goals, no matter how lofty.

DON'T BE AFRAID TO FAIL. In my life, I've learned some of my most important lessons as a result of failing. It's easy to hold back from going for something—or to stop in the middle—because you don't want to fail. But if you ask me, failing at something is better than never try-ing it at all. Often, when you push through the discomfort and doubt, you're amazed at what you can achieve.

TALK TO YOURSELF NICELY. We are our own worst critics. But, really, why? The next time you start to tell yourself, "You're so stupid" or "You can't do this," or another self-defeating phrase, stop. Instead, switch it to positive self-talk. Try things like, "No one is perfect and I'm no exception" or "Learning from my mistakes makes me a better person."

Nine

Be Fit and Trim

As Steve and I spoke with one amazingly healthy person after another, a common theme emerged. None of them were overweight.

This makes sense, as excess pounds increase your risk for just about everything that can kill you off long before your time: diabetes, high blood pressure, heart disease, stroke, some cancers, sleep apnea, fatty liver disease, kidney disease...you name it. Excess body fat can also rob you of your vitality by putting pressure on your joints and siphoning your energy.

Yet, becoming too obsessed with your weight can backfire too. If you focus too much attention on your body, for example, you may rob yourself of vitality in different, more subtle ways. For example, you may put off doing things—such as a beach vacation—until you've lost the weight and look "good" in a bathing suit. Or, you may generally feel awkward, uncomfortable, and self-conscious, no matter where you go or what you are wearing. And, you may develop a love-hate relationship with food: craving certain foods only to feel terrible about eating them. That's *no* way to live!

Thankfully, our interviews with several of the World's Healthiest People showed us that there's a better way—a much better way. Some of our interviewees are trim because they battled weight in the past and learned what works for them to lose weight and keep it off. Others have been trim their whole lives. All of them are slim because of their lifestyles—the good habits they put into practice every day. None of them crash diet, binge on exercise, or obsess about the numbers on the scale. By virtue of being healthy, they stay fit and trim.

Okay, let's meet them.

Kari Dougan's Secret

Adjust Your Fitness and Nutrition Goals As Your Body Ages

. . . .

Make breakfast or lunch your biggest meal

Eat blueberries every day

Work out like you're 20 years younger—but don't skip the warm-up

. . . .

When I worked as a writer at Prevention 20 years ago, Kari Dougan's kickboxing and spin classes at the company gym were the talk of the office every morning: "Did you go to Kari's class last night? What a workout! I can barely move today!"

Apparently, not much has changed. Today, at 58, Kari is still tough as nails, busting asses at fitness centers and working out 6 days a week without fail. Kettlebells, sleds, heavy ropes, weighted bars, and dead slam balls are all part of her regular workout routine. "I love a good challenge," she says. Her latest was a "push-up challenge," for which she did 22 push-ups a day for 22 days. "Push-ups are still my favorite," she says.

Kari embodies an energy that is tough to describe. All I can tell you is this: She's one of the most fully alive people I've ever known. She walks with purpose. Her posture commands respect. Her skin glows. She's happy to see just about everyone who crosses her path. And, a joyful perkiness seems to pervade every one of her cells. Because of all this, it's easy to mistake her for someone in their twenties or thirties—until she starts telling you about her three grown boys and new grandbaby. Then, all of the sudden, you're like, ma-a-a-aybe she's in her late forties? Early fifties?

When she reveals that she's pushing 60, all you want is her secret.

"I work out for a living," she says, when I ask her how she has managed to stop time. Her other important secret: her eating habits.

"I keep it to lean proteins and vegetables. I don't eat processed foods or sugar (except around the holidays)," she says. And she eats blueberries. "Eating blueberries is the one thing I consistently do every single day," she says. She also practices intermittent fasting, which isn't as drastic as it might sound. "I frequently eat my dinner at lunchtime and go until the next morning without eating," she says, adding that this is the secret to keeping her weight down. She still weighs 120 pounds, the same as she always has.

"I have never in my life counted calories or gone on a formal diet," she says. "The intermittent fasting works great for weight control," she says.

Letting Her Mind and Body Go

Talking to Kari, it's obvious that she's stronger than the average person, which gives her the discipline and will to get through her active days and eating regimen, as well as the interpersonal challenges she has faced. Her day starts at 4:30 a.m. and ends at 8:00 p.m. In between teaching classes, Kari runs home to help care for her 28-year-old son Jake who has VATER syndrome, a birth defect that affects one in 10,000 to 40,000 babies. VATER stands for the different areas affected—vertebrae, anus, trachea, esophagus, and renal (kidneys).

"When Jake was born, he had to have a tracheal esophageal fistula repair surgery right away. This operation closed the connection between his trachea and esophagus," she says. "He also has severe congenital scoliosis and had three spinal fusion surgeries to stabilize his spine."

Unfortunately, the surgeries failed, and the severity of the curves in his spine impacted his lungs and led to pulmonary hypertension, a form of chronic lung disease. As his heart strained to do the work of his lungs, the right ventricle of his heart stopped functioning properly, a condition called right heart failure. Now under the care of a pulmonologist, Jake uses a machine at night to ensure that he continues to breathe during sleep. Called a BiPAP (bilevel positive airway pressure), the machine delivers pressurized air through Jake's airways, which helps keep his throat muscles from collapsing.

He has a serious disease for sure, but today, at age 28, Jake is doing well. He is learning to drive. He has a part-time job working at a local grocery store. He's an avid collector of antique toys, and a fan of old-school rock and country music. He loves to spend time with his twin brother and older brother, and he enjoys being an uncle and godfather to his oldest brother's son. "But, this is a progressive disease," Kari says.

Kari admits caring for her son has been trying at times, but she deals with the situation in healthy ways. She has avoided the stress reliever far too many people turn to: unhealthy comfort food. "I would choose exercise over a pint of ice cream any day," she says.

When her sons were younger, she ran to cope. "Going for runs was my stress reducer—it gave me time to solve problems and put things back into perspective," she says. "Once you are in the right pattern of breathing, you are free to let your mind go."

Unfortunately, Kari had to stop running in 2013 due to nagging back injuries from a car accident, but she's found other ways to relax her body and mind. "One of my favorite things to do is to go for a walk—it's not the same as running, but it feels good, and I've convinced myself that I can walk for fitness," she says.

She also uses prayer and meditation to keep her stress at bay, and she turns to her friends. "I have some really close friends who have seen me through a lot. It is so important for every woman to have a strong support group—as women, it's how we operate," she says.

Almost Time to Take a Bow

To stay "trainer fit," Kari teaches most of the same classes she did 20 years ago, uses weight machines, and jumps rope. "When I am teaching classes I am always on, I am always up—it's high energy, and I want to bring that to people, because it helps them stay motivated," she says. "It's almost like a performance."

She admits that the performance is winding down. "I'm starting to notice that I need more down time. My chiropractor just told me the other day, 'You aren't 25 anymore!'" she says. "The good news is I'm more okay with down time than I've ever been."

She has also had to adjust her workouts—both in and out of the instructor role—as she's gotten older. "When you get close to 60, things are less supple than they used to be, so your warm-up has to be longer than your actual workout," she says. She prepares her body for exercise by using foam rollers and good dynamic stretches. "And, of course, I do a decent cool down after I'm done," she says.

She's also a firm believer in rest days. "You have to give your body time to recover, especially as you age. I try to take the weekends off from exercise," she says.

Yoga also helps. "All it takes is 20 minutes of a yoga class to get my hips open and that feels really good," she says.

"And, then there's this thing called gratitude. For a hot shower, a cup of tea—gratitude for the big and little things is so important," she says, "Otherwise, you can start to become a martyr and say, 'woe is me,' and that's not healthy."

So, she's thankful for everything in her life, big and small—her husband, Bob, who has given her love, support, and parenting partnership for 38 years; her children; her new grandson, who is 18 months old; her energy level; and, of course, her blueberries. "Because I don't eat a lot of sugar, certain fruits and vegetables taste sweet—blueberries are a treat!"

Why It Works

If there's one food we should all eat every day, it's blueberries. In addition to being a good source of fiber, vitamin C, and vitamin K, blueberries contain flavonoids called anthocyanins, which are what give them their characteristic blue hue. Anthocyanins have antioxidant powers that may help prevent numerous conditions associated with aging, including heart disease, cancer, stroke, and memory loss. The flavonoids in blueberries also help skin appear younger by improving blood circulation and assisting with the formation of collagen, the tissue that holds skin together.

Women who ate the most blueberries and strawberries—at least three servings of a ½ cup of berries per week—were 34 percent less likely to suffer a heart attack than the women who ate the fewest number of these fruits, found researchers at the Harvard T. H. Chan School of Public Health. Blueberries also appear to have positive effects on the brain. Older adults with memory decline experienced improvements when they drank wild blueberry juice at breakfast, lunch, and dinner for 12 weeks, according to a 2010 study done at the University of Cincinnati Academic Health Center and published in the *Journal of Agriculture and Food Chemistry.*

A more recent 2016 study, also done at the University of Cincinnati, found that older adults with mild cognitive impairment did better on cognitive tests after taking a blueberry powder supplement equivalent to a cup of berries a day for 16 weeks.

If we were writing this book several years ago, the research probably would have cautioned you against skipping meals, as Kari does. Since then, however, studies have begun to pile up to support the practice, which is known as intermittent fasting. There are many different types of intermittent fasting. Some people, like Kari, squeeze all of their eating into a short culinary window: usually 8 hours or less. In other words, they fast for at least 16 hours out of every 24. Other people fast by keeping calories very low (usually about 500) every other day or for just 1 or 2 days a week. Much of the research on intermittent fasting has been done on animals, but there are a few human studies that look solid. Those studies show that the practice can lead to weight loss at a healthy rate of 2 to 3 pounds per week, reduce oxidative stress, improve cholesterol and triglyceride levels, and even boost learning and memory.

Another bonus: Because the body chews through glucose stores in about 10 hours, weight loss from intermittent fasting comes 90 percent from fat—that's 15 percent more fat than what is lost from traditional diets. By preserving muscle, intermittent fasting can lead to weight loss without a slow-down in metabolism.

There are a few different theories as to why intermittent fasting has health benefits. The most popular is that, during the fasting period, cells undergo stress. They respond to that stress by enhancing their ability to deal with it and, possibly, by resisting diseases. In other words, just like exercising flexes muscles, fasting flexes cells.

Steve's Secrets

Let's face it: Some of us have trouble fasting long enough for a routine blood test, let alone for part of the day, every day. And, gobs of fruits and vegetables don't make their way into everyone's busy lifestyle. Thankfully, there is some flexibility in Kari's eating plan. Use these tips to make it work for you.

PICK THE FASTING METHOD THAT FITS YOUR LIFESTYLE. Kari practices intermittent fasting 5 days a week, making sure to consume all of her calories between an 8- to 10-hour window (for example, between 7:00 a.m. and 3:00 p.m.). This type of fasting is called time-restricted feeding (TRF). There are variations of TRF, where you skip breakfast and push back your 8- to 10-hour window to later in the day, but the science on skipping breakfast has never been positive.

Another fasting protocol involves consuming just 500 calories every other day and eating normally on the nonfast days. Realistically, you don't have to be as strict as either one of these plans. Even doing a fast as infrequently as once a month can provide benefits. Technically, when you're not fasting, you can eat whatever you want. But, we don't recommend doing that because eating the wrong foods can interfere with general health.

EAT CLEAN. A diet rich in fruits and vegetables also helps to lower blood pressure, reduce the risk of heart disease, improve digestion, and helps keep blood sugar and appetite under control. To do this:

- Eat a variety of fruits and vegetables in a rainbow of colors—red, orange, yellow, green, blue, and purple.
- Keep fruits and veggies visible on the counter so you will grab a piece as a snack or on the go.
- Incorporate fruits and vegetables into every meal. Use them in pasta sauces, stir-fries, sandwiches, soups, and sides.

Filomena Warihay's Secret

Be Grateful

. . . .

Count your blessings every day

Don't be afraid to put on that bikini

Eat most of your calories in the form of fruits and vegetables

. . . .

Every day, Filomena "Fil" Warihay writes something that she's grateful for and drops the note into her gratitude jar. "It's clear and looks like

Aladdin's lamp. I let it fill up so I can see how much I have to be thankful for," she says.

Fil has quite a few blessings to count. She runs 5 miles 2 or 3 days a week. She started a very successful consulting company—Take Charge Consultants—to which she still contributes 20 hours a week. She and her husband live in sunny Florida, where they enjoy the beach and pool. She's raised four children she's still close with. And, she is in fantastic shape. At nearly 80 years old, she still proudly sports a bikini. (I haven't worn a bikini since my third child was born, when I was 36. This woman has had four children and is almost four decades older than I am. She has guts...and abs.)

"I have an abundance of energy, and for someone who is 78, I think I look pretty good!" Fil says. "I don't say it arrogantly, but I am proud of my body and my looks," she says, adding that she thinks the secret resides in her head. "I wake up every morning with drive and a sense of purpose. I've been blessed with energy and talent and a desire to help others be all that they can be, and I'm truly grateful."

Running Life Begins at 40

One of the things that Fil is most thankful for is her running, something she didn't start until she was 40. "My middle daughter got an athletic scholarship, and when she received her training schedule before freshman year, she saw it included running 3 miles 3 days a week. She said, 'Mom, will you run with me?' How could I say no?!"

The first time Fil ran, she felt miserable. "I made it around the track with my daughter once and said, 'We have to do this how many more times?!'" But, after a few months, she could go much farther. She was in such good shape, she decided to try a 5K. "Well, didn't I win the gold in my age group? That was it—I was hooked," she says. "I made a commitment to myself: 'You will win the gold in your age group every year until you are 75.'"

Believe it or not, she's done just that. Every year, from age 40 to 75, she won the gold for her age group in a 5K. With that mission accomplished, she decided to hang up her competitive running shoes and save the miles for more recreational runs that keep her in shape.

These days, she mixes running with gym sessions, where she uses the stair climber and elliptical machine—½ hour on each. "Then, I bike the next day, walk the next, and keep rotating through that schedule, so I'm doing something different every day," she says.

Taking the Pritikin Prescription

To stay bikini-ready, Fil eats a diet that focuses heavily on plant foods and lean proteins. She and her husband attend the Pritikin Longevity Center for a 2 week stint every 1 to 2 years. While there, they immerse themselves in healthy eating and exercise, with Fil working out a stunning 3 hours a day.

"Our stay at the Pritikin Center sort of gets us back on track—it's a wonderful experience," she says. "The food is tremendous—the chef could make dog doo taste good."

When they get home, Fil and her husband, Dan, employ the fresh, healthy eating and exercise tips they learned. "I eat 70 percent of my calories from fruits, vegetables, and grains; 20 percent from proteins like chicken and fish; and 10 percent from fat," she says. The only fats she will eat are those that "come from the ground."

Fil also stays away from processed foods. "It's a lot of chopping and food prep, which is a challenge, but it's worth it," she says. She admits that her greatest downfall is eating out. "We live in a social community where a lot of people like to go out and dance, which usually involves going to dinner. But, other than that, we eat pretty doggone healthy."

Watching her husband and others come through the Pritikin program, Fil is convinced that food is medicine. "I've seen people who were so arthritic they couldn't walk into the Pritikin Center without the aid of a walker. Two weeks later, they stroll out with ease on their own—it's amazing."

No Substitute for Challenging Your Brain

Another piece of Filomena's gratitude goes toward her consulting career, which is still thriving as she approaches her ninth decade.

Filomena has been so successful because, in addition to her keen business sense and dynamic personality, she continues to expand her knowledge. "I'm taking a copywriting course right now; one of my big clients sells financial products online and copywriting is critical to his success. I decided to take the course to learn more about what he does," she says.

She also took the course because she loves writing. "It has struck me that most of the people who are really happy in their retirement are doing things that gave them pleasure when they were, like, 9 years old," she says. "When I think back to being a kid, I was always making up stories and recording things in a diary—for me, that joy came from writing."

In addition to her copywriting course, she writes proposals and blogs for her company, Take Charge Consultants. Fil is also the author of several books including *Anti-Aging Habits: 137 Smart and Sassy Ways to Add Years to Your Life and Life to Your Years.*

Working remotely at Take Charge, she's also collaborating with her daughter/coworker on a new application for leadership development. From her Florida location, she coaches 20 executives. "I talk with each of them once or twice a month and visit them quarterly in person," she says. And, she loves every minute of it. "Helping others is the reason I wake up in the morning—it keeps me going, it's energizing, and it's satisfying."

She adds that she's watched a lot of retired former execs throw themselves into the world of Florida golfing. "They think it is going to be the be-all and end-all, but you can see that they aren't getting what they thought they would out of it—there is no substitute for challenging your brain."

Fil says a key part of her healthy body is her healthy mind and vice versa. "The mind-body connection is so clear," she says. "I don't consider myself a religious person, but I am a person who has strong beliefs and I feel blessed," she says. Her gratitude jar is full, but still has lots of space for thankful thoughts in the future. "I have enough room for another 5 years in there!" she says.

Why It Works

There is something to be said about being thankful for what you have. Gratitude seems to reduce toxic emotions and boost the positive ones. In a study published in the *Journal of Personality and Social Psychology*, psychologists asked study participants to write down a few sentences a week. One group wrote about the things they were thankful for during that week and a second group wrote about the things that irritated them. A third group wrote about events that took place, with no emphasis on being irritated or grateful. At the end of 10 weeks, the grateful group was more optimistic and felt better about their lives. They also exercised more and went to the doctor less than the group that focused on things that displeased them.

Research also shows that gratitude can boost self-esteem, improve sleep, and make you more sensitive and empathetic toward others. People who practice gratitude are also less likely to retaliate and seek revenge, even when given negative feedback, finds research.

And yes, it can also help you to stay fit and trim—to the point that you can proudly wear a bikini at age 78. When we're thankful we tend to be more positive and happier with ourselves, which makes us more likely to lose weight if we need to, and control our weight if we're already at a healthy number. Participants in a cognitive therapy treatment program—which encourages positive responses—lost more weight than those who did not participate in cognitive therapy, and they were more likely to keep it off too, according to a 2005 Swedish study published in *Eating and Weight Disorders*.

Steve's Secrets

Use these tactics to boost your own sense of gratitude.

MAKE IT MEASURABLE. It helps if you can count and visualize the things that you are thankful for. Try writing in a gratitude journal each day, recording a few things that you're thankful for on your desk or wall calendar, or, like Filomena, on pieces of paper to fill up a vase or jar. When you write down your blessings, be specific and think about how you felt when the good thing happened to you. As the Swedish study showed, gratitude and resultant optimism can help support weight control. When you see all of the things that you have to be thankful for, you will be more positive and more likely to take the best possible care of your health, including maintaining a healthy weight.

WRITE THANK YOU NOTES. In this digital age, written thank you notes and cards have fallen out of practice for some. But, the act of physically sitting down and writing what you are grateful for and thanking the person who gave you that gift will benefit both you and the receiver.

MEDITATE. Mindful meditation helps cultivate positive thoughts and forces you to be present in the moment. Some people focus on a particular word or phrase when they meditate. You can also try focusing on things that you are grateful for, such as the health of your family, the warm sun, or a nice long walk that you took.

Deb Gordon's Secret

Push Yourself

. . . .

Use healthy competition as a motivator
Strength train for stronger physical and emotional health
Continue to add a little more distance and weight to your exercise routine

. . . .

For the first four decades of her life, Deb Gordon would have sworn she was "allergic to exercise." She hated anything that made her feel uncomfortable and she often joked that, "Of course, I got an epidural when my kids were born. Duh—I hate pain, remember?"

She disliked the pain of exercise too. In fact, she played hooky from the gym for much of her life. "I hated exercising and came up with every excuse in the book not to do it," she said.

Then, at about age 40, she gained 30 pounds. "I had always been naturally thin so it was a shock," she says.

To fight back, she began working out. "I started with a spinning class, partially to lose the weight, and partially so I could drink more wine and still fit in my clothes." She then moved to TRX, a suspension strength-training system that uses straps, body weight, and gravity. When the TRX coach started CrossFit about 3 years ago, she decided to give it a try.

CrossFit is a high intensity, extremely demanding fitness program that often involves many of the classic exercises that most of us hated to do in gym class. Thus, it was a shock to Deb, but she sort of *liked* it. "I was someone who was never the least bit athletic—*ever*," she says.

Within a few months of doing CrossFit, Deb did her first handstand. Then, a handstand push-up, then a pull-up. Today, at age 54, she has deadlifted more than 200 pounds, hoisted more than 115 pounds of steel over her head, and pushed herself mentally and physically harder than she ever thought she could. "Each day I have four goals—don't get hurt, don't quit, don't cry, and don't throw up," she laughs.

Despite often being on the verge of all four, she loves every minute of it, mostly because CrossFit has unleashed her competitive spirit and taught her to push herself. A nice bonus: It has completely transformed her body. "In CrossFit, you are constantly trying to take things to the next level," she says. Some days that means beating the previous day's row, number of burpees, or clean and jerk.

"Other days it becomes not 'did I lift more weight or go faster,' but, 'did I not quit?' A lot of times the challenge is simply to be there and push through it," she says.

From Hooky to Hooked

Deb had no idea how much a workout could change her body and mind. You can hear the confidence in her voice as she describes her new athletic self.

"I have bigger muscles than I ever have and I get complimented on them by complete strangers when I am sleeveless (which is so *awesome*). My body fat is less than 14 percent. When I had my mammogram recently, the tech could see my pecs!"

The rest of her body is in great shape too. "My blood pressure is so low that sometimes they think I'm dead," she laughs. "I'm not surprised though—I have more stamina and strength, and feel better than ever."

That strength bolsters her emotional health too. "I struggle with chronic depression, which used to sideline me in the past. Now, when I'm having a bad day and just want to curl up in bed, I make myself go to CrossFit and walk out feeling 100 percent better. I mean *100 percent*."

Part of the reason that she feels better is the dopamine rush from the exercises. The other part is the sense of community. "I've never been good at working out by myself. Every day I get to go hang out with people of all shapes, sizes, and confidence levels, who are all doing the same thing and supporting each other—it's so gratifying," she says.

It's also been great for her marriage since her husband, Keith, also does CrossFit. Together, they have participated in several competitions. "We have this fun hobby we share together," she says.

Today, instead of coming up with excuses *not* to go to the gym, Deb reminds herself to take rest days. "I'm at the gym 5 or 6 days a week—I'm hooked," she says.

A Healthy Push and Pull

One of the things Deb loves most about CrossFit is that not only does it make her push herself but it also teaches her when to pull back. As someone who has struggled with workaholic tendencies, she's found it hard to juggle her life and career at times. Deb was one of my first editors and mentors when I started my writing career, and on the days I would come in early or work late, she was *always* sitting at her desk, chugging away.

But thanks to CrossFit, she's given herself more room in her schedule for the workouts, as well as other things. "I started going on 2½-hour bike rides with my neighbor when the weather is nice." She also does hot yoga (yoga performed in a heated room, usually above 100 degrees) once a week, which she swears really helps with her mobility.

"And, I run a mile or so every other day. I've always hated running so this is huge for me." She can now complete the 800-meter sprints in CrossFit—"without having to stop and walk—yay!"

And, after she's pushed through a tough few hours at the gym, she returns to her desk with a renewed perspective. "The workout routine keeps me calmer and much more balanced...I don't get as frustrated with clients or want to quit like I used to."

Perhaps most importantly, CrossFit has taught Deb that she can do anything; the impossible has become not only possible, but achievable. "At my age, it's so satisfying to see that I can still move forward physically and mentally, and do things I've never done before," she says. "I could never do a pull-up...now I am continuously adding more to my routine. I'm athletic now!"

This open-minded sense of adventure has carried over to her personal life as well. "About a year ago, my husband and I moved halfway across the country from Virginia to Chicago when he took a new job. We didn't know anyone, but today, we have a fulfilling life here full of fresh experiences and wonderful friends."

The Transformation of a Fitness-Hater

Before talking with Deb, it had seemed to us that the world contained two types of people: People who love fitness and people who hate fitness. Was it really possible for a fitness-hater to become a fitness-lover? We asked, "What's your secret? How did you get from being anti-exercise to someone who craves it?"

"Push yourself," she says without hesitation. "If you are walking every morning, try a run/walk. If you are working out with 5-pound weights, take a stab at 10," she says. "Don't ever assume that you can't do anything because of your age, and don't be afraid to challenge yourself, because no one has been more surprised by what I am doing than me."

Deb recalls the day that she knew her love affair with CrossFit was the real deal—the day she first tackled her nemesis: the rope. She had been inching up that rope for months as part of her routine, but she couldn't seem to get past the middle. Then, on that miraculous day, her coach said, "You're not supposed to be using your *arms*, you're supposed to be using your *legs*." Then, it clicked and she scooted to the top. Like that moment when the perfect sentence comes to her as a writer, she just got it.

It now stands out as one of the best days of her life. "I was 52 years old and climbing on a rope was something I thought I would never do—but I did it!"

Why It Works

Exercise routines like CrossFit are designed to get people to try to beat their most challenging rival—themselves. Pushing yourself is the best way to get results, both in the gym and once you leave, research shows. Short bouts of intensive exercise changes the body and muscles in ways milder exercise does not, found a study conducted at the Scripps Research Institute and published in *EuroMediterranean Biomedical Journal*. Over time, higher intensity activity leads to increasingly better athletic performance. This positive feedback cycle is what helps athletes like Deb continue to lift more weight, run faster, and add repetitions—even into their fifties and beyond.

By extending her workouts, Deb may also be extending her life. Scientists have found a link between higher exercise intensity and lower risk of death. In a 2013 Austrian study published in *PLOS ONE*, researchers found a decreased risk of death in people who walked at a brisk pace (faster than a 24-minute mile) when compared with people who walked at a slower pace (slower than a 24-minute mile).

As Deb notes, these benefits continue long after the gym lights go dark. Higher intensity workouts carry over into other areas of your life. When, like Deb, you realize that you *can* climb a rope in your fifties, other previously unattainable goals seem more within reach.

Steve's Secrets

CrossFit isn't for everyone, but you really don't know how you will react to a workout until you try it, right? If the mental and physical challenges of CrossFit sounds appealing to you, here are some secrets on how to get started.

START SLOWLY. If you plan to try a high intensity workout like Cross-Fit, don't jump in too fast. It's important to ease into it for a few weeks or months to let your body adjust to the intensity. When you do start to move forward, do so at a reasonable pace. Don't try to jump from 20 push-ups to 50 push-ups in the same week, for example.

BEWARE OF TOO MUCH BURN. By its nature, CrossFit teaches people to constantly improve upon their previous performance by adding more reps, weight, or speed. As such, injuries can happen.

In a study published in the *Journal of Strength and Conditioning Research*, researchers surveyed 132 CrossFit athletes and found that 73.5 percent of them had sustained an injury. Nine required surgery. The good news—this injury rate is about the same as that for general fitness workouts. The take-home message: If you are going to do Cross-Fit, don't add too many reps or too much weight too fast.

And, listen to your body. If something hurts beyond the normal post-workout soreness, lay off of it for a while.

Delayed onset muscle soreness (DOMS), which can happen any time you increase the duration or intensity of a workout, is harmless (it is actually a sign that you pushed yourself—yay!). It usually hits 12 to 24 hours after the workout and can worsen for up to 3 days before it starts to ease up. During this window, make sure that you stay hydrated and get plenty of sleep. If the pain lasts longer than 5 days, it could be an injury, such as a tendon or muscle tear. Seek medical attention for this kind of persistent pain.

Natalie Jill's Secret

Keep Things Simple

. . . .

Visualize a healthier you

Use your body weight to grow stronger

Eat a diet composed primarily of things that grow

. . . .

Natalie Jill will never forget the day nearly 10 years ago when she realized that it was time for a *big* change. She was not in a good place. Hit with multiple life stressors—a divorce, childbirth, job loss, and depreciation of her retirement funds—all at once, she'd become depressed and had coped by eating comfort foods. As she walked her dog and newborn daughter, she caught a glimpse of her reflection in a store window.

"The person I saw was *not* me. I had always been fit, and there were all these bulges and things sagging...." She walked straight home, put her daughter down for a nap, and began mapping out a plan.

"I grabbed a stack of magazines and cut out photos of fit women; healthy, happy moms; and scenarios I wanted in my future, including my dream house—images that I knew would motivate me," she recalls. She kept it realistic, choosing photos of women she could relate to. "I cut out petite brunettes, not tall blondes," she says.

With these cut-outs displayed on a vision board in front of her, Natalie researched how to achieve these goals. She knew that she had to find a different, healthier way to cope. What she found was nothing groundbreaking, and it didn't involve a crazy diet, running a marathon, or investing in fancy fitness tools.

"It comes down to moving your body and eating clean, healthful, unprocessed foods," she says. "I said to myself, 'If I start moving more, eating more natural foods, and drinking more water, it has to work.'" She incorporated these changes, adding a little more every day.

"I promised myself that I would give it 4 months and see what happened—no obsessing, no scale," she says.

The plan worked wonders.

At the end of 4 months, she climbed on the scale, and held her breath. "I wasn't at my ideal weight, but I had lost 50 pounds and completely changed my body—it was so motivating," she recalls. "It made me want to keep going. So, I did."

Having recently relocated from Washington, D.C. to California, Natalie didn't have a support system of friends close by. "So, I used Facebook," she says. She posted pictures of what she ate and talked about her exercise routine. "People were interested—they would say, 'oh, what is that? I want to try it,' which was motivating. Plus, it kept me accountable," she says.

True to her philosophy, the eating plan was simple. "Everything was based on natural foods and worked on balance. Each meal had a protein, a carb, and a fat, and I had to be able to pronounce all the ingredients," she says. "It included lots of salads and protein, and I added olive oil or avocado for the fat." For a snack, she would have an apple and a few chocolate morsels. And, she drank tons of water.

To measure her foods, Natalie used her fist for carbs, her thumb for fats, and her palm for proteins. "Veggies and berries were unlimited—the more, the better," she says. "I never counted calories, and the big rule I stressed—and still stress to myself and others—was eat the good things first, and you'll have less room for the bad."

Natalie used her body for more than just measuring portion size. "I thought, 'You are a 170 pound woman; that is 170 pounds that you can move and work with.' I started using my own body weight for exercise," she says. Her workout included lots of plyometric exercises like pull-ups, tricep dips, and planks. "I got really creative with my body weight and I didn't spend hours working out." She adds, "If you are exercising daily and making it intense, you really don't need more than 20 minutes."

Over time, the social media interest in Natalie's eating and exercise plans grew. "People asked me for recipes and a recipe book, so I took a week and made a PDF with my blackberry," she says. Then, people requested a meal plan, so Natalie created her *7-Day Jump Start*—a culmination of her vision board, goals, meals, and workouts—and sold it for $35. Whatever her followers asked for, she gave them. "The cool thing was, people were getting results. Women were posting pictures of themselves on my Facebook page to show off their weight loss." The next thing she knew, Natalie had a full-fledged business.

All the while, Natalie continued to improve her own fitness and health. At the age of 39, she started fitness modeling. She felt happier and healthier than ever before.

Today, at 45, not only has Natalie lost 50 pounds, she's helped thousands of others get healthier too. Her fitness program—Natalie Jill's Fitness—includes functional body-weight training; nutritious, unprocessed foods; and lots of positive messages. Now a Licensed Master Sports Nutritionist and functional fitness trainer, she has more than two million social media followers around the world, she published her *7-Day Jump Start* (a national best-seller!) as well as several other books, and she's put out four fitness DVDs.

Perhaps even more impressive, Natalie has become the person she created on her vision board. She's 50 pounds lighter and in great shape, physically and emotionally. "Every single thing on that vision board has come true for me," she says. "I met and married the perfect husband I always dreamed of; I am that healthy, happy mom; and the house with a golf course view I cut and pasted—I'm looking at that view out my window right now."

Why It Works

Natalie's approach to weight loss and fitness is simple yet effective.

Processed foods are higher in salt, added sugar, preservatives, and other chemicals—nothing nutritious your body will miss if you skip them. If you replace these with healthful fruits, vegetables, healthy fats, whole grains, and lean protein, you are doing your body good. If you take it too far beyond that, however, clean-eating plans can be somewhat ambiguous and hard to follow, setting people up for obsession or failure.

The best version of a clean eating program is the Mediterranean diet, which is based on foods in Mediterranean-style cooking—olive oil, fish, fruits, vegetables, whole grains, limited healthy fats like those from fish and avocado, and moderate amounts of red wine.

And, though it may sound a tad decadent compared to other diets, it works. In a 2008 study published in the *New England Journal of Medicine*, researchers assigned 322 obese people to different diets, including a calorie-restricted low-fat diet and a calorie-restricted Mediterranean diet. At the end of 2 years, the Mediterranean diet participants had lost more weight than the low-fat group—9.7 pounds, compared to 6.4 pounds for the low-fat group. The individuals on the Mediterranean diet also saw improved insulin and glucose levels compared to those on the diet low in fat.

Clean eating may help Natalie's mental outlook too. When researchers compared clean diets such as the Mediterranean diet to the typical Western diet, which is more processed, they found that the risk of depression is 25- to 35-percent lower in those who ate the Mediterranean diet.

In addition to boosting weight loss and mental health, the Mediterranean diet may also prevent cardiovascular disease, cancer, Parkinson's disease, and other diseases.

Regarding Natalie's workout plan, body weight based exercises yield the following benefits, all of which are fantastic for older people.

THEY COMBINE CARDIO AND STRENGTH-TRAINING INTO ONE. When you alternate planks, push-ups, and mountain climbers, you keep your heart rate up and strengthen your muscles at the same time.

THEY IMPROVE BALANCE. Functional movements such as isometric leg holds and single-leg squats improve body awareness and stability.

THEY ARE EASY. Because body weight based exercises don't require equipment, you can do them anytime, anywhere. If you're not a fan of gyms, you can do a body weight based program in the comfort of your own home.

THEY WORK. Within weeks of starting a body weight based program, most people see results in the way they look and feel.

You may wonder if you aren't losing out by only using your body weight rather than dumbbells and barbells. According to research, the answer is no. Despite the lack of weights and other equipment involved, body weight based exercises, when done correctly, are enough to make muscles stronger. Instead of increasing the amount of weight over time (which is impossible because you are using your own body weight), you can increase the number of reps and sets, or add more difficult variations of exercises.

In addition, a weight loss vision board can be a powerful motivational tool, provided you use it the right way. Negative phrases like "you're gross," or "fat girl" or unflattering photographs of yourself can actually be detrimental to your weight loss plan. Positive images like the ones Natalie used—images of fit girls, photographs of places she'd like to visit or live, and visions of a supportive, loving husband—on the other hand, can be inspiring. Although we can't find any formal research on positive vision boards for weight loss, intrinsically, the concept makes sense and it certainly can't hurt.

Steve's Secrets

To reshape her body—and, as a result, her life—Natalie didn't reinvent the wheel. Most of what she does and teaches to her followers is simple and straightforward. And, it works. Here's some advice from Steve on how to incorporate some of her tips into your own life.

PRACTICE PORTION CONTROL. If you force yourself to measure your foods using cups and scales, you will be more likely to quit. This isn't practical on a long-term basis. Instead, do it the Natalie way: For each meal, use the size of your fist to measure carbs, your thumb for fats, and your palm for proteins. And, allow yourself unlimited vegetables and berries. If you are in a restaurant or other setting where you can't easily measure, fill as much of your plate with vegetables as you can.

REPLACE BAD FOODS WITH GOOD. It's a simple concept, but it works. Fill up on fruits and vegetables, and you will be less hungry for processed foods and snacks. Be proactive with this approach. If you want a slice of pizza, eat a plate of grilled vegetables or a large spinach salad first. And, each time you are about to eat a food, ask yourself, "Will this nourish my body?" If the answer is no, avoid it. Also, drink lots of water—aim for 91 to 125 fluid ounces per day.

GET STRONGER WITH BODY WEIGHT BASED EXERCISES. Both Liz and I regularly do body weight exercises. You'll find them in Chapter 10. Liz does about 30 minutes of them after her 45 minute jog in the morning, 5 days a week. I do them 5 days a week, and follow up with 30 to 60 minutes of swimming or running 5 days a week too (on some days, these workouts overlap, and I do both). I also surf an average of once a week for 2 to 3 hours at a time.

Liz and I do all of this not because we're vain (okay, maybe we're a little vain), but primarily because we want to keep our bodies in the best possible shape we can so we can continue to do the things we love—surfing, running, hiking, playing beach games with our kids, etc. We've found that body weight exercises are a quick, effective, and inexpensive way to keep our bodies toned.

Gary Tarola's Secret

*Discover a Bigger, More Powerful Purpose
to Stay Fit and Trim*

. . . .

Move while you work

Enjoy everything you love—in moderation

Eat anti-inflammatory foods

. . . .

Each day, Gary Tarola cracks, twists, and moves objects that are on average about 180 pounds. "I'm almost always moving, walking, bending, and changing positions," he says. Gary is a chiropractor, which keeps both his body and mind in the health and nutrition game.

"The body is designed for motion," he says. "People who have jobs that require staying in one position for prolonged periods—especially sitting—are at a disadvantage."

Gary is at a clear advantage, not only because of the active nature of his job, but also because he practices what he preaches. He eats a primarily anti-inflammatory, whole foods diet, works out most days of the week, and lives by the motto, "everything in moderation."

"Obsession in any facet of life is destructive," he says.

As a result, Gary embodies what he teaches his patients. He's small but mighty—a muscular, fit guy with a body that moves more like someone 30 years his junior.

He also actively attends conferences, engages in research, and promotes his chiropractic practice. "It's important to immerse yourself in something larger than yourself, something that could have an impact on others," he says. "When you are productive, it boosts your sense of self-worth."

Staying Flexible and Functional

As one of Gary's patients, it's obvious to me how much he cares about his job and the people he treats. Steve saw Gary's passion too, so when his patients need a chiropractor, Gary's name is the first he gives. It's also clear how much Gary believes in the healing power of his practice, as well as the activities that help prevent chiropractic problems in the first place.

"Physical movement protects all the tissues in our bodies that help us move properly—bones, muscles, ligaments, spinal discs, and all connective tissues," he says. He believes in reasonable, moderate activity, and avoiding exercises that are high impact or likely to overstrain. "Following these rules helps most people stay flexible and functional throughout their lives, with fewer problems."

To keep his own tissues in good shape, Gary performs resistance and aerobic exercises 3 to 5 days a week for 20 to 40 minutes. He does this with variations of cable resistance utilizing the Total Gym; some free weights and floor exercises; aerobic exercises utilizing a treadmill, short bursts of rope skipping, and kickboxing with a heavy bag.

Because he treats people who are inflamed, he's also a big proponent of anti-inflammatory foods. "Systemic inflammation is largely to blame for most chronic health conditions—arthritis, heart and vascular disease, and even cancer," he says. "And, diet is a significant contributor to inflammation in our bodies."

For Gary, the diet takes the form of whole foods as much as possible: lots of fruits, nuts, and vegetables. He eats fowl or fish three to four times a week. "Salmon is my favorite," he says. He rarely eats fast food, and stays away completely from red meat and carbonated beverages. He allows himself an occasional dessert and two to three social drinks a week. "You have to cheat sometimes!" he says.

He may not be doing anything radical, but what Gary does works well for him and for his patients. "In terms of quality of life and longevity, it all comes down to the state of your body and mind," he says.

Why It Works

No doubt, people who move as part of their jobs have a leg up in the fitness department. This is especially true of individuals who couple their active occupation with other forms of physical activity and a healthy diet. That's no surprise.

Another habit worth highlighting is Gary's preference for foods that fight inflammation. Some of the age-related diseases linked to inflammation include cancer, heart disease, arthritis, depression, and Alzheimer's disease. In a 2016 study published in *Food and Nutrition Research*, participants who increased their intake of long-chain omega-3 polyunsaturated fatty acids (such as the ones found in salmon and other oily fish) had lower levels of the inflammatory marker C-reactive protein than those who did not boost their intakes.

Steve's Secrets

By the nature of his work, Gary gives people guidance on how they can move better and become healthier overall. As a bonus, he follows his own advice. Use these tips to incorporate some of Gary's words of wisdom into your own life.

BUILD FITNESS INTO YOUR WORK DAY. Most people with sedentary jobs aren't in the position to change careers simply to become more active. If you are already in an active occupation, great. If you aren't, look for ways to be more active during your work day.

- *Take short fitness breaks—inside the building or outdoors.* You can stop for I minute every hour and do something active: a plank, some push-ups, a few stretches. Or, if you have a little more time, take a short walk around the building or outdoors.

- *Make meetings mobile.* Suggest that your company hold meetings on a walking trail rather than in a conference room. To bolster your case, mention that active employees tend to get more done. A study done at Leeds Beckett University in England looked at the influence of daytime exercise on workers who had access to a company gym. The researchers asked more than 200 employees in a variety of companies to self-report their productivity on a daily basis. Then, they looked at the differences within individual employees on the days they exercised versus the days they did not. On the days employees exercised, they reported managing their time more efficiently, being more productive, and having smoother interactions with their coworkers than on the days that they didn't exercise.

EAT SOOTHING FOODS. Try to eat as many anti-inflammatory foods as you can. Load up on these standouts:

- Avocados
- Berries
- Broccoli
- Cherries
- Green tea
- Soy (such as tofu)
- Tomatoes
- Walnuts

Also avoid the worst pro-inflammatory foods. These include fried foods like doughnuts and French fries, trans fats in commercial baked goods and coffee creamers, white bread, sugary foods, and bacon.

TREAT YOURSELF RIGHT. Life is too short to deprive yourself all the time. The key is finding the right balance between healthy habits and treating yourself now and then. If you are like Gary in that you like an occasional dessert, go for an anti-inflammatory piece of dark chocolate. You'll get the sweetness you crave and lower inflammation at the same time.

Steve's Prescription for Being Fit and Trim

Okay, so you've heard stories from the World's Healthiest People on how they have lost weight or maintained a healthy weight throughout their lives.

• •

At a Glance: How to Be Fit and Trim

→ Get enough sleep to feel rested. That's 7 to 9 hours nightly.

→ Drink up to 4 cups of unsweetened green tea a day.

→ Do 30 to 60 minutes of cardio 5 times a week, plus strength train 2 or 3 days a week.

→ Build fitness into your day by always taking the stairs, taking short walking breaks, and generally trying to stay mobile as much as possible.

→ Fill up on veggies and berries. Include 2 or 3 vegetables and 1 fruit in every meal.

→ Keep your portions of carbs (potatoes, rice, pasta) to no more than the size of your fist, proteins (meat, fish) to the size of your palm, and fat (oils, butter) to the size of your thumb, at each meal.

→ Prioritize anti-inflammatory foods such as berries, cherries, avocados, broccoli, grapes, and tomatoes.

→ Nix all sugary drinks. Instead, guzzle 91 to 125 fluid ounces of water a day.

→ To keep weight off, make dinner your smallest meal of the day. Or, skip it altogether.

→ Practice gratitude by writing in a gratitude journal each day, placing gratitude notes in a jar, writing thank you notes, or meditating on how fortunate you are.

No doubt, these are fantastic pieces of advice. Beyond these tidbits, I have some additional tips—from my own personal weight loss experience (at one point, I was 190 at 5'9"; today I'm 160), what I've seen work in my patients, and what research shows is most effective when it comes to slimming down for good. I recommend that you give your body a little jump-start by focusing on one of these tips per day and building on them each day.

So, it will look something like this:

DAY 1: Juice fast

DAY 2: Increase water

DAY 3: Drink lots of water and quit drinking all sugary drinks

DAY 4: Drink lots of water, ban sugary drinks, and eat things that grow

DAY 5: Drink lots of water, ban sugary drinks, eat things that grow, and add exercise

DAY 6: Drink lots of water, ban sugary drinks, eat things that grow, exercise, and guzzle green tea

DAY 7: Drink lots of water, ban sugary drinks, eat things that grow, exercise, guzzle green tea, and make sure to get 7 to 8 hours of sleep

DAY 1: JUICE FAST. When it comes to effective weight maintenance, Kari Dougan (page 190) has it right. Fasting is a great way to give your body a jump-start when it comes to losing weight. I actually do this myself every time I feel myself getting a little too thick in the middle or I've overindulged more than usual. I do a little fast now and then, probably every 4 months or so. I do 1 to 3 days of a juice fast, followed by 3 to 4 days of eating only vegetables and fruits. For the juice day, I consume 16 ounces of organic juice in place of each meal, choosing juices that include fruits and vegetables, and nothing else. At the end, I feel fantastic, and I usually drop the extra 5 pounds that were weighing me down.

DAY 2: DRINK LIKE A FISH—WATER, THAT IS. Most weight loss programs tell participants to increase their water intake—with good reason. Water aids in weight loss and weight control by keeping us feeling full and aiding in digestion. Plus, studies show that it can actually speed up your metabolism. In fact, resting energy expenditure (aka calorie burning) rises 24 to 30 percent within 10 minutes of drinking 500 milliliters of water—and this effect lasts for about an hour. So, how much should you drink? The exact amount depends on your activity level, size, and gender, but in general, the Dietary Reference Intake of water for adults is between 91 and 125 fluid ounces per day.

DAY 3: SURRENDER ALL OF YOUR SUGARY DRINKS. When I ask overweight and obese patients about their eating habits, 99 percent mention some sort of sugary drink—usually soda or sweet tea. These beverages are the kiss of death when it comes to weight control. Sweetened drinks have been a major contributor to the obesity epidemic, concluded a 2004 study done by the American Society for Nutrition. If you want to maintain a healthy weight, you must ban soda, sweet tea, juice, sweet iced coffee, and all other sugary drinks from your beverage repertoire. For good.

DAY 4: EAT THINGS THAT GROW. I like Natalie Jill's (page 205) tip here. People who eat more vegetables and fruits—especially vegetables—tend to weigh less. I've seen it in my practice and at home. In our house, we try to include a few vegetables and one fruit in every meal. We snack on them too. We belong to a community-supported agriculture (CSA) operation, which supplies us with an abundance of veggies and fruits. When we run out, we head to the organic produce section of our local grocery store. My advice when it comes to fruits and vegetables is that you can't eat too many, so incorporate them whenever you can. Make a smoothie with frozen blueberries, mangoes, and bananas for breakfast, paired with yogurt with fresh strawberries. For lunch, have a spinach salad with green apples, chopped broccoli, carrots, and grilled chicken. Then, for dinner, stir-fry some red and yellow peppers, green squash, and cauliflower mixed with tofu for a power-packed meal. Make vegetables and fruits a priority in your diet and a main staple in your meals, and your waistline will thank you.

DAY 5: COMBINE WALKING WITH WEIGHTS. I recommend doing 30 to 60 minutes of aerobic exercise (brisk walking, light jogging, biking, swimming, etc.), at least 5 days a week. On top of that, I recommend doing at least 2 or 3 days of resistance exercises, like the ones shown in Chapter 10. These exercises can take the form of weight training or body weight exercises (my preference).

DAY 6: GUZZLE GREEN TEA. We can add yet another health benefit of green tea to the already long list—it helps you burn calories. Thanks to both its catechin polyphenols and caffeine, green tea boosts thermogenesis, and, therefore, drinking it may be an effective weight loss tool, reported a study published in *Nature*.

So instead of making it sweet, take your tea green. Drink up to 4 cups of unsweetened green tea a day.

DAY 7: GET YOUR Z'S. You might think that more hours awake equals more calories burned. Not so. In fact, short sleep duration is associated with higher rates of obesity in both adults and children. Adults who sleep fewer than 5 hours a night are significantly more likely to be obese than adults who sleep the recommended 7 to 8 hours per night, according to a review published in the journal *Sleep*. For the sake of your weight, energy level, and almost every other element of good health, make it a priority to get good sleep. Aim for 7 to 9 hours nightly.

Ten

The World's Healthiest 9-Week Plan

Our time with the Healthiest People in the World is about to end, but for you, the voyage is just beginning. Now, it's time for you to put the knowledge and advice you've gained into practice.

This plan will act as your guide. Step-by-step, the plan will tell you what to do to strengthen your body, stimulate your mind, and enlighten your spirit. Each week for 9 weeks, you'll focus on one secret of healthy aging and cumulatively build on your actions from the previous weeks. At the end, retake the quiz in Chapter 3, and see how many years you've shaved off your Health Age.

Week 1: Embrace Your Age

> *"As we age, there are going to be challenges to our bodies, minds, and emotions –it's how we respond to them that matters."*
> *–Jeannette Alosi, age 67*

An important part of successful aging is admitting that you are getting older. After all, only by first accepting reality can you age in a healthful way.

You don't want to start with acceptance. You want to start with change. We get it. But, this is important, as acceptance lays the path that you will walk upon in your journey to a fitter, healthier you. In a study published in *The American Journal of Geriatric Psychiatry*, researchers set out to investigate the true meaning of "successful aging." They interviewed 22 adults over age 60, with a mean age of 80. At the end of the interview process, two main themes emerged as being key for successful aging. The first was self-acceptance/self-contentment. The second was engagement with life/self-growth.

Armed with science, this week, focus on boosting your self-acceptance by doing the following:

Take an honest look at yourself. Literally. Stand in front of a mirror and take a good look. Do you like what you see? Chances are that you don't love everything. When we spoke with Deb Gordon (page 200), she flat out admitted, "Lately, I look in the mirror, and I *don't* like what I see." That's a normal reaction. Part of accepting the aging process is admitting that you don't look the same as you did 20 years ago and you *definitely* don't look the same as you did 40 years ago. And, that's okay. This week, take a good look at yourself in the mirror each day and make note of something positive you like. Then, say it out loud to yourself. It could be something like, "I have beautiful eyes," or "I'm having a good hair day."

Let it go. Let go of the notion that youth equals power and beauty. If you've been mourning the things you used to do and the way you used to look in your younger days, let that go too. Put simply, say goodbye to your younger self and hello to the older one. To drive this point home, this week, each day, write down a piece of wisdom you've learned as you've gotten older. Examples include, "I've learned not to sweat the small stuff, I value time with my friends more than ever," or "I love the people my kids have become; I owe myself a pat on the back."

See yourself like a fine wine. You may not be able to run as fast as you used to or ski a black diamond; but chances are your interpersonal skills, relationships, wisdom, and knowledge are at their peak. Focus on the positive aspects of getting older and you'll be more upbeat about your age. To focus on this point, try to keep your eyes and ears open, and notice one person each day who is like you (same age, same weight, same background) who has done great things. Pick out the parallels in your own life, both the past and where you would like to be in the future.

Week 2: Change Your Diet

"Good nutrition is like the ultimate endurance race because it lasts a lifetime."
–Amy Morosini, age 48

To shift your diet, use the advice in this section along with Chapter 11, which provides you with simple mix and match menu options. Both the menus and food recommendations on the following pages are based on our interviews with the Healthiest People in the World. We asked them what they ate each day and begged them for their favorite recipes. Then, Prevention's test kitchen developed mix and match menus based on what they told us.

The menus and food recommendations are also based on the cuisines consumed in the world's Blue Zones. These areas of the world breed longevity. These regions—termed Blue Zones by Dan Buettner, the explorer and author who discovered them—have the highest concentrations of centenarians in the world. The people in these areas of Latin America, Europe, Asia, and the U.S. have numerous healthy habits; one of the most salient is their diets. Many of their eating habits overlap with the habits of the World's Healthiest People.

Use the following guidelines to shift your eating toward the foods that the World's Healthiest People eat and also start incorporating the menu options in Chapter 11 into your daily repertoire. If it's too much to make all of these changes in one week, it's okay to adopt them gradually over multiple weeks, as long as you incorporate as many as you can.

Eat mostly plants. Not many of the people we interviewed eat a lot of meat. In fact, many of them are vegetarian. However, you don't have to completely give up meat if you love it. This week, aim to limit meat to a 3- to 4-ounce portion size, no more than once a week. This allows you one small burger or steak per week (if you want it).

- **Eat 2 to 3 cups of vegetables a day.** You cannot overdo this. Who says you can't have veggies at breakfast? Make a smoothie with frozen blueberries, spinach, banana, and papaya for breakfast. Drink that, along with an egg white omelet with spinach and roasted red peppers. For lunch, have a romaine salad topped with carrots and snap peas. Make a tasty stir-fry with green, yellow, and red peppers; broccoli; cauliflower; and green beans for dinner. The key is making a conscious effort to slip veggies in here and there. Once you start to do it on a regular basis, it will become a habit you enjoy.

- **Consume 3 cups of beans and legumes a week (or about ½ cup per day).** To get more beans in your diet, slip them in wherever you can. Toss a handful of cooked lentils onto your salad. Substitute hummus (mashed chickpeas) for mayonnaise on your sandwiches. Add a variety of beans to your favorite chili recipe and replace half the amount of ground turkey or ground beef in recipes with black beans or white beans.

- **Eat 1½ to 2 cups of fruit a day.** Make at least 1 cup berries. These are high in disease-fighting, anti-aging compounds called antioxidants. The berries that are highest in antioxidants are blueberries, strawberries, blackberries, and raspberries. Have a blueberry, strawberry, and raspberry yogurt parfait for breakfast, an apple, orange, or pear (or all three!) with lunch, and a salad topped with strawberries and salmon with a mango chutney for dinner.

Eat light at night. Blue Zoners eat their smallest meals of the day in the late afternoon or evening. A number of our interviewees mentioned practicing the same eating style. Coincidence? We don't think so.

Your biggest meal doesn't necessarily have to be breakfast; just make sure it's not dinner. A good rule of thumb is to avoid eating at least 2 hours before you go to bed. This is a good excuse to go out for brunch on the weekend and then eat lighter the rest of the day. Or, if you can't imagine giving up dinner as your main meal, plan it right. If you typically go to bed at 10:00 p.m., finish eating your dinner and all after-dinner food no later than 8:00 p.m. For more specifics on how to practice this way of eating, see Chapter 9. Also, use the mix and match menus in Chapter 11—as we've made sure to front-load some of the lunches with more calories, while keeping some of the dinners on the lighter side. Just use the nutritional analysis that appears with each meal suggestion to guide your choices.

Enjoy alcohol in moderation. The definition of moderation depends on where you are in the world, in part due to serving size, alcohol content, and cultural norms, but in general, the recommendation is no more than one to two servings of alcohol per day. In the United States, a standard drink contains about 14 grams of alcohol. This amount is in one 12-ounce beer

(5 percent alcohol), 8 to 9 ounces of malt liquor or stronger craft beer, 5 ounces of table wine, or 1.5 ounces of distilled spirits (gin, vodka, rum, whiskey, etc.). Preferably, to avoid habits that lead to problem drinking, consume alcohol with friends and/or food. Also, spread the drinks out over all 7 days in the week; this doesn't mean that you avoid alcohol all week and then have 7 to 14 drinks on a Friday night!

Eat superfoods. Call them what you will, certain foods seem to pack a more powerful nutritional punch than others, and many of these foods are favorites of those who live a long time. Foods that we heard interviewees talk about the most include the following: garlic, beans (all kinds are good, but fava, soy, black, and lentil are best), almonds, avocados, salmon, honey, berries, broccoli, spinach, and yogurt. The menus in Chapter 11 showcase many of these foods. In addition, use these strategies as well.

ALMONDS

- Use slivered almonds as a topping for oatmeal or yogurt
- Add almonds to any muffin recipe
- Substitute almond milk for regular milk in your cereal or coffee
- Use almond flour instead of regular flour
- Toss your salad with some almonds

AVOCADOS

- Spread mashed avocado on toast
- Use avocado instead of mayonnaise on a sandwich
- Top an omelet with sliced avocado
- Add avocados to your smoothie
- Use avocados instead of butter in brownie recipes

BEANS

- Make chili and double the amount of beans you usually use in the recipe
- Mash beans into a homemade bean dip
- Substitute chickpeas instead of tuna or chicken in tuna or chicken salad
- Replace half of the ground beef with kidney beans or black beans in tacos
- Mix beans and rice for a tasty side dish

BERRIES

- Add strawberries to your oatmeal or yogurt
- Make a smoothie by blending frozen blueberries, raspberries, and blackberries with a banana and almond milk
- Use strawberries or blueberries as a salad topper
- Eat dried blueberries or strawberries as a snack
- Cook blueberries with a touch of maple syrup and pour over pancakes or waffles

BROCCOLI

- Use fresh broccoli as a salad topper
- Roast broccoli with garlic for a tasty side dish
- Blend fresh broccoli into smoothies
- Add broccoli to a soup recipe
- Dip raw broccoli into hummus or ranch dressing for a healthy snack

GARLIC (RAW MINCED GARLIC IS BEST)

- Add it in fresh homemade salsa
- Stir it into ranch dressing
- Use it and olive oil as a topping for toast
- Mix it with hot sauce
- Mash it into guacamole

HONEY

- Add honey to smoothies
- Drizzle honey on top cereal or oatmeal
- Add honey to your salad dressing or marinades
- Sweeten iced or hot tea with honey

SALMON

- Add salmon to your morning omelet
- Top your bagel with lox
- Top a spinach salad with grilled salmon
- Use canned salmon instead of tuna and make salmon burgers or a tasty salmon salad
- Grill a piece of salmon for a quick, healthy dinner

SPINACH

- Add it to smoothies
- Use spinach in your salad instead of lettuce
- Mix fresh or thawed frozen spinach into your ground beef for a tasty, healthful burger
- Stir spinach leaves into hot pasta
- Sprinkle spinach on top of pizza

YOGURT

- Use yogurt as a dip for fruits and vegetables
- Marinate chicken in Greek yogurt and spices
- Add vanilla or plain yogurt to smoothies
- Substitute plain yogurt as a healthful alternative to sour cream
- Layer yogurt with berries and granola for a parfait

Week 3: Boost Your Brainpower

"One of the best things about bridge is that, no matter how many times you've played, you're always learning. New things always come up, which helps keep me sharp as I'm getting older."
–Peggy Kaplan, age 65

In a 2017 study published in *JAMA Neurology*, researchers found that adults age 70 and older who engaged in mentally stimulating activities at least once or twice a week for 4 years were less likely to develop mild cognitive impairment (MCI). MCI is a condition where people are still able to perform their everyday routines but experience problems with thinking and memory.

In this study, it didn't matter if the participants started doing the mentally stimulating activities after age 70—clear evidence that it's never too late to start.

So, try at least two new brain-bending activities this week. Look for activities that challenge you *and* bring you joy.

Here's how:

Brainstorm brainbenders. To start, sit down and think about some of the activities that challenged you as a child. Maybe you loved to build things with blocks, play the violin, paint pictures, or solve puzzles. Make a list of the activities that still intrigue you and try at least one of them this week.

Make it merrier. Look for mentally stimulating activities that involve other people, such as board games, bridge clubs, book groups, or a creative arts class. Gathering with like-minded people stimulates the learning and empathy centers of our brains, as well as our abilities to discern. Socializing also causes our brains to release feel-good hormones that help support long-term memory.

Take it online. In this technologically advanced era, you can easily stimulate your mind without having to leave the house. To find challenging activities you can fit in here and there, explore what's available on your smart phone and online. The American Association of Retired Persons (AARP) web site (aarp.org) offers a range of online games. Or, stick with what's popular, like Words with Friends, What's the Phrase, and Draw Something.

Week 4: Get Moving

*"Physical activity is so good for your body
and your mind. When I skip my run because
it's raining or I'm on vacation or something,
my day doesn't go as well."*
–Rick Connella, age 80

Nearly all of our interviewees get regular physical activity. Some, like Deb Gordon (page 200), Steve Colwell (page 46), Charles Eugster (page 37), and Natalie Jill (page 205), have even made exercise a main focus in their older years.

This week, focus on incorporating more physical activity into your routine. You don't have to do it all at once (in fact, doing so may be a recipe for an injury), but make it your goal to work your way up to 150 minutes (2½ hours) per week. That's the magic number of minutes of weekly movement that drops your risk of an early death by 31 percent. Are you an overachiever? Well, it has its benefits. If you exercise for 450 minutes (7½ hours) per week (a little more than an hour a day), you can drop your risk of death by 39 percent.

As you work up to 150 minutes (and beyond), use this advice.

Start where you are. Every little bit helps when it comes to exercising, so start by doing a little more than you were doing before. Maybe you start by walking about 10 minutes a day and adding a few minutes each day until you reach 150 minutes (or more) for the week. And, talk to your health-care provider before making any changes to your physical activity plan.

Change it up. Most of our interviewees have varied workout routines focusing on balance, flexibility, strength, and cardiovascular health. Bob Morris (page 34) goes to a different set of classes at the YMCA almost every day. Ed Shimer (page 137) runs, bikes, swims, surfs, plays tennis, and enjoys body weight workouts. Tom Servais (page 97) plays tennis, windsurfs, or board surfs—or all three—depending on the weather. To prevent boredom and maximize benefits from exercise, keep your workouts interesting. If you are already at 150 minutes and want to take things to the next level, aim to try a new type of exercise class, or, at the very least, one new stretch or move each day this week. For example, your week might look like the sample below.

Monday: Go for a hike in the woods

Tuesday: Take a Zumba class with friends

Wednesday: Play golf and walk instead of taking the cart (even if you've never played before)

Thursday: Try aqua aerobics at a local gym or Y, or if the weather is nice, try some water exercises in a pool or lake

Friday: Play doubles tennis (again, even if you've never tried before)

Saturday: Do a 5K run or walk for charity

Sunday: Take a leisurely walk with a neighbor

Exercise for enjoyment and achievement. Another common theme among our healthiest exercisers is that they're not suffering through a treadmill walk, constantly checking the time. Instead, they choose activities that they enjoy. They hike, do yoga, run on the beach, and practice martial arts. Some of them also use goals, like triathlons, 5K races, and competitive tennis with friends, as motivation. Charles Eugster (page 37) says, "With exercise, one should have a goal—it's extremely important to know what you are aiming for," he says. "Not just to have a beach body."

Include strength-training. Walking and other forms of cardio will only get you so far. To keep your metabolism humming, you'll also want to strength train, preferably by using your body weight as resistance.

To get started, use the routine below. Keep in mind that some of these body weight exercises are fairly advanced. If you can't complete the full set, start with as many as you can do and work your way up.

If you do all of them, you will hit all of your major muscle groups. Do as many of these exercises as you can 5 days a week. If you skip some one day, make sure that you do the ones you missed the next day. It's fine to build your way up in terms of the number of exercises and the number of sets. Here's a sample week that will show you how you can include these exercises along with your cardio.

Monday: 30 minutes of cardio
Straight arm plank, push-up, mountain climber, side skate, chair dip

Tuesday: 45 minutes of cardio
No body weight exercises

Wednesday: 30 minutes of cardio
Try to do the whole list of body weight exercises

Thursday: 30 minutes of cardio
Forearm plank, downward dog split with knee drive, Russian twist, burpee, air squat, side/back lunge

Friday: 30 minutes of cardio
Try to do the whole list

Saturday: 45 minutes of cardio
No body weight exercises

Sunday: Your choice. Rest if you need it. Or, if you don't, do push-ups, side skate, Russian twists, downward dog with knee drives, chair dips, and burpees

To get the most benefits from body weight based exercise, it's important to pay attention to your form. Closely follow instructions on how to do the exercises and keep the following in mind: vertical shins for lower-body moves to take pressure off your knees and vertical forearms for upper arm moves to take pressure off your elbows.

Forearm Plank

Place your forearms on the floor with your elbows aligned below your shoulders and your arms parallel to the body about shoulder-width apart. Close your hands into fists. Push your toes into the floor and squeeze your glutes to stabilize the bottom half of your body. Be careful not to lock your knees. Neutralize your neck and spine by looking at the floor, about a foot in front of your hands. Your head should be in line with your spine. Hold this position for 20 seconds to start. As you get more comfortable and your core gets stronger, hold the plank for as long as possible without sacrificing form or breath.

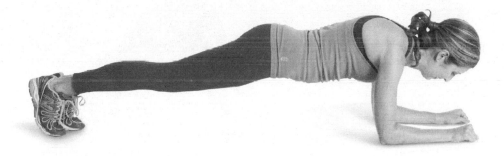

Straight-Arm Plank

On the floor, place your hands slightly wider than shoulder-width apart, like you are about to do a push-up. Push your toes into the floor and squeeze your glutes to stabilize the bottom half of your body. Be careful not to lock your knees. Neutralize your neck and spine by looking at the floor, about a foot in front of your hands. Your head should be in line with your spine. Hold this position for 20 seconds to start. As you get more comfortable and your core gets stronger, hold the plank for as long as possible without sacrificing form or breath.

Downward Dog Split with Knee Drives

Start in downward facing dog.

1. To do a downward dog, start on your hands and knees with your wrists directly under your shoulders and your knees directly under your hips. Spread your fingers wide apart and press firmly through your knuckles and palms, distributing your weight evenly across your hands. Tuck your toes and lift your butt toward the ceiling as you extend your legs, without locking your knees. Bring your body into the shape of an upside-down V.

2. Raise your right leg to move into down dog split.

3. Bend your right knee and pull it toward your tummy and then toward your forehead.

❸

4. Straighten and raise your leg back up toward the ceiling. Then bend your knee and, this time, bring it in toward your tummy and eventually toward your right elbow.

Straighten your leg again, then bring your knee across your tummy and toward your left elbow. Repeat three times. Switch legs and repeat.

❹

Push-Ups

In the push-up position with your arms straight, butt clenched, and abs braced, slowly lower yourself until your elbows are at a 90-degree angle. As you go down, keep your elbows close to your body; if they start to fly out, you're getting tired. Once your chest touches the floor, or your arms go down to a 90-degree angle, pause slightly and then explode back up until you're back in the same position. Complete as many push-ups as you can without sacrificing your form.

If you find traditional, full-body push-ups too challenging, start by doing them against a wall. Once you can do 12 repetitions comfortably, move to doing them while holding on to the edge of a countertop.

Once you can do 12 repetitions on the edge of the countertop, move to doing them on the floor, supporting yourself with your knees on the floor. Once you can complete at least 12 repetitions on your knees, try full-body push-ups.

Russian Twists

Sit on the floor with your knees bent and feet slightly hovering off the ground. Keep your back straight, with your thighs and torso forming a V shape. Twist from side to side using your arms, holding your hands together as if you are gripping a weighted ball. Perform this exercise for 30 seconds.

Mountain Climbers

Place your hands in a push-up position. With your arms straight, bend your knees and raise your hips slightly, bringing most of your body weight into your hands, draw one knee in toward your chest and jump to switch legs, as if running in place on your hands and feet. Do two sets of eight.

To make this exercise a little easier, try doing it while resting your hands on a bench.

Side Skate

Start by standing with your legs apart, your weight on your right foot, and your right knee bent. Lift your left leg off the floor behind you, as if you were pushing off as you were ice skating.

Bound to your left leg by pushing off with your right leg. Land on your left foot, lifting your right leg off the floor behind you.

Continue hopping back and forth for 30 seconds. If needed, touch your back foot on the floor behind you for balance.

Burpees

1. Start in a standing position.

2. Drop into a squat position with your hands on the ground.

3. Next, kick your feet back so you're at the top of a push-up.

4. Jump your feet back into the squat position.

5. Stand up to complete one rep. Do eight reps. If you lack the strength to do a burpee, try doing it while elevated. Rather than placing your hands on the floor, place them on a sturdy table or bench when you squat.

Air Squats

Stand with your shoulders rolled back, chest facing forward and chin up, feet shoulder-width apart. Rest your weight in your heels (you can lift your toes slightly off ground to serve as a reminder). Swing your hips back. Don't bend your knees into the squat position until your hips are all the way back.

Stick your butt out and aim to have your thighs parallel to the ground. Repeat 15 to 20 times.

As a slightly easier alternative to air squats, try doing them while holding on to the back of a sturdy chair.

Side/Back Lunge

Stand with your feet hip-width apart. Step one leg out to the side, bending that knee at 90 degrees so that your knee is directly over your toes. Lower your butt back and down, while keeping your other leg as straight as possible.

Push off with your bent leg and return to the standing position.

Next, step straight back with the same leg you lunged to the side with, bending both of your knees to 90 degrees, front knee over your toes.

Push off the floor with your back leg and return to the starting position. Complete 10 reps for one set and then repeat on the opposite side. Do two sets.

Chair Dips

Sit on a sturdy chair. Place your palms against the seat of the chair next to your hips and scoot your rear forward until it comes off the chair and you are supporting your body weight with your arms and legs. Bend your legs at a 90-degree angle.

Bend your elbows back and slowly lower your butt toward the floor. Keep your elbows tucked in. Your body should just clear the seat. Push back up until your arms are straight; don't use your feet for help. Do 8 to 15 reps.

Week 5: Rub Elbows

"There are acquaintances and there are friends.
I have been lucky in my life to have many I would call friends."
–Barbara Packman, age 87

Another factor ubiquitous to the World's Healthiest People—they have strong, active social networks. This is true of people who live in the Blue Zones too. For some, like Honey Kimball (page 83), that network includes mostly family members. For others, like Kari Dougan (page 190), it consists of loving friends. Some interviewees talked about celebrating milestone birthdays by climbing mountains or hiking the Grand Canyon with old pals. A 2016 study published in *Proceedings of the National Academy of Sciences* found that the more social ties people have, the better their health. It is the first study to link social relationships to markers of physical health such as obesity, high blood pressure, and inflammation.

With that in mind, this week, focus on your social network. Pay attention to how often you see and talk to others especially people you like. Also take note of how often you help others and how much they offer to help you. Specifically, consider trying these tactics:

Accept every invitation for the next 7 days. See what happens. You might be surprised. If you continuously turn people down when they invite you to do things, they will eventually cross you off their social list. Starting this week, whether it's for a family birthday party, a casual coffee date with a friend, or a community potluck, accept every invitation you receive—even the gatherings you would typically skip. Then, go into the event with a positive attitude and an open mind.

Take the lead. Life is too short to wait around for the phone to ring or your text alert to chime. So, why not initiate plans yourself? Before the end of the week, organize a spontaneous happy hour, game night, or museum trip with friends. Or, suggest that you and a group of friends meet monthly for lunch and schedule six months' worth ahead of time. Follow Kathy Shaffer's (page 111) advice: "You have to schedule time with the people you enjoy, especially as you get older. Even if you feel like you are always the one doing the planning—stop pitying yourself and just do it! I'm always happy I did."

Remember, old is gold. As you expand or strengthen your social circle, look inward, at your oldest and dearest friends. This week, try to connect with at least one old friend, more if you can. If he or she lives close by, schedule a time to meet. If he or she lives faraway, call to arrange a summer road trip or a weekend at the beach.

Week 6: Discover Happiness

"I pray that things will work out for the best.
So far, they have. It's been a good life."
–Honey Kimball, age 97

If there is one thing all of the people we interviewed for this book have in common, it's happiness. We could spend an entire chapter delving into the definition of happiness and what it means for individual people, but to keep things simple, let's go with a popular definition among psychologists: Happiness is a mood or emotional state brought about by generally positive thoughts and feelings. In short, it's the opposite of feeling down.

Some, like Honey, talk about general optimism in the form of expectation that things will work out for the best, and gratefulness that they have.

Others talk about bumping up their optimism when they need it the most. In the middle of running a marathon—in her nineties!—Harriet Thompson (page 43) uses positive self-talk. "This is easy! You can do this," she tells herself.

So, you may be wondering, "If I'm not as happy as the people I read about, am I doomed?" The answer is no. Happiness is fluid and there are things you can do to boost it, including the following:

Do one good deed a day. When you give to others, you make them feel good, and in turn, you make yourself happier. In a 2008 study published in the journal *Science,* researchers gave participants a gift of $5 or $20 and asked them to spend it on others or themselves. They found that the amount of money had no effect on their happiness, but those who spent the money on other people felt happier at the end of the experiment.

Your good deeds don't have to be huge. It can be something as simple as emailing a friend to tell her what you appreciate about your friendship or stopping to help an elderly lady cross the street. Just make a concerted effort to be nicer and more giving, and see how you feel.

Connect with a friend or family member who lifts you up. Emotions are contagious, so the more positive, sunny people you can interact with, the happier you will be. Just living within 1 mile of a happy friend or family member can boost your happiness by about 25 percent, research shows. The contagiousness of happiness spreads far and can influence the happiness of others up to three degrees of separation from the positive person at the center.

Obviously, you can't change your residence solely based on being closer to happy people, and you can't choose your family members. But, you *can* try to spend more time with the people who lift you up. Pay attention to how you feel after spending time with someone—are you energetic and upbeat or drained and pessimistic? If it's the latter, think twice about whom you invite to your next social event. Each day this week, make a plan to get together with a friend or family member who makes you feel good.

Week 7: Give Thanks

"...there's this thing called gratitude.
For a hot shower, a cup of tea–gratitude
for the big and little things is so important."
–Kari Dougan, age 58

Gratitude is a recurring theme among the World's Healthiest People, and research shows that it can help you to become more enthusiastic, optimistic, attentive, and energetic.

To be more grateful, try the following.

Write down your blessings. Filomena Warihay (page 195) likes to write them on small pieces of paper that she can see filling up a jar. Other people prefer to write in a journal. No matter what the medium, try the act of physically writing about the good things in your life to reinforce positive thoughts. Set aside at least 10 minutes for some form of gratitude writing every day this week.

Go on a negativity diet. To be more mindful of negative thoughts and actions, go an entire day without complaining or passing judgment. If it works and you feel yourself becoming more grateful, stretch it to 2 days, and so on, with the ultimate goal of doing this for the entire week.

Say "thank you" as much as you can. They say that you can't thank someone too many times. In your "thankfulness week," thank people for all of the kind things they do for you, from bigger favors to simply holding the door open. No gesture is too small to deserve thanks and appreciation. Count the number of times you say thank you each day this week.

Week 8: Volunteer

"As long as I am here on Earth,
I want to be useful, engaged, and productive."
–Walt Hoffman, age 91

Hoffman and his wife started taking missionary trips to third world countries in their seventies. Sandra Ramos (page 92) has devoted her entire career to helping battered women. And fueled by his own experience, Dan Berlin (page 160) created an organization that helps blind children around the world. Formally and informally, a number of our World's Healthiest People volunteer their time to help others in need.

When you volunteer to do something nice for someone else, it lowers your blood pressure, decreases stress, boosts happiness, increases self-esteem, and ultimately, prolongs life. Plus, volunteering gives you a sense of accomplishment and provides an opportunity to meet like-minded friends.

This week, focus on volunteer opportunities. Whether you've never volunteered or are looking for something new, here are some tips.

Follow your heart. As you decide where you want to donate your time, consider your passions. Do you love animals? Call your local animal shelter, aquarium, or zoo to see if they need help. Some shelters use volunteers for tasks as simple as periodically petting the cats. Do you want to do something to help struggling individuals and families in your area? Spend some time in a homeless shelter, women's center, or food bank. If you love working with kids, see if there is a daycare, library, or children's hospital that could employ your skills. Or, you can spread your time between a few different charities or groups. This week, make a phone call or search the internet for a different charity every day. At the end of the week, write down the three you liked the most, and make a commitment to spend time at one or two of them.

Go on a volunteer voyage. Been thinking of volunteering and planning a trip? Why not combine the two and volunteer abroad? Look into one of the following organizations to help pair volunteering with seeing different parts of the world.

Peace Corps (peacecorps.gov)

CrossCultural Solutions (CCS) (crossculturalsolutions.org)

Global Vision International (GVI) (gviworld.com)

Global Volunteers (globalvolunteers.org)

Habitat for Humanity (habitat.org)

American Red Cross (redcross.org)

Think outside the box. Many volunteer opportunities fall outside of the typical activities that usually come to mind. Volunteers can fill important, enriching positions such as after-school program coordinators, tutors, and museum guides. As you brainstorm volunteer ideas this week, look for open positions near you on volunteermatch.org.

Week 9: Try Something New

*"We are often a lot more than we think we are—
the secret is trying new things with the
right attitude, effort, and discipline."*
–Dan Berlin, age 47

Whether it is hiking the Grand Canyon, doing martial arts, or skydiving, many of the people we talked to are open to new challenges in their lives, and they're not letting their physical handicaps or challenges get in the way. By taking this adventurous attitude, they are keeping their minds young and sharp.

As many of the stories demonstrate, you're never too old to try new things. The newer an activity is to you, the more powerful its health benefits. So, step outside your mental comfort zone this week, using this advice:

Do something you've always wanted to do. There was something so inspiring about Louise Gooche's (page 133) decision to form her own cheerleading squad at the age of 62. In honor of Louise and some of the other people we spoke with, look at your retirement years as an opportunity to seize the day. This week, sit down and make a bucket list if you don't have one, or expand it, if you do. Then, make plans to do at least one of the things on that list. It could be something as simple as trying sushi, painting your first portrait, or planning your first ski trip or ascent in a hot-air balloon. The key is to do something that pushes you out of your comfort zone.

Think about traveling to a faraway place. A number of our stories focused or touched on travel—in some cases, adventure travel. Pat and Alicia Moorehead (page 30) talk about excursions to more than 200 nations, including Iran, North Korea, and their favorite—Bhuton. Ann Jarrett (page 78) has traveled to more than 65 countries, some multiple times. And, Jim Yenckel (page 141) and Diogo Teixeira (page 174) went on challenging hiking adventures to celebrate their 65th and 70th birthdays, respectively.

To expand your mind, try expanding your horizons. If you can, this week plan a trip to a place you've never been, or a country you've always dreamed of seeing. If you prefer traveling in a group, check out the Road Scholar program (roadscholar.org), a travel organization for adults that travels to 150 countries.

Make a list of your adventurous friends. Doing new and exciting things is particularly good for your brain when you do those things together with people you like. Plus, trying a new activity with a trusted friend is more fun! As you focus on embarking on innovative and stimulating endeavors this week, make a list of the people in your life who are most likely to join you for the ride. Then, contact them and gauge their interest in going on various types of adventures.

We have only one chapter left in this book and it's one that we hope you'll find yourself referring to over and over again. It showcases dozens of mix and match meal options to help guide your eating choices.

As we draw to a close, hopefully you will feel inspired by the tales you've heard and will be empowered with advice from the World's Healthiest People. Our goal as a husband and wife writing team—who are also facing some of the challenges of aging—has been to arm you with scientific facts and practical tips to help you embrace your older years and make them some of the happiest and healthiest of your life. This is the end of our journey together but just the beginning of your journey to becoming one of the World's Healthiest People!

Eleven

The World's Healthiest Meal Options

As we interviewed dozens of amazing people for this book, we noticed that they shared several common eating habits. They eat mostly plants—especially veggies and beans—and limit red meat to 3- to 4-ounces a week. They also ate lightly at night. Some had their smallest meal of the day in the late afternoon or evening, with their biggest meal at either breakfast or lunch. They enjoyed one or two daily drinks with friends too.

Science also backs up all of these nutritional strategies.

The problem can be actually putting these healthy nutritional strategies into practice. That's what this chapter is all about. To eat like the World's Healthiest People, choose from the assortment of meals on the following pages. As you'll see, some of these menu options come straight from the kitchens of the people we interviewed. Others were created by Prevention's test kitchen, based on what the World's Healthiest People told us they ate.

What the World's Healthiest People Eat
for Breakfast

These breakfasts will help you to love every bite of great health. If you pre-fer to wake-up with a jolt of caffeine, pair any one of these options with the Kicked-Up Coffee on page 251.

If you'd like to front-load your calories for breakfast (and eat a light dinner or skip it completely), the Bacon-Onion-Pepper Omelet (page 249) is your friend. You can also easily double any of the smoothie recipes, and you can also bulk up other breakfast options by consuming them with half a sliced avocado (130 calories) or avocado toast (230 calories), ¼ cup nuts and seeds (160 calories), and/or a couple of hard-boiled eggs (140 calories) on the side.

• • • • • • • • • • •
Liz Shimer's All-Day Energy Smoothie

Blend 1 banana, ½ cup frozen berries, ½ cup baby spinach leaves, 1 scoop vanilla protein powder (or 1 tablespoon peanut butter), and 1 to 1 ½ cups unsweetened vanilla almond milk until smooth. Serves 1.

NUTRITION (PER SERVING WITH 1 CUP OF MILK): 305 calories, 26 g protein, 41 g carbohydrates, 7 g fiber, 21 g sugar, 6 g fat, 1 g saturated fat, 251 mg sodium

• • • • • • • • • • •
Amy Morosini's Feel-Great-All-Day Smoothie

Blend 1 cup ice, 1 cup baby spinach leaves, ¾ cup green grapes, ¾ cup pineapple chunks, 1 small apple, 1 small banana, ½ cup water, 1 tablespoon chia seeds, and 1 tablespoon of powdered greens, hemp protein, powdered fiber, or apple cider vinegar until smooth. Serves 1.

NUTRITION (PER SERVING WITH HEMP PROTEIN): 398 calories, 9 g protein, 90 g carbohydrates, 16 g fiber, 58 g sugar, 5 g fat, 0.5 g saturated fat, 57 mg sodium

Fruit-and-Veggie Smoothie

Blend ½ cup frozen mixed berries, ½ cup fresh baby greens, ½ frozen banana, 3 baby carrots, ¼ cup fresh orange juice, and ¼ cup low-fat vanilla yogurt until smooth and frosty. Enjoy with 1 hard-boiled egg. Serves 1.

NUTRITION (PER SERVING): 255 calories, 11 g protein, 41 g carbohydrates, 5 g fiber, 28 g sugar, 7 g fat, 2 g saturated fat, 146 mg sodium

Rick Connella's Breakfast of Champs

Combine 1 serving of your favorite low-sugar, multi-grain cereal (such as Great Grains), with 2 tablespoons raisins and 2 tablespoons almonds. Top with 1 cup unsweetened cranberry juice and 1 sliced banana. Serves 1.

NUTRITION (PER SERVING): 542 calories, 14 g protein, 111 g carbohydrates, 13 g fiber, 68 g sugar, 11 g fat, 1 g saturated fat, 148 mg sodium

Poached Eggs on Buttered Toast

In a small saucepan, bring 4 cups of water to a simmer over medium-high heat with a dash of apple cider vinegar. Crack 2 eggs into a bowl. Gently pour the eggs into the simmering water and gently stir. Reduce the heat to medium-low. Meanwhile, toast 2 slices whole-grain bread and spread each with 1 teaspoon butter. When the egg whites are opaque but the yolks are still soft, about 2 minutes, scoop them out with a slotted spoon and let them drain a bit. Place the eggs on top of the toast, and season with salt and pepper, to taste. Serves 1.

NUTRITION (PER SERVING): 349 calories, 20 g protein, 24 g carbohydrates, 4 g fiber, 4 g sugar, 20 g fat, 8.5 g saturated fat, 648 mg sodium

Almond-Blueberry Oatmeal

In a medium microwave-safe bowl, combine ¼ cup steel-cut oats with ¾ cup low-fat milk and microwave on high for 2 minutes. Remove from the microwave, stir, and continue to heat in 30 second intervals until the oats are cooked through, 3 to 4 minutes. (Alternatively, you can make this on the stovetop by bringing the mixture to a boil and then reducing the heat to low for 5 minutes.) Mix in ¼ cup blueberries, 1 tablespoon sliced almonds, 1 tablespoon ground flaxseeds, and ¼ teaspoon cinnamon. Serves 1.

NUTRITION (PER SERVING): 299 calories, 15 g protein, 46 g carbohydrates, 7 g fiber, 14 g sugar, 9 g fat, 2 g saturated fat, 81 mg sodium

Shredded Wheat Bowl

Combine ¾ cup no-sugar-added shredded wheat cereal, ½ cup mixed berries, ¼ cup bran cereal (such as All-Bran), 2 tablespoons wheat germ, and 1 tablespoon toasted walnuts or almonds. Top it off with 1 cup of low-fat milk. Serves 1.

NUTRITION (PER SERVING): 427 calories, 20 g protein, 69 g carbohydrates, 14 g fiber, 25 g sugar, 10 g fat, 2 g saturated fat, 154 mg sodium

Keep It Moving (High-Fiber) Cereal

Combine 1 cup low-sugar, high-fiber cereal, ½ cup raspberries, ¼ cup toasted pumpkin seeds, 1 tablespoon chia seeds, and 1 tablespoon unsweetened shredded coconut. Top it off with 1 cup of low-fat milk. Serves 1.

NUTRITION (PER SERVING): 542 calories, 14 g protein, 60 g carbohydrates, 16 g fiber, 23 g sugar, 26 g fat, 8 g saturated fat, 383 mg sodium

Bacon-Onion-Pepper Omelet

In a medium bowl, whisk together 3 large eggs with 3 tablespoons chopped onion, 3 tablespoons seeded and chopped green bell pepper, and 3 tablespoons shredded carrot. Coarsely chop 3 slices of cooked turkey bacon and stir them into the egg mixture with a pinch of black pepper. Heat I teaspoon of canola oil in a small, nonstick skillet over medium heat, and pour in the egg mixture. Cover and cook until the omelet is almost set in the center, about 4 minutes. Flip and cook 2 minutes more. Serve with a fruit parfait of I banana, I apple, and I orange with ¼ cup low fat Greek yogurt and 2 tablespoons granola. Serves I.

NUTRITION (PER SERVING): 732 calories, 47 g protein, 86 g carbohydrates, 13 g fiber, 53 g sugar, 26 g fat, 4 g saturated fat, 852 mg sodium

Scrambled Egg Plus

In a medium bowl, whisk together I large egg and I large egg white with a pinch of salt and black pepper. Heat ½ teaspoon olive oil in a small nonstick skillet over medium heat. Add the eggs and cook, stirring until soft curds form and are done to your liking, about 2 minutes. Serve with I slice of high-fiber bread and ½ cup of blueberries. Serves I.

NUTRITION (PER SERVING): 198 calories, 13 g protein, 22 g carbohydrates, 5 g fiber, 8 g sugar, 8 g fat, 2 g saturated fat, 364 mg sodium

Eggs, Mushrooms, and a Side of Fruit

Heat ½ teaspoon olive oil in a medium nonstick skillet over medium heat. Add I package (about 3.5 ounces) of mixed wild or exotic mushrooms. Cook, undisturbed, until the mushrooms release their liquid and start to turn golden. Sprinkle with a pinch of salt and black pepper. Scoot the mushrooms toward the sides of the skillet and add ½ teaspoon olive oil in the open space. Crack 2 eggs into the skillet, and cook until the whites are opaque and the yolks are still soft, about 4 minutes. Sprinkle with a pinch of salt and black pepper. Serve with ¼ cup blackberries, ¼ cup raspberries, ¼ cup strawberries, and ¼ cup blueberries. Top with 2 tablespoons of sliced almonds. Serves I.

NUTRITION (PER SERVING): 349 calories, 19 g protein, 26 g carbohydrates, 9 g fiber, 12 g sugar, 21 g fat, 4 g saturated fat, 393 mg sodium

Whipped Peanut Butter Toast

Whisk together 2 tablespoons low-fat Greek yogurt and 1 tablespoon natural peanut butter until completely combined. Spread over 1 slice of high-fiber, multi-grain toast and top with 4 halved grapes and 4 raspberries. Serves 1.

NUTRITION (PER SERVING): 186 calories, 8 g protein, 20 g carbohydrates, 5 g fiber, 6 g sugar, 9 g fat, 1.5 g saturated fat, 127 mg sodium

Spinach-Maitake-Egg White Omelet

Heat ½ teaspoon olive oil in a medium nonstick skillet over medium heat. Add 2 cups baby spinach leaves, 2 cups chopped maitake mushrooms, 1 minced clove garlic, ¼ teaspoon crushed red pepper flakes, and a pinch of salt. Cook, stirring until the spinach wilts and the mushrooms are tender, about 5 minutes. Scrape into a bowl and wipe out the skillet. Heat another ½ teaspoon olive oil in the skillet over medium heat. In a small bowl, whisk 4 egg whites with a pinch of salt, pour into the skillet, and cook until almost set, about 2 minutes. Pour the spinach mixture over half of the omelet and fold the other side over the spinach. Serves 1.

NUTRITION (PER SERVING): 182 calories, 19 g protein, 16 g carbohydrates, 6 g fiber, 4 g sugar, 5 g fat, 1 g saturated fat, 779 mg sodium

Cottage Cheese and Fruit Bowl

Combine ½ cup low-fat cottage cheese with ⅛ teaspoon ground cinnamon and ⅛ teaspoon ground cardamom. Top with ½ cup blackberries and raspberries, 1 segmented orange, and ¼ cup diced cantaloupe. Sprinkle with 2 tablespoons of sunflower seeds and 1 tablespoon of ground flaxseeds. Serves 1.

NUTRITION (PER SERVING): 330 calories, 20 g protein, 35 g carbohydrates, 9 g fiber, 21 g sugar, 14 g fat, 2 g saturated fat, 382 mg sodium

Yogurt-Cereal Parfait

In a tall glass or dessert cup, layer ⅓ cup low-fat plain Greek yogurt, ⅓ cup granola, and ¼ cup strawberries, then repeat again. Top with an additional ⅓ cup of yogurt and ¼ cup of strawberries. Serves I.

NUTRITION (PER SERVING): 402 calories, 24 g protein, 63 g carbohydrates, 8 g fiber, 29 g sugar, 8 g fat, 3.5 g saturated fat, 204 mg sodium

Kicked-Up Coffee

For every scoop of ground coffee, add ¼ teaspoon of either ground cinnamon, cardamom, or turmeric to the filter.

NUTRITION (PER SERVING): 4 calories, 0 g protein, I g carbohydrates, 0 g fiber, 0 g sugar, 0 g fat, 0 g saturated fat, 5 mg sodium

What the World's Healthiest People Eat
for Lunch

Loaded with veggies, fiber, healthy fats, and protein, these lunches fuel your body with everything you need for great health. If you're front-loading your calories so you can eat a light dinner or skip it altogether, gravitate toward these higher-calorie options: Turkey and Cucumber Sandwich Halves with Lemon-Quinoa Salad (page 252), Roasted Vegetable Salad with Lemon-Dijon Vinaigrette (page 255), Potato-Crust Quiche (page 255), Simple Chicken and Veggie Stir-Fry (page 256), and Colorful Quinoa Bowls (page 258).

Jeannette Alosi's Kitchari

Heat 2 tablespoons ghee (clarified butter) in a heavy-bottomed soup pot over medium heat. Add ½ teaspoon black mustard seeds and ½ teaspoon cumin seeds. Cook, stirring until the seeds begin to pop, about 3 minutes. Stir in I cup rinsed, drained, and split mung beans, ½ cup rinsed and drained basmati rice, I tablespoon minced or grated fresh ginger, 1 teaspoon salt, ¾ teaspoon ground coriander, and ½ teaspoon turmeric. Pour in 6 cups of water and bring to a boil over high heat. Reduce the heat to a simmer, cover, and cook until all of the liquid has been absorbed, about 20 minutes. Serves 4.

NUTRITION (PER SERVING): 341 calories, 14 g protein, 56 g carbohydrates, 9 g fiber, 4 g sugar, 8 g fat, 5 g saturated fat, 499 mg sodium

. . . .

Pesto Ham and Cheese Sandwich

Toast 1 whole-wheat English muffin and spread with 1 tablespoon of store-bought pesto. Top with 2 ounces baked ham, 1 slice provolone cheese, ½ sliced plum tomato, and 1 large romaine lettuce leaf. Serve with 1 cup of grapes. Serves 1.

NUTRITION (PER SERVING): 429 calories, 25 g protein, 56 g carbohydrates, 6 g fiber, 31 g sugar, 15 g fat, 5 g saturated fat, 1,145 mg sodium

. . . .

Turkey and Cucumber Sandwich Halves with Lemon-Quinoa Salad

In a medium bowl, toss together 2 tablespoons mayonnaise, 1 teaspoon prepared horseradish, ¼ teaspoon garlic powder, and ¼ teaspoon black pepper. Mix in 1 cup chopped cooked turkey or chicken breast and 1 chopped scallion. Divide the mixture between 2 slices rye bread, spreading it to the edges. Thinly slice half a small seedless cucumber and shingle the slices over the turkey mixture. Top both with another slice of bread and slice the sandwiches in half. In a large bowl, combine 3 cups cooked quinoa, 2 cups halved cherry tomatoes, 1 small, thinly sliced seedless cucumber, ¼ cup sunflower seeds, and 2 sliced scallions. In a small bowl, combine ¼ cup fresh lemon juice, 2 tablespoons olive oil, and ½ teaspoon salt. Drizzle the quinoa mixture with the lemon dressing and toss to combine. Finish the meal with 1 ounce of dark chocolate per person. Serves 4.

NUTRITION (PER SERVING): 635 calories, 23 g protein, 66 g carbohydrates, 11 g fiber, 13 g sugar, 32 g fat, 10 g saturated fat, 563 mg sodium

Salmon Salad Sandwich and White Bean Soup

In a large, heavy saucepan, heat ½ teaspoon olive oil over medium heat. Add ¼ cup chopped onion and 1 minced clove garlic. Cook, stirring, until translucent, about 3 minutes. Add 2 cups low-sodium chicken broth, 2 cups water, 1 can (15 ounces) rinsed and drained unsalted cannellini beans, 1 peeled and diced potato, and 1 teaspoon chopped fresh oregano. Cover and bring to a boil. Reduce the heat to medium-low and simmer until the potato is soft, about 15 minutes. Transfer about three-quarters of the soup to a blender and puree. Return the pureed soup to the saucepan and cook over medium-low heat until heated through. Season to taste with salt and black pepper. Stir in ¼ cup finely diced tomatoes and 2 tablespoons fresh basil just before serving. Meanwhile, drain 2 cans (6 ounces each) of wild-caught salmon and flake. Mix in 1 finely diced rib of celery, ½ minced small shallot, 1 tablespoon drained capers, 1 tablespoon extra-virgin olive oil, 2 teaspoons chopped fresh dill or tarragon, juice of ½ a lemon, and a pinch of salt and black pepper. Divide among 4 small whole-wheat pitas and serve each with a bowl of soup alongside ½ cup carrot sticks and 1 kiwifruit. Serves 4.

NUTRITION (PER SERVING): 432 calories, 27 g protein, 63 g carbohydrates, 10 g fiber, 12 g sugar, 10 g fat, 1.5 g saturated fat, 915 mg sodium

Apple-Peanut Butter Stacks

Slice an apple width-wise into ½-inch-thick slices and discard the core. Spread 1 teaspoon natural peanut butter or almond butter on each slice. Sprinkle each slice with ½ teaspoon chia seeds and 1 teaspoon dried unsweetened coconut flakes. Serves 1.

NUTRITION (PER SERVING): 315 calories, 7 g protein, 35 g carbohydrates, 9 g fiber, 21 g sugar, 18 g fat, 6 g saturated fat, 5 mg sodium

Kale Caesar Salad with Chicken

In a large bowl, whisk together 1 tablespoon fresh lemon juice, 2 minced anchovy fillets, 1 minced clove garlic, and ½ teaspoon Dijon mustard. Slowly whisk in ¼ cup extra-virgin olive oil. Add 1 large bunch chopped kale and toss in the dressing. Toss in 2 cups shredded rotisserie chicken, 1 cup halved cherry tomatoes, and 1 tablespoon grated Parmesan cheese. Serve with 2 apples cut into slices. Serves 4.

NUTRITION (PER SERVING): 374 calories, 29 g protein, 30 g carbohydrates, 5 g fiber, 11 g sugar, 17 g fat, 3 g saturated fat, 321 mg sodium

No-Bun Bratwurst with Sauerkraut and Broccoli

Heat the oven to 450°F. Slice 4 standard bratwurst down the center but not completely through to the other side. Push open slightly and place on one-half of a baking sheet. On the other side, toss 4 cups broccoli florets with 1 tablespoon olive oil, 1 minced clove garlic, and a pinch of salt and black pepper. Roast the brats and broccoli until the brats are cooked through and the broccoli is tender and lightly charred, about 15 minutes, flipping the brats and tossing the broccoli halfway through cooking. Transfer the bratwursts to a plate and spread 1 teaspoon spicy brown mustard down the center and top each with ½ cup drained store-bought sauerkraut. Serve alongside the broccoli. Serves 4.

NUTRITION (PER SERVING): 310 calories, 11 g protein, 11 g carbohydrates, 4 g fiber, 2 g sugar, 26 g fat, 9 g saturated fat, 1,379 mg sodium

Hummus and Veggie Wrap

Spread ⅓ cup hummus over a 6- to 7-inch whole-wheat tortilla. Add ½ cup baby arugula, ¼ cup chopped roasted red peppers, and ¼ cup chopped marinated artichoke hearts. Fold in the sides and roll. Serves 1.

NUTRITION (PER SERVING): 253 calories, 8 g protein, 40 g carbohydrates, 6 g fiber, 5 g sugar, 10 g fat, 0 g saturated fat, 877 mg sodium

Roasted Vegetable Salad with Lemon-Dijon Vinaigrette

Heat the oven to 425°F. On a rimmed baking sheet, toss 6 baby carrots, cut into matchsticks; 6 small red potatoes, halved; 3 parsnips, cut into matchsticks; 4 shallots, halved; I cup Brussels sprouts, trimmed and halved; and I cup shiitake mushrooms, stemmed, with I tablespoon olive oil. Roast until tender and golden, 25 to 30 minutes. Remove from the oven and let cool to room temperature. In a small bowl, whisk together 2 tablespoons fresh lemon juice, I tablespoon white-wine vinegar, 2 teaspoons Dijon mustard, ¼ teaspoon kosher salt, and ¼ teaspoon black pepper. Slowly whisk in 6 tablespoons extra-virgin olive oil in a steady stream. In a salad bowl, toss 3 cups arugula and vegetables with the dressing. Season with ½ teaspoon salt and ¼ teaspoon black pepper. Serve sprinkled with ½ cup crumbled feta cheese. Serves 4.

NUTRITION (PER SERVING): 609 calories, 13 g protein, 81 g carbohydrates, 10 g fiber, 14 g sugar, 29 g total fat, 6 g saturated fat, 738 mg sodium

Potato-Crust Quiche

Heat the oven to 400°F. In a large bowl, stir 4 cups thawed frozen shredded hash brown potatoes, 2 eggs, ¾ cup all-purpose flour, ½ teaspoon salt, and ¼ teaspoon black pepper until well-combined. Press into the bottom and up the sides of a greased 9-inch deep-dish pie pan. Bake until the edges begin to brown, about 15 minutes. Remove from the oven and set aside. Decrease the oven temperature to 350°F. Heat I tablespoon olive oil in a large skillet over medium heat. Add I large thinly sliced onion and cook, stirring occasionally, until deep golden brown, about 15 minutes. Increase the heat to medium-high and add 6 cups torn kale in handfuls, stirring until just wilted. Stir in 4 slices cooked and crumbled turkey bacon. Transfer the mixture to the crust in the pan. In a medium bowl, whisk together 8 eggs, I cup half-and-half, ½ teaspoon salt, and ¼ teaspoon black pepper. Pour into the pan. Scatter I ounce goat cheese evenly over the top, and bake until lightly golden and set, 45 to 55 minutes. Let stand for 10 minutes. Serves 4.

NUTRITION (PER SERVING): 751 calories, 40 g protein, 71 g carbohydrates, 6 g fiber, 2 g sugar, 36 g fat, 14 g saturated fat, 1,468 mg sodium

Trout Ratatouille en Papillote

Heat the oven to 375°F. Lightly season four 4-ounce trout fillets on both sides with salt and black pepper. Cut four pieces of parchment paper, each measuring approximately 12 x 18 inches, and lay them on a clean work surface. Fold each in half crosswise, then open and lay them flat. Divide 1 thinly sliced zucchini, 1 thinly sliced yellow squash, 1 thinly sliced Japanese eggplant, and 2 thinly sliced plum tomatoes onto each sheet of parchment, shingling them in alternating layers on one side of the fold. Drizzle each with 1 teaspoon olive oil and sprinkle each with 1 teaspoon fresh chopped thyme, and a pinch of salt and black pepper. Lay a fillet on top of the vegetables and drizzle each with ½ teaspoon oil. Fold the parchment over to form a half-moon shape. Beginning in one corner, make small overlapping pleats all the way around to seal the edges completely. Transfer the packets to 2 rimmed baking sheets and bake until the parchment puffs up, about 10 minutes. Immediately place a packet on each of 4 plates and use kitchen shears to cut the packets open at the table. Top with whole fresh basil leaves. Serves 4.

NUTRITION (PER SERVING): 270 calories, 26 g protein, 9 g carbohydrates, 3 g fiber, 6 g sugar, 15 g fat, 2.5 g saturated fat, 132 mg sodium

Simple Chicken and Veggie Stir-Fry

In a small bowl, whisk together ⅓ cup low-sodium soy sauce, 2 tablespoons honey, 2 tablespoons cornstarch, and 1 teaspoon toasted sesame oil. Set aside. Heat 2 teaspoons peanut oil in a wok or large skillet over high heat. Add 1 pound thinly sliced boneless skinless chicken breasts and thighs and cook, stirring often, until browned and cooked through, about 5 minutes. Transfer to a plate. Add another 2 teaspoons peanut oil to the pan. Add 1 inch fresh ginger, thinly sliced, and 2 thinly sliced cloves garlic and cook until fragrant, 30 seconds. Add 1 chopped red onion, 1 seeded chopped bell pepper, 1 cup broccoli florets, 1 cup cauliflower florets, and 1 cup halved sugar snap peas. Cook, stirring constantly, until bright and crisp-tender, 2 minutes. Return the chicken to the pan, pour in the soy sauce mixture, and cook, stirring constantly, until the sauce has thickened and the flavors have melded, about 2 more minutes. Garnish with 2 thinly sliced scallions and ½ teaspoon sesame seeds. Serve over 1 ½ cups cooked long-grain brown rice. Serves 2.

NUTRITION (PER SERVING): 727 calories, 57 g protein, 78 g carbohydrates, 8 g fiber, 24 g sugar, 21 g fat, 4 g saturated fat, 1,699 mg sodium

Chicken and Green Veggie Pot

In a medium pot, heat ¼ cup olive oil over medium heat. Add ½ chopped onion and cook until translucent and soft, about 7 minutes. Add ¼ cup all-purpose flour, and cook until it bubbles and smells nutty, about 30 seconds. Stir in I tablespoon chopped fresh thyme, I tablespoon chopped fresh sage, ½ teaspoon salt, and ½ teaspoon black pepper, and cook until fragrant, another 30 seconds. Whisk in 4 cups low-sodium chicken broth and cook until thickened, about 5 minutes. Stir in 2 cups shredded rotisserie chicken, 2 cups torn kale leaves, 2 cups broccoli florets, and I cup frozen green beans, and cook until the broccoli is tender, about IO more minutes. Serve with crusty whole-wheat bread. Serves 4.

NUTRITION (PER SERVING): 499 calories, 36 g protein, 5I g carbohydrates, 5 g fiber, 5 g sugar, 18 g fat, 3 g saturated fat, 769 mg sodium

Spinach, Berry, and Goat Cheese Salad

Toast ¼ cup walnut halves in a small, dry skillet over medium heat until fragrant and just beginning to take on color, about 8 minutes. Meanwhile, in a small bowl, whisk together I ½ tablespoons extra-virgin olive oil and I ½ tablespoons red-wine vinegar, 2 teaspoons blackstrap molasses, zest of ½ lemon, and ¼ teaspoon freshly grated ginger. Place 6 cups baby spinach leaves or baby kale, I cup sliced strawberries, and ½ cup blueberries in a large bowl. Toss gently to combine. Pour the dressing over the salad and toss gently to coat the spinach or kale. Divide the salad between 2 plates or bowls. Top each salad with half of the walnuts, 2 ounces of crumbled goat cheese, and freshly ground black pepper. Serves 2.

NUTRITION (PER SERVING): 479 calories, I7 g protein, 27 g carbohydrates, 7 g fiber, I3 g sugar, 36 g total fat, I4 g saturated fat, 4I3 mg sodium

Colorful Quinoa Bowls

Press a 16-ounce block of firm tofu between two flat surfaces for 1 hour. Whisk together ⅓ cup canola oil, ⅓ cup white or yellow miso paste, ½ cup rice-wine vinegar, and 1 tablespoon grated fresh ginger until combined. Heat the oven to 425°F. Lightly spray 2 baking sheets with cooking spray. Toss the tofu in ⅓ cup of the miso dressing, then arrange in an even layer on a baking sheet. Cut 2 large sweet potatoes into 1-inch cubes and 4 medium beets into ½-inch wedges. Arrange them in a single layer on the other baking sheet, and season with salt and black pepper. Roast until the tofu is golden and crisp on the outside, and the beets and sweet potatoes are tender, about 25 minutes. Meanwhile, cook 1 ½ cups quinoa according to the package directions. Divide the quinoa equally among 4 bowls and top with the tofu, sweet potatoes, and beets. Divide 2 cups shredded red cabbage, 1 cup halved snow peas, 1 cup cilantro leaves, ½ cup thinly sliced scallions, and 2 teaspoons sesame seeds among the 4 bowls and drizzle each with the remaining dressing before serving. Serves 4.

NUTRITION (PER SERVING): 732 calories, 26 g protein, 94 g carbohydrates, 16 g fiber, 24 g sugar, 29 g fat, 2.5 g saturated fat, 815 mg sodium

What the World's Healthiest People Eat **for Dinner**

As you'll see, many of these dinners came straight from the people we interviewed. For the rest, Prevention's test kitchen worked true culinary magic, creating hearty, stick-to-your-ribs options that pack in the super-foods, while setting you back only a minimum of calories.

Middle-Eastern Chopped Chicken Salad

Whisk together ¼ cup extra-virgin olive oil, 2 tablespoons red-wine vinegar, 1 minced clove garlic, ½ teaspoon salt, and ½ teaspoon black pepper in a large bowl. Add 3 chopped tomatoes, 2 cups chopped cooked chicken, 1 seeded and chopped cucumber, 1 seeded and chopped green bell pepper, 1 seeded and chopped red bell pepper, ¼ chopped red onion, 2 tablespoons chopped fresh parsley, and 2 tablespoons crumbled feta cheese. Toss thoroughly to combine. Divide among 4 bowls. Toast 2 whole-wheat pitas, cut into quarters, and place 2 wedges in each bowl. Garnish with lemon wedges. Serves 4.

NUTRITION (PER SERVING): 362 calories, 27 g protein, 22 g carbohydrates, 5 g fiber, 6 g sugar, 19 g fat, 3.5 g saturated fat, 525 mg sodium

Rosemary Roasted Chicken and Vegetables

Heat the oven to 425°F. Coat a large rimmed baking sheet with cooking spray. Add 2 small sweet potatoes, cut into 1-inch chunks; 2 red bell peppers, seeded and cut into ¾-inch chunks; 1 sweet onion, cut into ¾-inch chunks with layers separated; 1 package (3.5 ounces) mixed wild or exotic mushrooms and 1 package (10 ounces) frozen artichoke hearts. Sprinkle with 1 teaspoon chopped fresh rosemary, 1 teaspoon olive oil, ¼ teaspoon salt, ¼ teaspoon black pepper, and toss to combine. Move the vegetables to the sides, and place 4 small boneless, skinless chicken breasts down the center of the baking sheet. Brush with another 1 teaspoon olive oil and sprinkle with 1 teaspoon chopped fresh rosemary and 1 teaspoon salt. Bake until a thermometer inserted into the thickest part of a breast registers 165°F and the vegetables are tender, about 30 minutes. Transfer the chicken to a plate. Stir 1 teaspoon lemon zest into the roasted vegetables before serving. Serves 4.

NUTRITION (PER SERVING): 293 calories, 30 g protein, 29 g carbohydrates, 9 g fiber, 10 g sugar, 7 g fat, 1 g saturated fat, 962 mg sodium

Amy Morosini's Goulash

Cut 2 large potatoes into 1-inch pieces and place in a microwave-safe bowl. Cook in the microwave on high until mostly tender, about 5 minutes. Transfer the potatoes to a large stock pot and combine with 2 cans (28 ounces each) chopped tomatoes (with juice), 2 cans (15 ounces each) drained and rinsed chickpeas, 2 bags (16 ounces each) frozen cauliflower florets, 2 cups frozen peas, 1 small chopped onion, 1 tablespoon curry powder, 1 tablespoon ground turmeric, 1 teaspoon ground cumin, and 1 teaspoon garlic powder. Cover the pot and cook over medium-low heat until simmering, stirring occasionally, for about 25 minutes. Add 2 cups baby spinach leaves and stir until wilted, about 2 minutes. Season to taste with salt and black pepper. Serve the goulash over 1 ½ cups cooked brown rice. Serves 8.

NUTRITION (PER SERVING): 388 calories, 15 g protein, 78 g carbohydrates, 14 g fiber, 10 g sugar, 2 g fat, 0 g saturated fat, 726 mg sodium

· · · · · · · · · · ·
Joan Connella's Cassoulet

Heat the oven to 350°F. In a large baking dish, combine 1 beef polska kielbasa, cut into ½-inch-thick rounds; 1 pound chopped grilled chicken; 2 cans (15 ounces each) rinsed and drained unsalted red kidney beans and 2 cans (15 ounces each) rinsed and drained unsalted great northern beans; 2 cans (14 ounces each) unsalted diced tomatoes; 1 red and green bell pepper, seeded and cut into strips; 1 thinly sliced medium onion; ½ cup red wine; 2 minced cloves garlic; 1 teaspoon dried sage; ½ teaspoon salt; and ½ teaspoon black pepper. Cover and bake for 40 minutes. Uncover and bake until thick and saucy, about 30 more minutes. Serve with crusty bread, if desired. Serves 6.

NUTRITION (PER SERVING): 532 calories, 42 g protein, 39 g carbohydrates, 10 g fiber, 9 g sugar, 22 g fat, 8 g saturated fat, 898 mg sodium

· · · · · · · · · · ·
Ed Shimer's Meat and Veggies

Heat 1 tablespoon olive oil in a large skillet set over medium heat. Add 1 chopped small red onion, 2 minced cloves garlic, and ¼ to ½ teaspoon crushed red pepper flakes. Cook, stirring, until the onion becomes translucent, about 5 minutes. Add 1 pint cherry tomatoes and a large pinch of salt. Cook, stirring, until the tomatoes burst, about 5 minutes. Add 1 pound trimmed and halved string beans and ½ cup low-sodium chicken or vegetable stock. Cover and cook until crisp-tender, about 8 minutes. Meanwhile, heat another large skillet and add 1 tablespoon olive oil. Season 4 (4 ounces each) boneless pork chops generously with salt and black pepper. Add them to the hot skillet and sear until golden brown on both sides and cooked to the desired doneness or until the internal temperature reaches 145°F, about 5 minutes per side. Serve with vegetables. Serves 4.

NUTRITION (PER SERVING): 265 calories, 29 g protein, 13 g carbohydrates, 4 g fiber, 6 g sugar, 11 g fat, 2.5 g saturated fat, 556 mg sodium

Split Pea and Ham Soup

Heat I tablespoon olive oil in a medium saucepan over medium heat. Add I cup diced baked ham, I chopped medium onion, 2 grated carrots, and 2 thyme sprigs. Cook, stirring, until the onion is translucent, about 5 minutes. Add 6 cups low-sodium chicken broth, I cup dry green split peas, and a pinch of salt and black pepper, and bring to a boil. Reduce to a simmer and cook until the peas are tender and the soup has thickened, about 45 minutes. Remove the thyme sprigs before serving with a mixed green salad and crusty, whole-wheat bread. Serves 4.

NUTRITION (PER SERVING): 3II calories, 25 g protein, 4I g carbohydrates, I4 g fiber, 7 g sugar, 7 g fat, I.5 g saturated fat, 834 mg sodium

Thai Green Curry Soup

Trim I pound asparagus, and coarsely chop the tough ends. In a medium pot, heat 2 teaspoons coconut oil over medium-high heat. Add I small chopped onion; a I-inch piece of peeled ginger, chopped; and the asparagus ends, and cook until the vegetables begin to soften, about 5 minutes. Add I tablespoon Thai green curry paste, I can (I4 ounces) light coconut milk, and I quart low-sodium vegetable broth. Bring to a boil, reduce the heat to a simmer, and cook until the vegetables are very tender, about 8 minutes. Add 5 ounces of thawed frozen peas and 5 ounces of fresh baby spinach, and cook until the spinach is wilted, about 2 minutes. Remove from the heat, blend in batches, and season with ½ teaspoon salt and ½ teaspoon black pepper. Cut the asparagus stalks into I-inch pieces. Heat 2 teaspoons coconut oil in a large skillet over medium-high heat. Add the asparagus, I cup trimmed and halved snap peas, and another 5 ounces of thawed frozen peas. Sauté until crisp-tender, about 3 minutes; season with salt and black pepper. Serve the soup topped with the sautéed veggies and ½ cup fresh mint leaves. Garnish with lemon wedges. Serves 4.

NUTRITION (PER SERVING): 258 calories, I0 g protein, 30 g carbohydrates, 9 g fiber, II g sugar, I2 g fat, 9 g saturated fat, 609 mg sodium

Pollo alla Calabrese

Heat the oven to 400°F. On a large rimmed baking sheet, toss to combine 8 bone-in, skin-on chicken thighs, I pint halved cherry tomatoes, I pound halved baby potatoes, I seeded and sliced green bell pepper, 2 sliced medium carrots, and I large sweet onion, cut into wedges. Add ¼ cup olive oil, 4 minced cloves garlic, I teaspoon dried oregano, I teaspoon sweet paprika, I teaspoon kosher salt, and ¼ teaspoon crushed red pepper flakes, making sure to rub the chicken with the spices. Arrange the vegetables underneath the chicken pieces. Roast, turning the chicken and tossing the vegetables halfway through, until the vegetables are tender and the chicken is cooked through, about 45 minutes. Serves 4.

NUTRITION (PER SERVING): 559 calories, 60 g protein, 33 g carbohydrates, 5 g fiber, 10 g sugar, 20 g fat, 5.5 g saturated fat, 736 mg sodium

Salmon Vegetable Parcels

Fold two I4 by I8-inch sheets of parchment paper in half. Open up the sheets and add 2 cups chopped broccoli florets, ½ thinly sliced medium bulb fennel, and ½ seeded and thinly sliced red bell pepper on one side of both sheets. Place I skinless salmon fillet (4 to 6 ounces) on top of the vegetables. Melt I tablespoon unsalted butter, and stir in 2 teaspoons orange zest, 2 tablespoons fresh orange juice, 2 teaspoons fresh thyme, ¼ teaspoon kosher salt, ¼ teaspoon black pepper, and ⅛ teaspoon cayenne pepper. Spread the orange mixture over the salmon. Fold the empty half of the parchment sheets over the salmon and vegetables and crimp them shut. Microwave each parchment packet on high for 4 minutes. Open a corner of the packet and check that the salmon flesh is cooked through. If not, microwave in 30-second intervals until the salmon is cooked. (Alternately, you may bake them at 400°F for 25 minutes.) Let the parchment packets rest, sealed, for 5 minutes. Slice open the packets to serve and sprinkle each with ½ teaspoon black sesame seeds. Serves 2.

NUTRITION (PER SERVING): 4I6 calories, 32 g protein, 22 g carbohydrates, I0 g fiber, 4 g sugar, 24 g fat, 7.5 g saturated fat, 4I4 mg sodium

Steve Bowers' Amazing Veggie Salad

Cook ½ cup brown rice and ½ cup quinoa as directed. Heat 1 tablespoon olive oil in a large skillet over medium heat and cook 2 cloves minced garlic until fragrant, about 30 seconds. Add 1 seeded and finely chopped yellow or red bell pepper, 1 finely chopped small yellow squash, and 4 cups shredded kale leaves (stems removed). Cook, stirring occasionally, until the kale is wilted and the pepper is soft, 8 to 10 minutes. In a large bowl, combine 1 can (15 ounces) drained and rinsed black beans with the cooked rice, cooked quinoa, veggie mixture, ¼ cup grated Parmesan cheese (if desired), juice of 1 lime, 1 tablespoon soy sauce, 1 tablespoon Worcestershire sauce, a few dashes of your favorite hot sauce, to taste, ½ teaspoon sea salt, and ½ teaspoon black pepper. Serve warm or cold with 2 chopped avocados on top. Serves 4.

NUTRITION (PER SERVING): 421 calories, 14 g protein, 60 g carbohydrates, 13 g fiber, 4 g sugar, 17 g fat, 2 g saturated fat, 833 mg sodium

Margherita Pita Pizza

Heat the oven or a toaster oven to 400°F. Set a 6-inch whole-wheat pita on a baking sheet. Arrange 4 slices of tomato on top and dot it with 2 tablespoons tiny mozzarella balls (ciliegine) and 6 small basil leaves. Bake until golden brown, 6 to 8 minutes. Remove from the oven, cut into 4 wedges, and top with ½ cup baby arugula drizzled with 1 teaspoon olive oil and a pinch of salt and black pepper. Serves 1.

NUTRITION (PER SERVING): 307 calories, 12 g protein, 39 g carbohydrates, 6 g fiber, 3 g sugar, 13 g fat, 5 g saturated fat, 307 mg sodium

Grilled Spanish Mackerel with Hearty Salad

Score the skin of 4 Spanish mackerel or Arctic char fillets (about 5 ½ ounces each) diagonally with a knife. Sprinkle the fish with I teaspoon ground turmeric, ½ teaspoon ground cumin, ¼ teaspoon salt, and ¼ teaspoon black pepper. Coat a grill pan or grill with cooking spray and heat to medium-high. Grill the fish, skin-side down, until well-marked, about 5 minutes. Flip and cook until the fish flakes easily, about 5 more minutes. Meanwhile, in a large bowl, whisk together ⅓ cup olive oil, 2 tablespoons balsamic vinegar, I tablespoon fresh chopped rosemary, I ½ teaspoons fresh thyme, I clove minced garlic, ⅛ teaspoon salt, and ⅛ teaspoon black pepper. Add 8 cups mixed salad greens and ½ red onion, thinly sliced, and toss to coat. Divide the salad among 4 plates and top each with I tablespoon toasted pumpkin seeds, chopped pistachios, or chopped walnuts, and I ounce crumbled goat cheese or feta cheese. Serve each with a fish fillet. Serves 4.

NUTRITION (PER SERVING): 576 calories, 4I g protein, 8 g carbohydrates, 3 g fiber, 3 g sugar, 43 g fat, I2 g saturated fat, 507 mg sodium

Fiesta Quinoa with Shrimp

Cook ⅓ cup rinsed white quinoa according to the package directions. In a jar with a lid, combine 2 tablespoons fresh lime juice, I tablespoon olive oil, I clove garlic, mashed to a paste, ¼ teaspoon cumin, ¼ teaspoon dried oregano, a pinch of salt, and a few grinds of black pepper, and shake until combined. Set aside. In a large bowl, toss together the quinoa, I cup rinsed and drained no-salt-added black beans, ½ cup thawed frozen corn kernels, ½ cup seeded and finely diced red bell pepper, 2 thinly sliced scallions, and the dressing. Let the salad sit to meld the flavors while you prepare the shrimp. Heat I ½ teaspoons olive oil in a medium nonstick skillet over medium heat. Add ½ pound peeled and deveined jumbo shrimp, and cook, tossing occasionally, until opaque and slightly curled, about 4 minutes. Toss in ½ teaspoon lime zest and I tablespoon chopped fresh cilantro. Divide the quinoa and shrimp between 2 plates and serve. Serves 2.

NUTRITION (PER SERVING): 432 calories, 28 g protein, 49 g carbohydrates, I0 g fiber, 4 g sugar, I4 g fat, 2 g saturated fat, 725 mg sodium

Pumpkin Curry with Cucumber Raita

Heat 2 tablespoons coconut or olive oil in a large skillet over medium heat. Add I teaspoon cumin, I teaspoon fenugreek seeds, and ½ teaspoon mustard seeds, and cook until the oil and seeds start to spatter, about 4 minutes. Add I chopped yellow onion, I finely chopped Serrano chile, 3 teaspoons minced garlic, I teaspoon grated fresh ginger, and ¼ teaspoon kosher salt. Cook, stirring frequently, until softened and browned, about 4 minutes. Add 4 cups cubed peeled kabocha pumpkin (or butternut squash) and ½ cup low-sodium vegetable broth. Bring to a simmer, lower the heat, cover, and cook until the pumpkin is extremely soft, about 20 minutes. Uncover, increase the heat, and stir in 2 cups baby spinach leaves, ¼ cup plain coconut water, and I tablespoon fresh lime juice. Cook until the spinach is wilted and the pan is nearly dry, 5 to 6 minutes. Meanwhile, mix together (by hand or in a blender) ¾ cup plain Greek yogurt, ½ cup diced cucumber, I tablespoon chopped fresh mint or cilantro, I tablespoon fresh lime juice, ½ teaspoon minced garlic, and ¼ teaspoon kosher salt. Serve the curry with the raita and warm naan. Serves 2 (or 4 as a side dish).

NUTRITION (PER SERVING): 593 calories, I9 g protein, 75 g carbohydrates, I0 g fiber, I8 g sugar, 27 g fat, 20 g saturated fat, 949 mg sodium

Chicken in a Pot

Place a 3- to 4-pound whole chicken in an 8- to I0-quart pot and cover with water by an inch. Bring to a boil, reduce the heat to a simmer, and cook for 30 minutes. Skim any foam that may form on the surface. Add 2 coarsely chopped yellow onions, 2 coarsely chopped carrots, 2 coarsely chopped celery ribs, I thinly sliced fennel bulb, 3 cloves garlic, 3 bay leaves, 2 thyme sprigs, 2 teaspoons kosher salt, and ¾ teaspoon black pepper. Bring back to a simmer, and cook until the broth is flavorful, about I hour. Transfer the chicken to a cutting board, remove and discard the skin, and either shred the meat or leave it in large chunks. Discard the thyme sprigs, bay leaves, and garlic. Add the chicken back to the pot. Season to taste with salt and pepper. Stir in either 2 cups cooked rice or 4 cups cooked egg noodles, ¼ cup chopped fresh parsley and/or dill. Serve with lemon wedges. Serves 6.

NUTRITION (PER SERVING): 246 calories, 26 g protein, 26 g carbohydrates, 3 g fiber, 3 g sugar, 4 g fat, I g saturated fat, 79I mg sodium

What the World's Healthiest People Eat
for Snacks

One of the traits of the World's Healthiest People: They do not deprive themselves of pleasure. These delicious snacks and desserts include healing spices and other healthful ingredients, but their main selling point is the party they start in your mouth. Enjoy!

• • • • • • • • • • •
Turmeric-Cinnamon Fruit Salad

In a large bowl, whisk together the juice of I lime with ½ teaspoon ground turmeric and ¼ teaspoon ground cinnamon. Toss in 2 cups cubed watermelon, 2 cups cubed cantaloupe, and 2 cups cubed honeydew. Serves 2.

NUTRITION (PER SERVING): 169 calories, 3 g protein, 42 g carbohydrates, 4 g fiber, 35 g sugar, I g fat, 0 g saturated fat, 58 mg sodium

• • • • • • • • • • •
Red Pepper Hummus with Carrot and Celery Sticks

Combine ½ cup chopped roasted red peppers, ¼ cup plain Greek yogurt, and I teaspoon finely chopped rosemary with 10 ounces plain hummus. Serve with 2 carrots, quartered and cut into 2-inch sticks, and 2 ribs celery, halved and cut into 2-inch sticks. Serves 10.

NUTRITION (PER SERVING): 60 calories, 3 g protein, 6 g carbohydrates, 2 g fiber, I g sugar, 3 g fat, 0.5 g saturated fat, 130 mg sodium

• • • • • • • • • • •
Honey Black Pepper Snack Mix

Heat the oven to 450°F. Line a baking sheet with aluminum foil. Toss ¼ cup almonds with 1½ teaspoons honey, ½ teaspoon extra-virgin olive oil, ½ teaspoon black pepper, and a pinch of kosher salt. Spread on the baking sheet and roast until deep amber in color, 6 minutes. Transfer to a bowl and toss with I tablespoon dried blueberries. Serves I.

NUTRITION (PER SERVING): 295 calories, 8 g protein, 23 g carbohydrates, 6 g fiber, 13 g sugar, 20 g fat, 1.5 g saturated fat, 149 mg sodium

Gremolata Parmesan Popcorn

On a cutting board, chop together ¼ cup chopped parsley, I small clove chopped garlic, ½ teaspoon lemon zest, and I tablespoon finely grated Parmigiano-Reggiano, until fine. In a large bowl, toss I0 cups air-popped popcorn while spritzing grapeseed oil with a mister. Add the gremolata and ½ teaspoon salt and toss until coated. Serves 2.

NUTRITION (PER SERVING): I9I calories, 6 g protein, 32 g carbohydrates, 6 g fiber, 0 g sugar, 5 g fat, I g saturated fat, 627 mg sodium

Baked Rosemary Apple and Manchego on Crackers

Heat the oven to 400°F. On a baking sheet, toss I cored apple (such as Braeburn or Jonathan), cut into 8 pieces, with I teaspoon fresh rosemary leaves and I tablespoon unsweetened apple cider. Sprinkle with a pinch of kosher salt. Bake, stirring once, until the apple is soft and golden, about I5 minutes. Cool slightly. Cut I ounce Manchego cheese into 8 pieces. To serve, top each of 8 shredded-wheat crackers (such as Triscuits) with a slice of Manchego and a piece of baked apple. Serves 2.

NUTRITION (PER SERVING): 204 calories, 5 g protein, 28 g carbohydrates, 4 g fiber, I3 g sugar, 9 g fat, 4 g saturated fat, 267 mg sodium

Natalie Jill's Ready-to-Eat Chocolate Chip Cookie Dough

Combine ½ cup packed almond flour, ¼ cup tapioca flour, I tablespoon agave nectar, ¾ teaspoon pure vanilla extract, and 5 tablespoons cold, unsalted grass-fed butter in a blender, and blend until smooth. Stir in I ounce chopped dark (85% cocoa) chocolate and a generous pinch of pink Himalayan salt. Serves 4.

NUTRITION (PER SERVING): 290 calories, 4 g protein, I6 g carbohydrates, 3 g fiber, 6 g sugar, 25 g fat, II.5 g saturated fat, 22 mg sodium

Chocolate Chip-Cranberry-Walnut-Oatmeal Cookies

Heat the oven to 350°F. In a large bowl, combine 2 cups rolled oats, ½ cup whole-grain pastry flour, ¾ teaspoon baking soda, ½ teaspoon ground cinnamon, and ¼ teaspoon salt. In a medium bowl, whisk together ½ cup brown sugar, ⅓ cup canola oil, 3 large egg whites, and 2 teaspoons vanilla extract until smooth. Fold in 2 ¼ cups chopped walnuts, ¾ cup coarsely chopped cranberries, and ½ cup semisweet chocolate chips. Gradually fold in the flour mixture and stir until well-blended. Drop the batter by tablespoons onto 2 large baking sheets coated with nonstick cooking spray. Bake until the cookies are golden brown, about 10 minutes. Transfer the cookies to a wire rack to cool completely. Makes 24.

NUTRITION (PER COOKIE): 172 calories, 4 g protein, 15 g carbohydrates, 2 g fiber, 7 g sugar, 12 g fat, 1.5 g saturated fat, 72 mg sodium

Quinoa Fruit Salad with Maple Dressing

Bring ¾ cup tri-colored quinoa and 1 ½ cups water to a boil. Reduce the heat and simmer, covered, until the grains are tender and the water has been absorbed, about 12 minutes. Set aside, covered, for 5 minutes, and then fluff with a fork. Meanwhile, in a small bowl, whisk together 2 tablespoons pure maple syrup, 1 teaspoon grated lemon zest, juice of ½ lime, ½ teaspoon ground ginger, and ¼ teaspoon salt. Place the quinoa in a large bowl and toss with 2 cups blackberries or blueberries, 2 cups diced pineapple, ½ cup dried tart cherries, ⅓ cup coconut chips, ⅓ cup unsalted pistachios, ⅓ cup sliced fresh mint, and 3 tablespoons hemp seeds (hemp hearts). Toss the dressing with the quinoa salad and serve. Serves 6.

NUTRITION (PER SERVING): 273 calories, 8 g protein, 43 g carbohydrates, 9 g fiber, 19 g sugar, 9 g fat, 0.5 g saturated fat, 104 mg sodium

Index

Underscored page references indicate boxed text.